A Day at the Beach

A Day
at the Beach

Recollections

Geoffrey Wolff

Alfred A. Knopf
New York
1992

Some of the essays included in this work were originally published in
Granta and *New Times*.
Esquire: "An Illuminated History of a Model Friendship" (now titled "The
Company Man and the Revolutionary"), May, 1977; "A Day at the
Beach," December, 1987.
Lear's: "Writers & Booze" (now titled "Drinking"), March, 1990.
The New York Times Book Review: "Advice My Brother Never Took" (now
titled "Apprentice"), August 20, 1989 (previously the Introduction to *Best
American Essays: 1989*, Ticknor & Fields).
The Paris Review: "The Sick Man of Europe," October, 1991.
Travel & Leisure: "It's the Top" (now titled "Matterhorn"), June 1989.

Library of Congress Cataloging-in-Publication Data
Wolff, Geoffrey.
    A day at the beach: recollections / Geoffrey Wolff.—1st ed.
    p. cm.
    ISBN 0-679-40333-7
    1. Wolff, Geoffrey, 1937–   —Biography. 2. Authors,
American—20th century—Biography. I. Title.
PS3573.053Z462   1991
813'.54—dc20
[B]   91-57916
         CIP

Manufactured in the United States of America
First Edition

For my deckhands
and yard-maintenance engineers:

you know who you are

Contents

A Day at the Beach

Apprentice

There arrived in my mailbox a *billet-doux* from my little brother Toby. More specifically, this was a five-page letter to him, from me, with his Post-it self-stick memo stuck to page 1. The letter was dated 13/xi/63—à la European mode—and postmarked Cambridge, England, mailed decades before to an eleventh-grader. Single-spaced elite, without margins, it was typed with such manifest urgency that words fly truncated off the right edge of the tissue-thin foolscap; the keys must have been righteously rapped—"o"s are little holes.

The tone of this document owes much to austere dogma, a religion of literary Art. It answers a letter in which Toby seems obscurely to have offended me by an expression of enthusiasm for his country and for some of its better contemporary and popular prose writers. Now Toby is himself one of our better contemporary prose writers, but at that time he was too young to vote, and I wasn't, so I took it upon myself to tell the stripling a thing or two.

"We live in an age when contraception and the Bomb and rejected opportunities usurp each other [sic] as negative functions . . . the cliché governs by executive function . . . in the ruined warrens are pockets of beautiful life . . ." The bulk of my letter consists of a suggestion that before Toby read another word of William Styron or Norman Mailer (for whom he had

confessed such provocative admiration) he turn at once to
Donne, Eliot on Donne, Sophocles, Aristotle, John Jones on
Aristotle, Racine, Hegel (on tragedy) and I don't know who
all else. In short: "Begin at the beginning and familiarize yourself with literature." To this end he was to write weekly essays
for me, and I would lead him across the ages, "working
through language and time until you learn how to read, and
may discover whether you wish to write."

Jeepers! Or, as Toby noted on the yellow Post-it: "I *still*
don't know half the stuff in here, and I'm a Full Professor,
Mr. Smarty Pants!! (I thought you might want this back.)"
Let's say Toby has me by the shorts on this one: it's in his
archive still—he sent a photocopy, damn him.

For a letter so passionately typed, mine has an oddly distanced air, save for its *ad hominem, ad extremum* and *ad ab-
surdum* assertion that "every backward glance at our family
tree reveals a body hanging from the withered limbs." I think
I understand the abstracted character of these declarations:
whatever the provenance of my athletically typed (and no
doubt plagiarized) maxims, all I can now say with confidence
is these were thoughts never thunk by me, or never in just
these words.

But there's more too on Toby's Post-it annotation: "It's a
sweet letter. I was touched by it." In the spirit of confession
may I disclose that I too am touched by my jejune gospel of
a literary calling? My correspondence with my brother
launched gaudy little vessels of language; my sentences didn't
go forth carrying cargo, but in a hope of netting something
out there on the vasty deeps. At the end I signed off: "I'm sorry
I have no news; I have little to talk of other than my work.
That is everything."

It's simple enough to poke fun at the patchwork boy I was,
the ill-matched concoction of attitudes and characteristics I
aspired to be. I dressed in motley: three-piece blue pinstripe

with gravy stains on the vest (a touch of Edmund Wilson in the waistcoat?), suspenders, wire-rimmed glasses to add even more years to my solemn face pallid from bad diet and irregular habits. (My God—I'd already had my first gout attack.) My Cambridge college tie beneath my Cambridge gown offset bohemian footwear, Army-surplus boots. The Greeks, Jacobeans, Metaphysicals shared my bookshelves with modern poets, William Burroughs, Harold Pinter, Jean Genet and *Europe on Five Dollars a Day*. Parked in front of my digs stood a cherry-red 750-cc Royal Enfield Constellation, with full racing fairing, hell of a bike. George Steiner, my Churchill College tutor, my reason for being at Cambridge, was satisfied by the (literary) books, but sore about the motorcycle. Let's call the ragout of my conflicting circumstances a mess.

But for all the hotchpotch of my circumstances and styles, for all the egregious posturing and borrowed sentiment and faked-up lingo of my lugubrious letter to my brother, there was also something there I won't disavow. In those overwrought homilies about the long littleness of life and eternal uplift of Art was a felt passion, a longing for something that mattered, might stay, be firm. To learn something, to master something, anything, is as sweet as first love. In fact, it may *be* first, preceding memory, the blissed-out grin that seems urged by the nervous system to accompany a baby's first solo steps, or a kid's first bicycle ride, or anyone's first unmonitored, unassigned, discretionary experience of reading. Don't you remember the first thing you read? Mine was *Donald Duck*, and I was sitting in the bay window of a boardinghouse in Saybrook, Connecticut, where a drunk husband and his drunk wife hectored my drunk father about a gambling debt unpaid for fifteen years, and the awful noise went through me like silence through space, because I was elsewhere, living otherwise. And like a great whistler, who can entertain himself at will, or a sixteen-year-old with license, car and gasoline, I had the keys to the cell. To read was to escape, at will, solitary confinement.

Later I was forever pressing books on friends ("Have you read this? You *must* read that!"); now I pitched woo saying poems by heart. I favored, for their periodic drive and lonely outcasts caught in implied sensual contact, the closing lines of *Paradise Lost*:

> *The world was all before them, where to choose*
> *Their place of rest, and Providence their guide:*
> *They hand in hand with wand'ring steps and slow*
> *Through Eden took their solitary way.*

I knew then that a life lived reading and writing could be a life well lived, in good company. That may have been all I knew, but I would not unknow it now.

I was an eager student back then, avid to please, twenty-six going on sixty. The teachers whose good reports I cherished were cultural and literary critics—R. P. Blackmur, George Steiner, F. R. Leavis—for whom it seemed to me (if not to them) that literature of imagination was a secondary artifact, the rough ore from which the precious alloy of criticism might be fabricated. To me, then, the self-consciously impenetrable essays in *Scrutiny, Encounter, Partisan Review* and *Kenyon Review* were primary texts, and to read them was to belong to an exclusive guild whose members shared a dense jargon, a chastening insistence on commitment to text, a call to arms in some arcane combat in which a solemn band of initiates guarded the True Faith's gates against a vulgar gang of middlebrow, mid-cult vandals.

I wished to stand stringent sentry among the few initiates. Why? I was a sucker for pulpit oratory (as long as it came delivered from a secular pulpit—say, a lectern), and I was a sucker for whatever was inside the place I was outside. Also,

I was skeptical of all faiths, save bookishness; I was bone-idle, except around books. Around books I worked like a Turk, reading with a pencil in my hand, reading three or four things at a clip. I had read headlong and helter-skelter since I'd plowed as a kid through Albert Payson Terhune simultaneously with the Hardy Boys. To read compulsively and to write about reading were my only appetites (of too many appetites) sanctioned as virtues rather than condemned as vices.

The poet Stanley Kunitz has remarked, reviewing his life's work for a collection of his poems, that evolution is a delusion. We change, but always at a cost: to win this you lose that. I feel sharp-witted these days, like to believe I know the score, would as soon laugh at myself as laugh at another, value lowlife idiom at least as preciously as high sentiment. When my brother forwarded to me that old letter, I paraphrased (shame would not countenance full quotation) its rhetoric and presumptions to a friend of many, many years who had herself been on the receiving end of my bygone puffed-up gravitas. I said to my friend, with what I took to be irony, "Boy oh boy, I sure was learned then."

"Yes," she said. "You were."

I paused quite a good pause there, and let this soak in, and realized that I was lingering in the dangerous domain of a truth, and I wanted to laugh my way to a comfier neighborhood. "What do you think happened?" I asked. "Wisdom, or just too much television?"

"Nah," she said. "You could say car payments. You could blame kids, but basically you eased up is all, wanted to relax."

She was part right, I'm afraid. To be the Man of Letters I aspired to be, avuncular at twenty-six, a virtuoso of the well-timed *harrumph*, able to contextualize, perspectivize, plumb the subtexts, incite chums and bully a younger brother to do the same—this was sober work, hard work. My friend was also part wrong, for a plunge into language was never joyless work.

A final note about that letter to my brother: it was mailed a little more than a week before President Kennedy was murdered. I know it's recollection's merest commonplace to suggest that what happened to him and to America had something to do with oneself, but it did have something to do with how at bedrock I hoped to regard myself. Fact is, on the stroke of Dallas I no longer wanted to be a knockoff of R. P. Blackmur, John Milton or even George Steiner. I inexplicably and all at once did a U-turn, ambitionwise. I meant to find a voice, apart from the remnants of conflicted idioms in my schoolboy collection, that I might convince myself was truly mine. Moreover, I aspired to act rather than meditate. In brief, an old story: I was an unhappy graduate student, woe was me. So I quit. Graduated. "Commenced," as they nicely say.

I had what seemed to me a dandy cee-vee: Choate, a postgraduate year at an English public school, Princeton (*summa cum laude*), a couple of years teaching literature in Turkey at Istanbul University and Robert College, Fulbright at Cambridge . . . Moreover, after having decided at Princeton that I was too exquisite to waste on that suburban New World my roughneck country, I was coming home. With arms outstretched. Willing to shake and make up. Put my shoulder to the wheel of American culture where my conspicuous gifts could count, as a journalist, in the nation's capital. How was it, then, that the Washington *Post* personnel office imposed on me a typing test, which I failed? Never mind, I taught myself to type fast enough to get an interview "upstairs," and was tentatively hired by a managing editor who had a soft spot for Turkey (he was building a vacation house there), and soon (despite my failure of a psychological test in which I declared—what *could* I have been thinking?—I would rather be a florist than a baseball manager, which I wouldn't rather be, but I had blackened the wrong rectangle on the answer sheet, and try explaining that to an alarmed personnel director while you're wearing an English shirt of peach broadcloth with a white detachable collar) I was at useful work, making a difference, writing about a dozen obituaries a day.

"I don't suppose you're secretly writing a novel during your time off?"

How could Bill Brady, night city editor, have guessed, my first afternoon on the death shift? Was it written on my face? The man was a seer. He saw more than I could possibly show because, yes, while I *meant* to dream up a novel when I wasn't retailing the death of civil servants and merchants, and who had survived them, and what kinds of Masons they were . . . while I had every intention—when I wasn't tracking down pix to accompany my little essays ("Wolff! Have we got art with the Makepeace obit?")—of doing art, I hadn't yet done art.

I was not, that is, after all, a Writer. I was a would-be Writer. Today such a distinction cannot exist. To want to be a writer is to be one, done and done. If I ask a dozen students in a fiction workshop how many think of themselves as writers, they are confused by the question. I read what they write, don't I? What else is writing? What's the question again? Not that they take everything for granted; quite a few ask, midway through their second semester as artists, whether they will someday be "first-rate." More than a couple have requested my warranty. Will I certify, if they work hard, read the books I have suggested they read, mend the errors of usage I have located, that they will—soon—become "great"? Because if labor were to make them merely "good," what's labor's point?

In my day we defined ourselves as Writers by no more logical a measure: when you were published by a disinterested, consequential (grownup) publication, then you were a Writer. By this measure a couple of stories in the Choate literary magazine, a couple of excerpts from a novel in the *Nassau Literary*

Magazine and some polemic from the left in *Cambridge For-ward* did not a Writer make. Lest I seem to claim for Kids Back Then proportion and humility superior to the feral am-bition of Kids Today, let me confide that I wanted to be a Writer long before I had the dimmest notion what story I wished to write. Let's call the phenomenon, then as now, careerism.

For someone not a Writer, however, I had sure done a gang of writing. In addition to piling up pages of all those school papers and independent projects and critical essays and book-length college theses, I had taken a year off from Princeton to complete a half-baked, doleful novel. But until I hit the glory hole of material that is any obituary essayist's estate, the principal vessel into which I poured my art was the letter. Love letters were best, but any letters would do. Letters were my apprenticeship: I used them as my commonplace book, as tryouts for characters, to get a purchase on what mattered to me and how I might articulate what mattered. I wrote weather reports and geography lessons, how snow touched the black waters of the Bosporus, how the sun bore down on Lindos, what a ninth consecutive day of rain did to Vienna. Hundreds of these letters, most unanswered. What was the recipient to say? This was not correspondence (as my amused brother now realizes); these were finger exercises, and just about as wel-come to my audience as a sixth, ninth, fifteenth run-through of "Heartaches" by a first-year student of the tenor sax.

Letters at least gave the illusion of a reader. Journals dis-couraged me, and for reasons more of character than of genre. Hidden by the privacy of a journal, I was too free to display my worst self. I look back over journal entries from years back—entries that I taught myself to write as though they were public, in which I obliged myself to develop characters as though I were meeting them every time for the first time, in which no information was shorthanded or privileged—and I discover a whiner. Awful. My characteristic voice is aggrieved or furious, condescending or monstrously generous. If that was my voice, who could want to listen?

My voice was of no interest to the Washington *Post*. Not that I didn't labor to make even that oldest of stories new: "The world yesterday lost a good man: 'There was never a better dad,' said Trixie A. of the gentle-fingered chiropractor lying this morning in Hulbert's Funeral Parlor."

"Come off it, Wolff! You've got the embalmer spelled wrong! *Hubert!* Get the stuff right, give me a new lede, hold it to eight inches, where's the art?"

They were like Masons, as abstruse in their idiom as New Critics: journalists spelled "lead"—for first or *leading* paragraph (what jargonmeisters today call "the attack")—"lede," and they referred to snapshots of the dead as "art." But being among them was good for me. The demented urgency of deadline discouraged my fear of blank paper (although sometimes, later, I should have feared it more, should have left more paper blank); the knowledge that every obituary is read with a jeweler's loupe by the survivors made me feel those few readers at my back, peering over my shoulder as I composed: "No, you moron! It's 2021 Hillyer Place, not 2201! And he was Deputy Assistant Secretary, not Assistant Deputy!" And so many dozens gone. The cry was still *they go*! So many little essays so quickly composed. As a result, to paraphrase the boast of a newspaper colleague who must have been thinking of me: "I can type faster than anyone who can write better, and write better than anyone who can type faster."

For the poet form is self-imposed, the parabolic net across which one plays Frost's legendary game. For the journalist form is mere circumstance. For me form was prison, and to be its hostage—in an obituary, a news story, book review, police report—was to long for breakout. I graduated from obit-

uaries to night police, and in a ceremony of initiation my
predecessor (freed by my elevation to tell stories of zoning in
Montgomery County) took me back to the clip files to intro-
duce me to the Gabbett Lede. Harry Gabbett worked night
rewrite. If you know your *Front Page*, I need tell no more of
him than that he was all five and a half feet an ace; that he
later, when I was on the cultural affairs desk and on final
probation at the *Post* and six weeks short of marriage, "re-
wrote" stories about events I neglected to attend because of
some small trouble with alcohol; that he got these stories
(about conventions of librarians and disputes between city
planners and how many meals can the Washington Hilton
prepare in how many minutes for a banquet) on the front page,
under my byline; and that he wore, in the newsroom, a Bor-
salino hat.

The Gabbett Lede began a story that had been phoned in
from police headquarters about a pissant holdup at a movie
theater. The desperado got away with small change. Gabbett
laconically requested details, perpetrator description, mode of
arrival, path of flight, the usual. The reporter, bored by the
tedious usual, eager to knock off at 3 a.m., gave Gabbett what
meager intelligence he had, and Gabbett wrote his lede: "A
man carrying a briefcase to show he was in business, and
pointing a revolver to show what business he was in . . ."

The ceremonial display of the Gabbett Lede was to suggest
that there's a great story in anything. It's an old American
notion. I was first told back in junior high that in each of God's
creatures is a great novel. Huey Long was wrong. Every man
is *not* a king; neither is each a Flaubert. Harry Gabbett, for
example, was not a Montaigne, or a Samuel Johnson, or a
John McPhee. Harry Gabbett wrote a honey of an introductory
sentence, not a great essay. He caught a reader's attention,
sure enough, but to what end? It is one thing to want and win
a reader's attention, quite another to have a reason to want

and hold the reader's attention. Ambition is ubiquitous, purpose rare.

Ambition showed a pleasant face at the Washington *Post*. To work there as a young would-be seemed honorable, was a hoot. I've not had a happier job of work, except writing in solitude. There was a largeheartedness to my colleagues, a pervasive decency. My friends among the reporters were greenhorns like me, and old pros, but they shared an appealing irreverence unsoiled by cynicism, a capacity to be surprised, an affection for newspapering. Out on the newsroom floor there was buzz and bustle and much laughter. Instructed by craft and inclination, daily journalists tell good jokes, good gossip, good stories. They narrate with speed, know how to hear and play back the swinging music of the revealing detail or unforeseen quote.

As dearly as I loved their company, among the beat reporters—people who gave a day's work for a day's pay—I mingled as an apostate, a curiosity. To a good beat reporter a story was not form but material. Good reporters didn't kick against the box of form except to make it longer by inches, so it could hold more facts, bring newer news. Pro newsmen had a relationship with time different from mine. For them augury was boss. Even more vital than what they knew was when they found it out. Divination was chronology, being wired in *pronto*, wised up *first*, having the *breaking* inside skinny, knowing now what the future held.

As a night police reporter, I, on the other hand, intended to write for the ages, labored to make a mark as a poet of the mean streets, long on the atmospherics of violent death, writing blowhard Miltonic sentences: "Beneath a spill of mustard light from the broken streetlamp, in a wet gutter choked with last week's racing forms, wearing a pair of mismatched shoes, lay the victim. Stabbed."

Bill Brady would shout across the newsroom: "Wolff! How

about a domicile for the stiff! And maybe an age. And perhaps an approximate time of death. And while you're digging, maybe you can let us know his name?"

This was not meant to be. When I got sent from police headquarters to chase ambulances, and sometimes caught the ambulances, I wouldn't—couldn't—do the next thing, which was to report. The *Post* had a yearlong crusade on its editorial page, exhorting drivers to buckle up. To support this campaign, reporters covering automobile accidents were instructed to learn whether victims had worn seat belts. I chanced on a catastrophe one night in a suburban Virginia emergency room, a mother and father dragged from a movie and brought to that hospital to be told that all three children—eldest fourteen, youngest eight—were dead. The eldest had taken his brother and sister for a spin in the family sedan. I was told to ask the parents whether their children had buckled up. I would ask those parents nothing. A reporter was sent to report, and I was fetched back to the newsroom and told how it was, that maybe this was for the best, maybe I'd get down to that novel after all.

"What novel?" I asked.

"Come on, Wolff," the city editor said, "every cub has a novel."

To tell the truth, I had stolen some time on the job to write a little fiction. Sent to cover the dead Herbert Hoover, lying in state at the Capitol Rotunda (and a stately thing he was in that place at that time, believe me), I had done some creative writing on the response aspect of the sober story. I was instructed to get "responses" from well-wishers passing puzzled by the late personage, and if you put a gun to my head I'll have to admit my college roommates weren't really there that afternoon, shaking their heads, saying, "This was a tragedy; they broke the mold when they made Herbert Hoover; the world is a poorer place without him."

So the city editor imagined fiction to be my destiny; if he had read Philip Roth's landmark *Commentary* essay in 1961, "Writing American Fiction," he'd have known that fact—awful, sensational, numbing, intimidating fact, the fact of the Bomb, the fact of Holocaust—was where it was at. Who better than a city editor to recognize the limitless bazaar of the bizarre *mondo weirdo* every morning? Roth wrote, famously: "The American writer in the middle of the 20th century has his hands full in trying to understand, and then describe, and then make *credible* much of the American reality. It stupefies, it sickens, it infuriates, and finally it is even a kind of embarrassment to one's own meager imagination." Maybe that was why this cub didn't have a novel to take up the slack of imminent unemployment.

I wasn't sacked after all. Ben Bradlee saved my bacon, and made me the *Post*'s book editor. I wrote hundreds of book reviews for the Washington *Post*, five years of book reviews, three a week, many hundreds. Add two years of book reviews twice weekly for *Newsweek*. Let's not forget five years of book reviews, every two weeks, for *New Times*. (Notice how *new* everything was?) A dozen or so for *The New Leader*. Book reviews for *The New Republic*. Have we hit a thousand yet? Oh, and *The New York Times Book Review*, and at the end of this sequence *Esquire*, who found my book reviewing—how may I put this more delicately than *Esquire* put it?—old hat, stale. For fifteen years without a break (except to teach, except to write three novels, essays, a biography and an autobiography), I wrote about writing.

I came to have opinions about writing, though casual opinion-mongering, standing hunch on stilts, is the curse of the critic and teacher, deepening his voice an octave, encouraging his vigorous nod of agreement with his own abruptly contrived axiom, lightning-bolt theorem. My overruling opinion was simple enough: I loved what I liked, and hated what

I didn't, and what I liked took as many forms as what I didn't—verse, short stories, novels, reporting, biography, autobiography, just about everything that came from the heart (as I understood the heart to have a location *close to the bone*), that came to the page felt. Yet eventually I realized I had not had much occasion to love my book reviews.

I look back now at those desiccated, pulpy clips, a quarter-century of them, and my heart leaps up and my heart falls. My God, I was always up to something; did I ever say no? Much of my longer, more arduous criticism was written in the early days for *The New Leader*. Calvin Trillin has boasted that his piecework fee from a similarly high-minded periodical was in the high two figures. *The New Leader* paid me less than a low one-figure wage. And telephoned collect to copyedit the work, and copyedited it skillfully and respectfully, as though what I had written and they would publish was for the ages. It wasn't. For this book reviewer, judgment was everlastingly interim, occasional, hedged by duty. Still the eager-beaver student, I boned up on Haiti, the fall of the Third French Republic, the fall of Algeria (the *Britannica* was my friend), Sir Walter Raleigh and Sir Walter Scott, a world of plenty or a stewpot of trivia, depending on my vantage; my vantage shifted glacially from serenity (*what a nice position I enjoy!*) to instability (*what am I doing here?*).

Not long after I didn't have a novel—not for what Philip Roth lamented but because I had nothing novelistic on my mind—bingo I had one. Looking back twenty-some years at *Bad Debts*, I think not of what that novel was but of what it wasn't: a book review. I recollect how pinched I felt by the chores that burden reviewers. I had the rudimentary sense to understand I was in print principally to listen, and translate. It is tautological to rehearse the review's iron imperatives: its obligation submissively to compress what is complex without dishonoring that book's integrity. Perimeter, the hedge, duty, equity, perspective . . . the high-mindedness (not to mention a limit of 800 words, plus or minus 2) can be suffocating. To progress (as it seemed) from pint-sized to bottomless, from institutional accountability to unimpeded will—that was the ticket! A novel was open-ended, obliged to no deadline, could be fresh, unfair, low-minded, new, mine alone. My early working title for *Bad Debts* was "Accounts Past Due," as though I owed it to an impatiently waiting world.

Remember when Miss Bartlett told us in seventh grade each of our lives would make a great novel, and how next year's homeroom teacher advised us to write only from experience, and how the very next year we were instructed *Never, never, never begin a letter or an essay with the first person singular?* Me, myself and I were tall in the saddle those late sixties; back then writers began many a sentence with "I." In those days, believe me, Willy Loman wouldn't have waited for his widow to insist: *Attention must be paid!* If you don't have a dog, Delmore Schwartz observed, bark for yourself. Mailer's *Advertisements for Myself* was merely the leading-edge zephyr of serial hurricanes of self-inflation, good tempests, fine furies, mischief. The writers I most admired then were working way, way up the register and a full crank of the volume knob beyond the Eric Sevareidish sonorities, all hush and long view, which Tom Wolfe described in his preface to *The New Journalism* as the voice of a "radio announcer at a tennis match." The sixties made a high-voltage, high-pitched corking great ruckus—confrontational, profane, immediate, assertive—and hooray for it.

What, after all, is the pleasurable purpose of this calling if it isn't music? What we agree to call voice? I read comic books for the noise that played in my inner ear, drowning the dead stillness of a rainy rural Connecticut afternoon, and by the time I got to Jim on his raft, Mr. Pickwick on his high horse, by the time I was learning poems and passages by heart, I was there to listen, to ride the riffs and changes, hear the solos. *Listen to me!*

Not every voice a great soliloquy makes, a truth at odds with
the education of many an American writer, with the education
of *this* American writer. At boarding school in England, writing
about Cordelia in the moment when she recognizes how mistaken is her father's measurement of affection, I spent the
greater part of my allotted space telling about a tangled mis-
understanding between my dad and myself: "So I understand
just how Cordelia felt." Of course my teacher wrote "Who
cares?" Of course he was right to write that: always to filter
data through the mesh of personal relevance is to translate
voice into a bully, licensing its tyrannical sway over listener
and speaker alike. Sometimes it should be okay to take facts
in, quietly manipulate them behind an opaque scrim and display them as though the arranger never arranged. It should
be all right to mediate, let another voice speak through your
spirit medium, pretend as a writer not to be front and center
on stage.

But the music that drew me to the club was the virtuoso
solo, the timed bomb of a joke, an unexpected change-up of
delivery, the driving cadence of a long list of nouns, a juxtaposition of the decorous with the vulgar, Hamlet on how to
deliver a speech, Hamlet on Yorick's skull, Bessie Smith singing "Up on Black Mountain" or Edward Hoagland's description of a leopard dropping from a tree on the dog hunting
him, "as heavy as a chunk of iron wrapped in a flag," good
Anglo-Saxon music, tough, weighty, cargoed with consonants.

Americans, having been to so many odd schools to get our
language, want to be heard. I want to. Why? Why write *Kilroy
was here*? Is the declaration selfish, designed to drown out
rival claims? (Kilroy was here and you weren't.) Is it mistakenly
self-important? (You'll surely wish to know Kilroy once stood
where you now stand; please note the plaque.) Is it generous,
an attempt to connect with who comes after? I don't know; I
do know that I return compulsively to the first person singular,
to read and to write.

Stanley Kunitz, wise man, has also written that "you can say anything as long as it is true, but not everything that's true is worth saying. . . . You need not be a victim of your shame, but neither should you boast about it." Of course he's right, and sometimes I feel so powerfully the simple truth of this judgment that I shut up shop, or simply shut up, or throw my voice to a fictional character, or get an exit visa to another world, anyone's life but this one. I know that the self can be too easy a subject, that candor without the restraint of reticence is so much cheap talk. I know that it's as ugly a lie to be disarmingly hard on oneself as to be charmingly easy.

Because: who *does* he think he is? Believe me, I hear the question; believe me, offering a private life to public view, I ask it of myself, and can't answer it otherwise than by blind faith in good faith. If cheap talk won't connect, careful candor might.

But why me, and why now? The practical consequences of this question are on everyday display in Morocco. In the marketplace of Marrakesh, the Place Jamma Al-F'na, are colorful entertainments: juggling, snake-charming, fire-eating. Scattered cross-legged on rugs among competing acts sit an honored cadre of storytellers, waiting to tell stories. If listeners gather—and you will not find in the Place Jamma Al-F'na storytellers for whom listeners do *not* gather—the storyteller begins his tale. When he gets to a good place in the story, he stops. He passes a hat. If listeners like what they have heard, and want to hear more, they give. If coins are put in the hat —a sufficiency of love, let's say—the storyteller continues. If coins are not put in the hat, the storyteller returns to his tale's beginning, and tries again. It's a graphic situation—no?— literary criticism in action: coined hat or hat uncoined. And when he begins anew? What then? What if his listeners wander off? Well, then he tries another line of work, an easier racket, tooting at cobras, eating fire, shutting up.

The Great Santa

What a moody cuss He was. Manic-depressive doesn't tell the half of it; recollect His haphazard nighttime unloading of His Christmas Eve cargo—an Omega wristwatch in my stocking one year, a lump of coal the next. The Great Santa, like circumstance itself, blew hot and cold; He was all caprice, chance, crapshoot. Christmas charts the wobbly course of the American Family Wolff, going to and fro on the continent, up and down the greasy pole. When we had a chimney, He slid down it. When we had a roof, He might land on it. So here's how Christmas past was for us, and how it was was unforeseen.

Upside: of Noël, Yuletide cheer, good will toward man, mistletoe, holly, the wreath, the candy cane, a sugar dust of snow, sleigh bells, Dancer and Prancer and Blixen, Tiny Tim, the roast turkey and cooked goose—Speak, memory! Let me jiggle recall's little glass paperweight and watch the snowflakes spread, settling on an earmuffed cub with wool mittens clipped to his snowsuit; he's dragging a sled. A blue spruce is tied to the sled, and a collie pup, Shep, racing circles around the boy and the boy's freight, buries his muzzle in the powdery flakes. Mom and Dad are giggling, tossing loosely packed, talcumy snowballs at each other. In yonder red barn-boarded farmhouse (with all modern appliances, copper pipes and wired to code), carolers are rehearsing. Mom and Dad and Shep and little Jeffie pause to cock an ear to "Hark, the Herald Angels Sing" and "Good King Wenceslas." Dad—not one teensy bit tipsy—pours hot buttered rum from a battered stainless thermos; the good cheer steams atmospherically from a mug.

"Merry Christmas, dear," he says.

"And Merry Christmas to you, honey," says Mom, her eyes misting from a near-excess of warm feeling.

And they, in unison, "Merry Christmas, Jeff."

Shep, wagging his tail, barks.

Utterly allegorical, right off memory's Hallmark card. Let me deal from a straight deck. My mother was a lapsed Irish Catholic, my father an unacknowledging Jew, the son of an atheist. My mother was as pretty as a picture, with dreamy blue eyes and an appetite for adventure. My father was bright, quick, musical, charming, a wonderful storyteller. He was also a bullshit artist who doctored his bloodline and fabricated his *curriculum vitae*, becoming the man he felt he should have been rather than the man his history had made. I heard it said of him (at an age when I thought the reference was to pets) that he could weave a pussy out of steel wool. His chosen field of work was aircraft engineering, and he was good at it, bogus academic degrees notwithstanding. Such a family as mine is not designed for constancy, but my single persistent expectation growing up was that Christmas would, by Jesus, be celebrated. My father, who bought on credit, liked to treat himself well, but he relished giving even more than getting.

1941: Farmington, Connecticut—Early December at the Elm Tree Inn. For gift-oriented celebrants of the Christ's birthday these weeks pre-Christmas are more memorable than those post-. So it is that I recall December 7 so clearly. Father is in England, selling P-51s, Mustangs, to the British, Lend-Lease. Mother and I have been batting aimlessly around the country in a new Packard convertible, and this morning she is in the bathtub and I am listening to the radio. I give her the news through the bathroom door that the Japanese have bombed Pearl Harbor. I am four; she doesn't believe me, but in the excitement of the moment forgets to remove from the bathtub the gift she has been test-driving under the suds, a windup submarine bought at the toy store F. A. O. Schwarz, which is, like the rest of America, on a war footing. I remember this because of the sub, a well-made and satisfying contraption, my first memory provoked by pleasure rather than by having a heavy Packard door shut on my thumb.

*

1944: Birmingham, Alabama—In an oversized, columned and ersatz antebellum house across the golf course from the Mountain Brook Country Club, I'm hanging around the edges of a Christmas Eve party of airplane designers, draftsmen, test pilots, model-makers, gunsmiths, expediters, grease monkeys— can-do men and women, performers. This is a company party; my dad is chief engineer of an airplane modification enterprise that installs refined bombsights, ordnance, armor, navigational equipment. The improved B-17 Flying Fortresses and B-24 Liberators and (later) B-29 Super Fortresses will be returned by ferry pilots to India or Guam or England, wherever the

---

* Note to the reader: I assay my experience of the Holy Birthday according to the convention established by Michelin in its judgment of eating and sightseeing and resting facilities. The quality and quantity of gifts received (by me) is bestowed one to four Santas. What I call quality of life (was an edible holiday feast served in a timely manner? did we live in a house with a fireplace? with a separate bedroom for me? was snow on the ground? was the snow clean? was Daddy shitfaced?), I rate with Frosty the Snowman (or men), one to four.

action's hot. In war, time is life, and the pressure on these improvers to perform is measurable even to a youngling; there's nervous static in this room. The crowd's impatient, noisy and raffish, and my father's in their midst making them laugh. He's telling stories I don't understand; I've just turned seven. I'm especially attracted to this one of our many house-guests. He's a carrier-based dive-bombing pilot who was shot down over Rabal and escaped the evil, dread Nips by wooden raft. Now he's a ferry pilot, delivering bombers from Birmingham to the Pacific Theater. He's got up as Santa Claus, the skinny devil. "Ho, ho, ho, my young flyboy. And what would you like to find under the tree tomorrow morning?" I think I still believe in the second-story man and chimney sweep, but I know who this is under the beard, wearing dark glasses, drinking Fish House Punch through a bent glass straw. The pilot's face, awfully burned, has been poorly re-paired; that face is the first strangeness I have come to take for granted. His face isn't what interests me. What interests me is his railroad empire of HO-gauge model trains he has set up in our basement. What a dream of a world he has contrived: Alpine villages with sheep and goats and cows by the tracks; tunnels, city terminals, fantastic loopy crossovers so intricately knotted that I can't credit the hairbreadth escape of the tightly timed trains vying for right-of-way. Oh, the lo-comotives whistle, blow steam. So what do I hope to find under the tree tomorrow? Puh-leeze. I remember that night, after the party, spying atavistically from the landing. ("I Saw Mommy Kissing Santy Claus"? Not yet, not this Christmas. My mother tonight looks swell in an Auxiliary Red Cross uni-form, nipped at the waist, a dove-gray worsted flattering to her curly blond hair.) I witness the tinkerers and wizards of electronics and hydraulics defeated by *my* little Lionel and its single, symmetrical oval, until they aren't, until they puzzle it out. I remember too the next morning when some hungover bravos of last night's revels, horsing around with my own toy train, pour too many watts into its transformer, till it derails. But what I value of this memory is not the electric train but an atmosphere of competence in the house where I live. This is not an illusion. Surrounding me everyone is busy, working and having fun. It is comforting to have people milling around with matters of more moment than Christmas and me on their minds. I am not starved for attention or affection. I am already overfed on attention, fat on affection.

1945: New York City—*Pacem in terris*, alas for the Wolffs. Dad's been sacked. Now I've got a baby brother, cute as a pin, but his diapers are washed in the toilet we share with a Dane (who fills the icebox with his stash, a block of dope as big as his head—personal use only), and with a turbaned Sikh jazz freak, and with the Dane's wife, who's Everyman's friend (but not Everywoman's, not my mom's—the diapers, I guess); she's a la-di-da childhood pal of my dad's and now an editor of the *Daily Worker*. The tenement ménage is a walk-up two-bedroom railroad flat on East Fifty-seventh, under the rumbling shadow of the Third Avenue El. Theatrically squalid, a crib—a damned manger, for Christ's sake. Dad looks for work, sort of, and drinks Black Horse Ale, paid for by the trust-fund Communist. Christmas Eve they listen to 78s of Fats Navarro and Bird and Pres. "Silent Night" my ass! There's a squabble among the communards, sparked by obscure tinder, division of labor. As I now understand, the to-eaches (from the trust fund) got out of synch with the from-eaches (to the Wolffs). The dispute's fueled by my father's prudish maledictions against reefer (which the flat-sharers call Mary Jane). Could

Dad have already caught on to the concept of ambient smoke? Whatever, the fight spills over; I get my first whipping ever for eavesdropping through the door. What door? I don't know yet but I'll know soon how to listen for the special music of my father's voice when spirits take him, when good cheer glooms him, when the o'er-brimming wassail cup drowns his sweetness. It's a trombonish sound, whiny but deep, long-playing, as welcome as an announcement from Herod that he's been thinking about babies.

(I got Lincoln Logs)

[No Frosties]

1946: Saybrook, Connecticut—Ground-zero bottomed-out misery. My father, hero of the Super Fortress soup-up center, is engaged in the manufacture of a fishing device he has co-invented and co-patented with another childhood friend, a would-be capitalist. The thingamajig is a red flag at the end of a steel spring mounted on a balsa square which floats on the surface of the water. From this bobbing platform depend fishing line, sinker, bait, hook. When the fish bites (which it doesn't), the flag unsprings (which it doesn't). A modification calls for the end of the flag rod to ring a bell, but this makes the gizmo top-heavy, and it capsizes. As I discover when the ice melts a little on the Connecticut River, where I am the invention's test pilot. We live in two tiny rooms of a boardinghouse, a bona-fide fleabag with genuine fleas. Our fellow tenants are old geezers limping down the home stretch; they walk their towel racks down the narrow, dark hallways, whispering our name: "Have the Wolffs paid their rent yet? I bet the Wolffs haven't paid their re-yent yet. Throw the bums out in the snow, they haven't paid their ray-yent. Why should we have to pay our rent when the Wolffs haven't paid their rahyay-ent yet? They never pay their rent, the Wolffs . . ."

[No Santas]
[No Frosties]

1947: Old Lyme, Connecticut—Dad got a job, "bought" a farmhouse (with the co-signature on the mortgage deed of another childhood well-to-do but ne'er-did-well). Noël will ne'er seem prettier. Here's the iconographic Yuletide scene, the Holy Birthday avatar. Here's the collie Shep, the snow, the wool mackinaw, the earmuffs, the pretty country lane. Here's the sled. Here's the sun low in the morning's cobalt sky after a sixteen-inch fall of fresh powder. Here I'm belly-down on the new Flexible Flyer at the top of Gin Mill Lane, about to shove off. Here Dad says don't do this, don't go there, don't especially put your tongue against that metal tie-rod. The metal tie-rod tastes okay at first, till I pull my tongue away. The blood tastes salty. It looks pretty, those little rubies set against white. Oh my, another screwed-up Christmas morning, a Wolff Xmas orthodoxy. The night before had started out okay, till Dad fell into the tree, after the chimney fire burned out, after eating the well-done meat. Doesn't every-one cook steak in the fireplace? Over logs? Soaked in gasoline?

(Before Christmas Eve dinner)

(Before the sled)

[No Frosties]   (In Dr. Von Glaun's office)

1948: Old Lyme, Connecticut—Singing "O Come, All Ye Faithful" in Miss Champion's fifth-grade homeroom, standing behind M———t D—n, kissing like a sneak thief her copper hair, growing a micro-boner in my cuffed blue jeans —will I burn in hell, oh ye faithful? "Angels We Have Heard on High." I'll say. I buy her older brother a Gilbert chemistry set. I've never exchanged a word with him, but I spend my Christmas allowance on a Gilbert chemistry set. I deliver it to him in sixth grade, tell him to tell her to love me. Okay, okay, what would you have done?

Dad consoles me in the bar of New London's Mohegan Hotel, where we celebrate having bought the best tree ever. He's up, high. Every year, every tree, best tree ever. Sweet calculus, who can fault it? The bartender misspeaks, calls Dad "baldy" or "buddy" or "pal" or "Duke," which is his name. It doesn't matter what the bartender calls him or says. At a certain point that I can now recognize, the score calls for the trombone. His voice slides down the scale, and we leave the bar—or, rather, we are asked to leave. Someone—bartender or Daddy—says, "I don't have to listen to that shit on Christmas Eve." Such words are being spoken in bars up and down the Christian world on this holy night. "Fuck you, buddy, and the horse you rode in on." Driving home in the '37 Ford station wagon, the old man shows me how to steer out of a skid, almost. Our hides are okay, and we wait in the cold front seat, in the shallow ditch, for the tow truck called by the merry Christmasers whose ditch it is, who have managed so to incense my father (with their "patronizing" invitation to have a seat and wait in their warm living room till the truck comes) that he "fuck-you"s them . . . While my dad has a free moment with me, he shares some observations he's recently made. He stares at me as though he's never noticed me before, and I think then maybe he hasn't. I don't feel it coming, this time. From tonight on I'll never not feel it coming, when I hear the trombone tuning. "Well, you're really something, aren't you? You're quite a number, don't you know? You never weary of kicking me in the ass, do you? You're bleeding me white. You're really something, aren't you?" (*Repeat chorus.*)

But: next morning there are sacksful of stuff. Stuffed stocking hanging from the mantel, stuffed clumsily wrapped boxes, heavy with promise, an Erector set, a Gilbert "Atomic" chemistry set in a metal traveling case, stuffed turkey with walnut stuffing. Also: apologies, let me make it up to you, how would you like a Raleigh bicycle, a Remington single-shot .22? I say I'd like them fine.

Christmas was my father's specialty season: it sanctioned impulse buying, excess, radical behavior, time out from work, lies. At Christmas I had my first inkling how dearly my father loved to lie. "Oh, we're so broke!" (This was true.) "Oh, please understand, there can't be any presents this year." Sure. The only doubt was, where had he hid them? Christmas called for deceit right down the line: bogus information on the charge-account application, a sham pre-inventory of the cornucopia that awaited discovery under the tree, a misleading presentation of the booty (camera wrapped in a box suited for a basketball). And, of course, the gifts were hidden. My mother always hid them on the top shelf of her closet, in hatboxes. My father went to extreme ends to protect his secrets: a drug mule couldn't take greater pains. I never found what he had stashed. Forget the attic, the mud-floored cellar. In Old Lyme I fished in an abandoned well, looking for the loot. I levered a manhole cover off our cesspool. Wherever the goods were, I wasn't.

1949: Sarasota, Florida—Father is in Istanbul, on the lam
from the creditors who paid for our redone farmhouse, his
sports car, my Christmas presents. He has been working the
Bazaar; he entrusts a flow of exotic oddities to my mother's
safekeeping. My mother, brother and I—also in flight from
those creditors—live in a moist, beaverboarded cabin on
Siesta Key. The floorboard splinters can penetrate thick-
soled black Keds. The tap water stinks of sulphur. There's a
storeroom back of the hovel, and this is where the stuff from
Turkey is stored. What will fit in hatboxes is in hatboxes, of
course. The ceremonial Turkish sword is under a blanket. Or
its hilt is. About a foot of blade is in plain sight. This is careless
hiding; like a clock striking thirteen, such desultory deception
upsets my sense of the order of things and makes me a little
crazy. My pathology expresses itself in unintended parody of
my old man's overextended conduct. I stockpile my allowance,
steal change and small bills from my mom's purse. I study the
Sears catalogue, accumulate Christmas presents for my
mother. These are of such a stunning inappropriateness—a
sun hat, costume jewelry, a heavy wool blanket, a cheapjack
redwood chest in which to hide the tawdry crap—that even
then I must have known this venture was bent. In downtown
Sarasota—where I cruise for goods to half-hide from my
mother, merchandise to surprise her with, stun her, overwhelm
her—the sun blazes unwholesomely. Forget snow, we're
greased with Coppertone. Tin stars and rubber angels droop
forlornly from the overhead phone lines and I hum along to
"Rudolph the Red-Nosed Reindeer" and "Frosty the Snowman." (Has "Jingle Bell Rock" been composed yet? If so, it
too.) For Mom, I steal a Christmas card, another icon, a
fuzzy simulacrum of our Old Lyme *tableau vivant* (snow,
pup, tyke, sled, perfect little tree). It is ornate, and stinks of
lavender cologne. "Too much of a muchness," in the oft-
repeated formulation of my stepmother, who will replace my

mother next year. My rich stepmother, by Santa! My at-first-
generous stepmother. My elderly stepmother. My under-
certain - misapprehensions - about - my - father's - history - and -
prospects stepmother.

1952: Boston—Holy smoke, a suite at the Ritz-Carlton. I've
got a privileged, unimpeded view of Boston Public Garden.
We dine in the second-floor dining room. A dinner-jacketed
and ball-gowned double quartet carols us with "God Rest Ye
Merry, Gentlemen" and "Away in a Manger." Master Wolff
wears rather a handsome wool suit. It's a well-made garment,
the wool neither too charcoalish nor too pale, the tailoring
unobtrusively unpinched at the waist, the trousers unpleated
(but cuffed, of course), the ensemble unwaistcoated. It shows
off to advantage my necktie, deep purple with the gold arms
of The Choate School, *quai sivi bona tibi*, we seeke to do thee
goode, which I have already learned to translate "we seek to
do thee: good." Oh-oh. My father and stepmother have selected my new wool suit on Newbury Street from Brooks Brothers, where a Chesterfield coat has been exhibited in a display
window, with snowflakes applied to its rich wool shoulders
and rich velvet collar. "It looks like dandruff," I'd said. Oh
heavens, this kind of thing is about to become a problem. Just
what Christmas needs, another wisenheimer.

I fly to Sarasota to visit my mother. She works in a Dairy
Queen. The night after Christmas her middle-aged boyfriend
tries to break down the tiny basement apartment's only door,
to get at her. We sit in silence, pretending not to be there. My
mother gives me an ivory plastic table radio with a dial lit as

mystery green as the middle depths of a tropical sea. Getting
into my father's new Jaguar at Boston airport, I drop this, and
it breaks. My father promises to replace it with a better radio.
This, for a wonder, does not console me.

(Sarasota)

(Boston)

[No Frosties]   (Sarasota)

1954: The Choate School; Wallingford, Connecticut—The
evening before vacation begins, in the Hill House dining hall,
the Reverend Seymour St. John intones grace most gracefully,
with an air of assurance that what we are about to eat is not
one calorie less than we deserve; we tuck into roast beef with
Yorkshire pudding, fruitcake and plum pudding afterward.
Then we go to chapel. I sing baritone in the choir, and put
my whole heart into Handel's "Hallelujah" Chorus. After
Christmas, back in my room, packing for the three-week jam-
boree ahead, I essay to entertain my roommate. Now, at last,
I wasn't born yesterday, I'm wise to the hustle. I monologue
him with a routine I've practiced on myself, my best audience:
"Face it, we're talking about a plug-ugly baby, aren't we? Can
we agree on this much? Tinted, rouged, lipsticked, as pink as
a boiled ham, pudgy little tits. Jesus! Even the masters—I don't
know, Bellini, Tintoretto, Rubens, all those—couldn't make
that boy cute. *Putti*, no? Doesn't even have a baby face! Frown-
ing like a wrinkled old codger. And why should His Little Self
be merry? How about those gifts? *Caramba, Kings, just what
I've always wanted. Frankincense! Myrrh!* I mean, do you know
what myrrh is? It's a spiny shrub, I looked it up. Merry Christmas! And how about those carols, blaring from loudspeakers

and rasping tinnily from the vents of elevators, as welcome as 'Happy Birthday' at the next table in an expensive restaurant. And tinsel strung from phone poles, and the Salvation Army putting the arm on you, and Santa Claus darting into an alley to take a hit off a pint bottle in a paper bag before he robs the bank of its Christmas Club deposits. No wonder it's the suicide season."

My roommate says: "Huh?"

I confuse him, confound myself, because I'm as soft as a baby too. What I'm soft for is a soft, satiny back beneath my sweaty hand at a fancy-dress ball. A soft breast against my fluttery heart. Soft snow falling past the softly lit streetlamps of Park Avenue, looking from uptown down, to Grand Central. A Checker cab sliding softly past the Central Park South entrance to the Plaza, where I'm about to fox-trot to waltz time (because my stepmother came along too late to have me educated at dancing school, but just in time to lever me onto The List). I'm on The List! I get invited to the Hols, Cols, Gets & Mets (Holiday Ball, Collegiate Dance, Get Togethers, Metropolitan Ball). I've managed, against all odds, to become a junior popinjay, parlor snake, tailor's dummy. I'm training my pipes to drawl Long Island lockjaw. I meet the girl whom I escort Under the Clock at the Biltmore, where we show off our glad rags. I leave after the dance with another, and take her to Jimmy Ryan's, where Wilbur and Sidney DeParis and their Dixieland Ramblers play "O Tannenbaum," Oh, Christmas Tree. I weep like a baby at the beauty of it all, the satin dresses, satin notched collar on my dinner jacket, satin breasts. At the fresh green Christmas-tree smell. I weep from nostalgia even before feeling the feeling that provokes nostalgia. The onset of nostalgia is a dire symptom: I'm now less a creature acted upon than an actor. With the onset of nostalgia I begin to accumulate a history, can contrast time was to time is. I'm responsible; gifts come not from Santa's little helpers but from

my own workshop. I'm an existentialist. Time flies: I'm growing old before I grow up. Boo hoo.

No Santas (He was off the case now. The only gift on
    my wish list was getting laid for free. Santa didn't read
    obscene mail.)
Frosties galore

The Sick Man of Europe

The Making of *Little Mary Sunshine*

It would be neat to claim I played Billy Jester, but in fact
I was just a forest ranger, Hank, in the chorus, Jester's
sidekick. I brought to my part a decent baritone voice and
peppy want-to. This was the spring musical at Robert College,
merry *Little Mary Sunshine*. A cynic might have called the
wholesome confection campy, if camp had been around in
1963. How did it go? Finishing-school maidens got sort of lost
in the woods, among Injuns, and the forest rangers sort of
calmed them and this led to low-key lovey-dovey. Sweet was
the ruling principle. In a note to his libretto, Rick Besoyan
warned would-be directors, "It is absolutely essential to the
success of the musical that it should be played with the most
warmhearted earnestness." A YOUNG LADY delivers the pro-
logue: "Hello: I'd like to take you back to a time when the
world was much more simple than ours is today. For instance,
good meant good, bad meant bad, virtue was all . . ."

I had only one line: during a bit of business with a camera
on a tripod, I was to instruct the hoopskirted maidens to say
"cheese." This evening was a closed dress rehearsal; my stutter
was wrestling the little speech to a draw—"s-s-s-s-s-ay
chuh-chuh-chuh-chuh-Camembert"—when I became aware
of a figure coming forward out of the darkness at the back of
the auditorium. The maidens were trilling a little tune, tra-la,

and then their song trailed off, and I squinted into the gloom.

"You've been fucking my wife!" The fellow waved a sidearm, a Webley service revolver, with its thong around his wrist. "You've been fucking my wife!" I dove to the stage. So did the wife in question. So did another forest ranger. And another. As many rangers as acted and sang in *Little Mary Sunshine* dropped like tenpins to the stage. A shot rang—as they say in stage directions—out. Before I was shot dead in Istanbul, my life flashed—as they show in movies—before my eyes.

The Socratic Method

Less than two years before, I had graduated from Princeton with a degree in English and a high degree of certainty in my high seriousness as a scholar and pedagogue. I came to Byzantium for exotic novelty and to teach. I could say I had chosen a calling as a teacher to evade the draft, but this would tell only the least portion of the truth. In fact, I saw myself as a missionary, crusading to Asia Minor to light a row of candles, the great works of Western Letters agreeable to the New Critics, whose apt and ardent student I was. (When I got word of my job at Robert College, where my Princeton adviser, Richard Blackmur, had lectured, I naturally sought advice. "Do not on any account have sexual congress with a Turkish melon," Blackmur advised. "It puts the foreskin in jeopardy.")

Robert College, eight miles from Istanbul and built into the ramparts of Bebek, overlooking Asia and the Bosporus, founded in 1863 by Cyrus Hamlin, an American missionary who had washed clothes for Florence Nightingale's hospital in Üsküdar, was the oldest American educational institution abroad. (*Was* because in 1971 it was returned to xenophobic Turks and renamed Bogaziçi Universitesi.) Instruction was in English, and most of the students were cosmopolitan Turks, together with students from ethnic minorities—Jews, Greeks and Armenians—whose parents cherished the visible sign of wealth and social position embodied in a degree from Robert College. During my first year, I was to teach in Robert Academy, a boys' secondary school on the campus of the college. Several of my colleagues were young, and a disproportionate number had been undergraduates at Princeton, where the headmaster of Robert Academy had studied. By an odd juxtaposition of circumstances, my father had lived and worked in Istanbul in the late 1940s, when I was living with my mother and brother in Florida, not quite a teen, easily impressed by the sword, Turkish harem slippers and fez he sent home at Christmas.

For romance, mystery, murky light, spiced and sour scents, novelty, menace, relentless beauty—nothing has compared. I fell in love, and falling in love with Istanbul was like falling in love with a whore, and in Istanbul I did that too. The city was decadent and worn; to Istanbul, everything had happened. Among its violent tourists had been Arabs, Huns, Tatars, Goths, Vlachs, Crusaders.

We crusaders on the faculty lived scattered around a hill (which I learned to call The Hill) in college housing, some grand indeed—Victorian houses with huge living rooms and formal gardens. My apartment had an unobstructed view of the Bosporus, and my first night in Turkey I was kept awake by ferries whistling as they steamed from the Golden Horn to the Black Sea, and by nightingales singing in the umbrella pines and cedars outside my window.

A couple of days after flying from New York to Turkey, the morning after the first in an exhausting succession of faculty parties uncompromising in their voluptuary and rakehell excess, I sat in the study of the highest academic officer of Robert College; I had been summoned to be welcomed to my first regular job, the calling for which my training and ambition had prepared me. The sturdy Protestant precepts of the college were given piquant expression by the drink I was offered, *çay*, tea served in a little hourglass shot glass. I felt abstracted: the long flight to an exotic setting, last evening's bender, this morning's awful hangover. The Dean made a steeple with his fingers; he cleared his throat; he looked directly at me; he sniffed the air; he cleared his throat again. We sat. He gestured toward the tea. I shook my head. We sat.

I said, "Sir, I'm glad to be at Robert College."

"Well," he said. "Well. This is the way of it: what you drink, how much, with whom—that is your business. What you teach, your opinions in the classroom—your department. Whether you teach, whether or not you appear at the appointed hour and in the appointed classroom—my department. Very. My bailiwick. Sexual preferences and energy—your affair. Sexual union with students—mine . . ." I cleared my throat now because, hang on just a New York minute here, my students were going to be men. Boys! Better to curse the darkness! The Dean welcoming me to my first teaching job was still speaking. ". . . and if I sack you, and believe you me I'd have no hesitation to sack you, there's no place beneath this place to which to fall. From this depth. Don't test the truth of my edict; welcome to Robert College."

If I got an odd greeting, it was no odder than the education I imposed on my students, who ran in age from sixteen to twenty. I was warned that many among them were cunning and rowdy, that they'd cheat me blind, that they'd hunt for the chink in my armor and exploit it mercilessly. In short, except for the cheating part, that they were schoolboys after my own heart. I heard horror stories about a teacher who had been laughed out of the country, about another who had pushed a wise guy out a second-story window. The boys didn't trouble me; I was indifferent to my students' esteem, and they seemed to like this. I found them as tame as pups, and I taught them whatever tricks I wished to teach them. May Allah be my witness, I press-ganged those young Turks into the ranks of the New Criticism.

During the three years they were our students, the boys were subjected to a course in literature that went from *Job, Book of* to *Jarrell, Randall*. We used a three-volume anthology of world literature, condensed as to contents and typography, densely printed on tissue paper. From this horn of plenty we assigned what whim or dogma dictated. Each year's class numbered more or less a hundred boys, and early every week the class would gather to be lectured by one of us. My colleague David Leeming was Professor Mythology: he lectured on the Greeks and the Icelandics. Charlie Klopp had spent a summer in Perugia: he did Dante and Machiavelli. I gave the guys the latest on Pope, Coleridge's *Biographia Literaria*, Arnold, Yeats, Eliot and Stevens. I've got some of my lecture notes before me, but candor has its bounds. Let me say this: there are a quantity of Turkish engineers broadcasting among their Near Eastern friends odd and insubstantial notions about what William Empson remarked to I. A. Richards about John Donne's conceits.

Using the lectures as points of reference, we met later each week in small discussion groups; in my discussion group all listened to one discuss, and the one was me, which was probably why I got along well with my students, who could never get in a word edgewise. Since I never gave them cause or opportunity to speak, how could I have known if they were contemptuous or insolent?

In discussion groups I'd ask Hasan Günzel: "What thread connects Goldsmith's 'Comparison Between Sentimental and Laughing Comedy' with Schiller's 'On Simple and Sentimental Poetry'?" Hasan, a deer caught by a jacklight, would stare at me. "Very good," I'd say. "Capital! I know what you're thinking, and agree entirely! Art in its highest form requires a certain . . . how should I phrase this, Seyit? How indeed, you may rejoin; well, let me venture, Halil, a certain . . . *expansiveness* of fancy. Just so!" I was a china shop in a bull corral.

Payday

I got less than two thousand a year, but in the early 1960s that was enough to finance winter, spring and summer holidays in Western Europe. In addition to my apartment and good meals in a faculty dining room, I also got an allowance in Turkish lira meant to cover incidentals and the odd restaurant meal. It was the custom among the faculty to take this money, paid in cash the first Friday of every month, Downtown. I say it was the custom of "the faculty"—I should amend this: the dissolute cohort to which I belonged comprised no more than ninety-seven percent of the American and English males teaching at Robert Academy and Robert College. Two percent were recluses and moral refugees hiding from the world, the law or themselves; perhaps as many as one percent were virtuous and moderate.

We'd gather in small groups at the bottom of The Hill, along the edge of the Bosporus near the castle Rumeli Hisar, at a dolmuş stop. Dolmuş means "stuffed," and these jitneys, big old florid tail-finned DeSotos and Hudsons, were overburdened with passengers picked up from stops along the route from the Black Sea to Taksim Square, the center of Istanbul's new quarter. The fare was cheap, the ride raucous with syrupy

Turkish love music sung in a wailing falsetto, played at distorting volume on portable 45-rpm phonographs by the drivers, who competed with one another for the flagrant flash of their overdecorated and overequipped pink-and-chartreuse taxis, for their audacity at the wheel, for their fighter-pilot ice-water nerves, for the excessive droop of their mustaches.

First stop was the Park Hotel, where my father had lived. From the hilltop of Pera the terrace had a commanding view of onion domes and minarets needling the smoky blue air and of Seraglio Point down in the Golden Horn and in all directions of water busy with shipping. The Park was favored by Western residents and spies, which is a redundancy because all Western residents, not excluding clergy and certainly not excluding teachers, were assumed to be spies. That I was not a spy was a discouraging index of the low degree of trust invested in me by the deans at Princeton, who routinely recommended foreign-bound graduates to the CIA. At the Park my friends and I would prime the pump with rakí, a licorice-based clear liquor, kin to Pernod and anís and ouzo, mixed with ice and water, which turns it buttermilk-yellow. Here we'd watch the sun set over the city, and hear amplified an inspired whine, a muezzin's call to prayers.

Next was a manageable walk to Taksim Square and along Cümhuriyet Caddesi to the Divan Oteli, where I might have my hair cut, beard trimmed, shoes shined. The Divan was small and luxurious in a less-is-more manner. Its cozy bar was favored by the wealthy and amiable Turkish intelligentsia, newspaper editors, bankers, importers, publishers and cosmopolitan layabouts educated at one of two English universities. I've never seen cigarettes smoked with such enthusiasm as they were smoked by Turks in that bar: the men's fingers were bright orange from tar, and the jokes and gossip in French and German and English were delivered hoarse-voiced, with hacking laughter.

I remember my first visit: Adnan Menderes, the increasingly despotic Premier who had been arrested several months earlier, was about to be hanged. Press censorship was tight, but the barflies at the Divan spoke freely about Menderes's coming execution, how excited he must be—how thrilled, really—how he'd been practicing for years by hanging himself with a silk stocking. I confessed bewilderment; the bartender regarded me with astonishment. Did I mean to leave the impression I had never hanged myself just a little? Not even for fun?

More rakí here, unless a Turk at the bar with a son studying at Robert College decided to buy a round of Johnny Walker Red Label for the indigent professors. I liked the Divan because it was the stopover for flight crews aboard KLM and BEA and SAS. I'd met a couple of stewardesses on the SAS flight that brought me to Istanbul, Finn sisters who didn't seem to compare notes, unless they did; they'd phone when they came to town, unless they didn't phone because they'd phoned someone else, but that was okay too, because they'd introduced me to other stewardesses, and for me—a survivor of what Richard Pryor has called The Great Pussy Drought of the Fifties—I didn't see how circumstance could have dealt me a better hand. We lived; we lived!

After barbering and sipping, our ragtag gang, less a couple of teachers who'd fallen from the pack for lack of stamina, plus a couple of pals gathered from the terrace of the Park and the bar of the Divan, made its way down crowded, narrow Istiklal Caddesi, noisy and raffish despite the old hospitals and libraries and embassy buildings in use before the capital moved to Ankara. The street attacked the senses: the Art Nouveau ironwork balconies were rusting out, and the buildings were falling in on themselves. Stray cats and dogs, thin to the bone, sulked in doorways. In the Ottoman days of empire, this main drag was known as the Grand Rue de Pera, and branching off it were alleys with fanciful names: Street of the Gate of the

Thumb, and Street of the Pine-Gum Tree. Along the way we'd stop for refreshments at the café attached to an art cinema, where bohemian intellectuals—painters and poets and movie directors and actors, dressed a hundred percent in black—drank black coffee. We Americans seemed always welcome in Turkey; American books and movies and clothes and cars and money and slang engaged the hip, and our mastery of nuclear fission engaged the warlike working-class Turks. Everyone hated the neighboring Soviets, so for that too we were celebrated. An American could grow spoiled in Istanbul.

Our destination was Rejans, also called The Old Russian Restaurant, run by three or four ancient sisters also dressed invariably in black, upstairs in a rickety wood building near the Fish Market and Galatasaray Square. Rejans had been memorialized in an early variant of "The Snows of Kilimanjaro," that soap opera in which Hemingway relentlessly misspelled all Turkish place-names. This was my favorite restaurant in Istanbul, which meant then it was my favorite restaurant anywhere. High-ceilinged, with posters on the grimy walls, the tables set far apart and covered with heavy cloth, there was nothing pretty or delicate about the place. I must have eaten thirty or forty dinners there, and I never had a bad time at Rejans. I invariably ate the same things: borscht, cold fish with mayonnaise, beef Stroganoff and—when they were in season—strawberries Chantilly. I don't order any of these dishes anymore, because Rejans, like the Turks, spoiled me. The Russian sisters made their own vodka. The state kept a monopoly on cigarettes and alcohol, and while the wine was excellent, and the beer was excellent, and the rakí was rakí, Turkish vodka was awful, awful, awful. We all made our own from 180-proof grain alcohol. This we'd boil and strain and dilute, according to various home recipes, bringing it down to 50 or 60 proof, making it barely suitable for mixing with juice or tonic. The sisters at Rejans, working with the same raw material, worked alchemy; they served their vodka chilled and straight in silver thimbles, and none smoother anywhere ever, with a hint of the Seville oranges they were rumored to grow for no reason other than to impart to their vodka a hint of Seville orange.

Well, now it was time to have some fun, drink a drink. For this we went to the Flower Passage, the courtyard of a building built to billet the Janissaries, elite troops of the sultans during the time of the Ottoman Empire. We meandered among fruit stands equipped with polished brass scales and fastidious arrangements of brass weights, found our way to a gallery of beer stalls where we sat at slate tables on high stools backed with cane, their seats worn smooth by the rub of workingmen's corduroy and whipcord. Or we stood beneath struggling black fan blades, at tables of common wood so many times varnished that the grain had disappeared beneath the shellac's dark luster. The table was pleasing to lean against, almost soft. Here we drank draft ale or dark beer in a quantity known as an Argentine, sometimes smoothed with a shot of vodka, often— too often—taken with a rakí chaser. The breweries had been designed and built by the Germans during World War I to supply the Kaiser's Janissaries with Bavarian pilsener, and to hell with the Germans, but they did know how to build a brewery that could make a beer a thirsty schoolteacher was happy to drink. We'd drink the beer in iced glasses as capacious as flower vases, and at each table fresh flowers were arranged in heavy beer mugs. We'd continue to eat, almonds and little meatballs and skewered spiced mutton grilled on charcoal braziers set within reach outside the big open windows, stuffed mussels and prawns from the Fish Market next door; the beer stalls were for the pleasure of the workers who stocked and serviced the Fish Market and the Flower Market; customers wore no neckties, and their shirts buttoned all the way up; the beer stalls were raucous with the static and hysteria of a radio broadcast of a football match. Inside were fights, brief but fierce. Outside, men strolled like baby brothers hand in hand, itinerant musicians played little steam calliopes, jugglers juggled, acrobats walked on their hands, magicians attempted tricks with transparent clumsiness that we nevertheless applauded, vendors sold lottery tickets and curiosities. I bought a plastic windmill and a helium balloon in the rough likeness of a cat. (I could have selected from the peddler's bouquet a mouse to go with it.)

After the Flower Passage, our paths divided. Some of my friends went to the Turkish baths, which were not necessarily in business to serve men looking for what some of my friends sought, but which were also not in business to deny what some of my friends sought. For "some of my friends" read "fifty percent, about." Robert College was a haven for or, depending on one's vantage, a nest of homosexuals. At about the time these friends would grow restless, and declare an intention to "round up some *boeuf*," I'd grow restless and declare my intention to go to the nightclubs.

There was a red-light district near the Flower Market, and I knew how to find my way to it, but my students patronized the whorehouses and reluctantly I had found the inner dignity to honor the bedrock decorum of my vocation; I had decreed the whores off limits to Meester Wolff. Bar girls were a different breed, of course, and I'd take my balloon cat and plastic windmill down an alley (Street of the Slave's Son) off Istiklal Caddesi to a hole in the wall lit fancifully by neon: Meksim or— my favorite—Fooles Bercer (pronounce the "c" as a soft "g," as in *Bergère*). The Istanbul Follies employed an entertainer, Veilah, and I loved her. She entertained me by letting me tell her how much and in what ways I loved her, and by telling me she loved me too, and by encouraging me to celebrate our abiding love with Turkish pink champagne. Veilah would promise to meet me after closing on a street corner to which she directed me with elaborate maps drawn on the backs of napkins. She spoke bar English and I spoke bar Turkish. We must have lost our way in the translation, because I'd stand on the slick cobbles of a street corner from 4 a.m. till dawn, smelling piss seep through the gutters, my heart beating passionately, and then it would be breakfasttime and Veilah would still be searching the city for me, without luck. (You can't know what I was up against, learning to speak her language. The first phrase book I bought taught me this: if I could just manage to say "*Sizden bir ricam var,*" I would have conveyed to my darling "I have a request to do you," or, as the language text renders it phonetically, "Ay hev a rikuest to du yu." On the other hand, I might say, "*Yüzümü kestiniz, kaniyor,*" and Veilah would understand me to have remarked, "You have cut my visage, it is bleeding." On the contrary, Veilah would retort, "*Hayir, bay, bir sivilce idi, onu.*" "No, I have not cut your visage, there was only a pimple and I have taken it away" ["No, ay hev nat cat yur vizeyc, der uaz onli e pimpil end ay hev teykin it evuey"].) I had seen *The Blue Angel*, and as drunk as I was I never didn't remember that Emil Jannings was a schoolteacher. But I wasn't a Foole at the Bercer because, as nearly as I can recall, I never crowed like a rooster, or not in public I didn't. It is true that, according to literal interpretation of the aphorism, I might have been mistaken for a Foole, inasmuch as me and my money were soon parted.

Hill Cocktails

We went to parties. Typically these were thrown on a week's notice in a young married couple's hillside house. The drink of choice, the Hill Cocktail, was served from a punch bowl and chilled by a block of ice. This was homemade vodka, orange juice and Turkish brandy. It was seductively smooth; it did the devil's work quietly, but by golly it did it.

Let's say there were fifty at the party, twenty or so of them Turks from Istanbul's lively theater community (which had been inspired by a few members of the humanities faculty at Robert College, especially a flamboyantly homosexual Englishman, Hilary Sumner-Boyd, who carried with him rumors of exile from home in the wake of great Oscar Wildean scandal). There would be a few teachers from the American College for Girls, our sister institution in Arnavutköy. The party would begin after dinner, build in jollity and veer toward lechery or mercurial rancor; sometimes the shouting matches were inspired by the warning signs of adultery (a husband finding his wife in the bathtub without water but brimming with his best friend), but some of the explosions were sparked by disagreements as to aesthetics. During a spring garden party, a Robert College dean, a sturdy fellow with a porcupine crew cut, insisted on reading aloud his poems in praise of Byzantium; these were singsong rhymed couplets; one pair married *feather* with *heather*, making a near-rhyme with *wherever* and *forever*. When he finished, the dean was weeping great salt tears.

Hilary Sumner-Boyd, who had stood listening with his eyes shut, which could have implied ecstatic transport or simple blackout, stirred: "Oh dear," he said.

"You like my lines," said the dean.

"Oh dear no," said Hilary. "They are odious verses."

"You faggot asshole," argued the dean, who was a Marine veteran of a foreign war. "I've killed Japs on beaches. You wouldn't know a sincere poem if it sucked your cock."

"How exactly," asked Hilary, "would that work? If I'd only known poetry could be so *useful*, my dear . . . why do you tell me only *now*?"

The dean disappeared. The dean reappeared with a bayonet, which he stabbed with appropriate exclamations into the tree against which Hilary leaned. Hilary snickered; he said to the dean: "How curious: you are a coward." The poet/dean wept.

Jimmy Baldwin came to live among us. He was trying to finish *Another Country*, and a Turkish theater director he had met in London offered the serenity of a room where he could live and write facing the Bosporus, a place where Baldwin wouldn't have to decide (for a change) whether he was principally a black activist or principally a writer. The first night I met Jimmy, he picked a fight with me. The first night Jimmy met anyone, he picked a fight. I don't recall the details of my quarrel, but from observing later bouts with others, I'm sure it went like this: I would have heard him railing against "The Man" or "Mister Charlie," and I would have tuned my ears. Jimmy would deliver a diatribe, a fierce preacherly polemic against white America. Then, with the Colonel Blimpery of a colonizer or a missionary far from the imperial heartland, I'd have protested some excess of rhetoric. I might have said that I wasn't sure I could agree that all white Americans, first to last, were bloodier than Hitler because Hitler at least had acted from passionate belief rather than standing by, smug and indifferent. I must have disagreed with something he declaimed, because I do recollect with perfect acuity Jimmy's astonishing soft eyes bugging out at me, his huge mouth twisting into a sardonic grin I might have mistaken for a sneer, a grin I knew later to have been provoked by the delicious prospect of an argument. How that man relished argument! He would dissent with anything: the excellence of Henry James's sentences (he loved them, unless you loved them), how to cook vegetables. He was a very Jesuit in debate. He talked fast and in complete sentences; his voice would grow louder and more emphatic until his opinion climaxed with a shrewd stare. Then he would theatrically lower his voice and—one or the other—laugh or cut you dead. If you had mentioned your dear Aunt Em, who considered her colored maid almost a member of the family,

Jimmy would consign you eternally to hell, and good for him. If he laughed, it meant not that he wasn't serious about white guilt, white shame, white lovelessness; if he laughed his ungoverned musical laugh, it meant that the argument would continue—forever, if he had his way. Meantime it was now recess; let's pour another drink and put Bessie Smith on the phonograph.

Jimmy liked Istanbul. It was a peculiarity of the Turks that they believed black people to bring good luck. This friendly bias may have been a payoff from the favored status of Nubian slaves among the Ottoman sultans' palace households. Whatever, Jimmy was free to kick back in Turkey, and he soon rented what had been a pasha's library, built above the towers and ramparts and crenellations of Rumeli Hisar. During the years he lived in Istanbul, years when he wrote *The Fire Next Time*, and visited home to witness Birmingham and the March on Washington, I'm not certain Jimmy knew or cared whether Turkey was ruled by a parliament or a pope or a king or a queen. He very well knew that the doorman at the Divan Oteli was a black man, and in Istanbul a personage, and if this combination of qualities troubled Jimmy, he and trouble were off duty.

At the tail end of parties there'd be a great pairing-off, or there'd be a Great Idea. Under the rubric *Great Idea*, maybe I'd persuade a teacher from the Girls' College to ride on the back of my fast, noisy English motorcycle out to the Black Sea beach at Kilyos where we would, conflating a Great Idea with a Great Pairing-Off, swim naked at sunrise. I spent the dawn after my first Hill party, which would have been my first dawn in Turkey, undertaking to swim the Bosporus with John Freely, a Brooklyn-born Irish-American mathematics teacher, a gravedigger's son with a doctorate in experimental physics, courtesy of the GI Bill. Freely knew Istanbul, particularly the Stamboul of mosques and Byzantine churches, better than any

Westerner. He wrote the authoritative *Blue Guide: Istanbul*, but dog-paddling across the full tidal bore of the Bosporus that night, egging me on with cries—Byron had fronted the Hellespont, how could I do less?—he neglected to guide me away from orange peels and fish heads. Seeing a Greek freighter steaming south toward the Sea of Marmara, on a collision course with my unhappy, bobbing self, I made for shore. Freely said the trouble with me was I always left the party before it really began. Since we'd known each other only since nine that night, I was determined to prove Freely a poor prophet, and I did. Who was it after all who drove with him and Bill Hickman across the border of Turkey into the no-man's-land of the Bulgarian frontier, bristling with mines and machine gunners? We'd decided to spend the weekend in Vienna, storm the goddamned gates successfully this time, to make up for Süleyman the Magnificent's miserable failure in 1529 to take that city. We had neither visas nor money, and Vienna was far, far away. The Bulgarian frontier police returned us to Thrace, dropping us across the border as though they held us with long tongs and we were turds being dropped into trash. They claimed we were drunk. What could we say?

John Freely said, "Consider Sultan Selim the Sot. He'd have a drink now and then. Behold his works!"

"He drowned in his bath," Bill Hickman said.

The Sick Man of Europe

That's what they called Turkey, and if Turkey wasn't, I was. I was in the infirmary. My relationship with the Robert College infirmary got off to a poor start when I put three Princeton friends in a sick ward with some students after a night at the Park, Divan, Rejans, Flower Passage and Fooles Bercer. I guess I'd misplaced my key to the infirmary, or maybe I'd never had one, so my pals had had to check into their room by way of a locked window. Then, as their dinner wore off, one of them sensed a wolf in his stomach and decided he needed a snack. He opened the refrigerator; he'd misplaced *his* key to the lock on the refrigerator door, so he had to pick the latch with a crowbar. Then he ate a loaf of bread and a beefsteak and a dozen eggs. How could you eat a dozen eggs? I'd asked him. "I just scrambled them up with cream and butter," he said.

Since then I'd been to the infirmary for a jumbo shot of penicillin (before I forswore the red-light district), administered by the Robert College doctor, a Turk so fastidious in his attitude toward the human body that he conducted his examination of my sorry condition while I remained fully dressed, with a sheet draped over my zipped trousers. His investigation of my symptoms was entirely anecdotal, and entirely conclusive, both that time and the next time, about four days after my beloved Veilah found me after all at the street corner to which she had sent me, because, taking a leaf from the spy's instruction manual, I had torn in half and kept one half of the very banknote that would be her banknote if she found me.

Now I was in the infirmary being treated for alcoholic poisoning. While I was there, the headmaster of Robert Academy paid me a visit.

"Have you ever heard of Dorian Gray?" the headmaster asked.

"You mean Oscar Wilde's Dorian Gray?"

"That Dorian Gray."

I said I guessed I had heard of him, saying this with the wariness a fellow might use if he'd been accused of plagiarizing *Moby-Dick* when in fact he hadn't read *Moby-Dick*. I mean, which would be the greater offense? Larceny or ignorance?

The (married) headmaster said if I hadn't read *Dorian Gray*, I should. I might also want to acquaint myself with *The Rake's*

Progress. With the picaresque in general—with *Gil Blas*, perhaps. And how about Boccaccio's *Decameron*? And perhaps
Under the Volcano. And by the way, I had been put off
limits—cast from Eden, as it were—by all single female teachers at the American College for Girls.

"Then that doesn't include wives, sir?"

The Unmaking of *Little Mary Sunshine*

As the gunshot rang out, as I chewed the scenery down there
on the stage, I was surrounded by wives. All the forest rangers,
mostly bachelors, were surrounded by wives. It had been a
merry production. There was no changing room; it was spring;
the high spirits backstage had been infectious (but not, thank
goodness, as infectious as Veilah). Given the facts, it was impossible to divine who was the subject of the sentence "You've
been fucking my wife!" In fact, it wouldn't have been possible
to know the object had not her husband made himself visible
in the rim of the floodlights.

He was British, which accounted for Her Majesty's Webley
with the thong. He fired again. There was silence, what I would
have to call an uncomfortable silence. It was broken by a
sibilant English schoolgirl's soprano, the very voice whose music had enraptured us these long days and nights of rehearsal:
"If I wasn't a virgin when we were married, I'm most surely
a virgin now!"

"How would that work?" whispered the fellow playing the
part of Chief Brown Bear, cowering beside me.

She called out again: "You go home, you silly boy! And
don't come back till you're all grown up, till you've learned to
behave yourself!"

Well, amen to that.

All Grown Up

I returned to Istanbul three years later with my wife. We stayed with Jimmy Baldwin and David Leeming in the pasha's library. The city was a shock to Priscilla; there's a gorgeous Thelonious Monk piece titled "Ugly Beauty," and for Priscilla Istanbul was like that. The Turks are ugly to animals, for example, and our first afternoon in the Old City she had to watch a beastly man beat his donkey nearly to death. And it wasn't beautiful to watch *hamals*, human pack animals, bear refrigerators on their backs.

Priscilla was surely bewildered, maybe shocked. It was not only that she was young and a Yankee, and six years earlier a Miss Porter's girl with a perhaps distorted understanding of what constituted sin. She was also newly married to someone she had been warned not to marry. Her defiance of those warnings had been built on her confidence that she knew me even better than I knew me. Now she wasn't so sanguine. Standing on the ramparts of Topkapi Palace with my friends, looking out toward the Column of the Goths and beyond to Seraglio Point, she heard what I believed to be charming stories of bygone human folly: wars, and religious persecutions, and devious eunuchs, and a sultan's wife who had her husband's grand vizier strangled by mutes, who had likewise poisoned her son. It was difficult to articulate how I could take pleasure from such Adamic history, why I'd wanted to do graduate work in depravity, why the stink of offal in the streets made me feel alive rather than ill. When I'd left Istanbul for the land west of Vienna, John Freely had warned me: "Terrible things will happen to you there. You will grow old. And serious. You will be crushed by falling canned goods in the supermarket. Your wife will join a book club. And I, my friend, will be thigh-deep in wine in the Sea of Marmara, or receiving admiring glances at the Divan, where I will drink with shrimp stains on my tropical suit."

A few days into our visit, Priscilla became one of us. It was difficult to locate the place and moment. Perhaps it was at a late-afternoon party given by Emin Bey, an infamously self-indulgent great-grandson of a sultan, at his swaybacked unpainted Palladian wood palace on the Asian shore of the Bosporus, just at the junction of the Sweetwaters of Asia. Emin Bey kept peacocks in his garden, and while they cooed and clucked we listened to him tell in his soft sinister Oxford-Constantinople accent about the palace across the Sweetwaters, with its façade removed one foggy spring night by a Soviet freighter. No one had repaired it, Emin Bey said. Why? He shrugged. There was the question of cost, of course. And liability. But really, it was possible, in Istanbul, to become used to anything. No?

Yes. That night Priscilla and I ate with old friends at a Bebek restaurant built out over the Bosporus. Along the shore bright blue fishing nets were stretched to dry. Priscilla saw rotten fruit floating in the black water among fish heads. But after stuffed grape leaves and cheese-filled pastries and pieces of lamb dipped in cold yogurt, Priscilla ate the fish whose heads now fed other fish. It was delicious *lufer*, bluefish, and while we ate we watched fishermen catching more, all anyone could want, from saffron and India-red double-ended rowboats lit by kerosene lamps. Now, at slack of tide, the boats converged from up and down the Bosporus, from the ruined palaces of Asia and from the Black Sea and from the Golden Horn. Then I persuaded Priscilla she had heard a nightingale, and that she smelled Judas blossoms, even though they were past their season, and so what if they were? Imagine.

The Company Man and
the Revolutionary

Friends? How does a friend behave? Will a pal survive in captivity? Friendship has inspired no want of homily. Ask Aristotle, he of rational First Principles: "A single soul dwelling in two bodies"; that's how you can recognize a friend. Sounds deadly as cancer, unsightly as goiter. *Two* souls? Show me one. Am I looking at friendship or its end? Gertrude Stein dreamed up a wonderful title: "Before the Flowers of Friendship Faded Friendship Faded." She had translated a friend's poem, and he felt she had taken liberties with it, and they fell out. Stein published her version and put her own title on it, and there they were, these friends, on the rocks. But I would like to tell of a case different from the one Stein's perception describes. Mine might have been titled "Before Friendship Faded, the Flowers of Friendship Faded." My title is neither as musical nor as interesting (grammatically); my title adumbrates an odd tale of odd times—a friendship that died after, rather than before, two friends wished it to die.

My friend—I'll call him Andrew—moves with deliberation and hydraulic ease, as though exploring underwater an eel-ridden cave. He is hipless and smooth, auburn-haired, with pale skin and a kutup kid's saucy freckles. He has the temperament of a cinnamon bear, by turns playful and sullen; people who have known him talk of him—he's an enticement for recollection, gossip, speculation. He has been a painter, sculptor, potter, photographer, actor, mischief-maker. Now he is a filmmaker, and such is his standing among experimental cameramen that one night in New York, when he came late to the screening of another man's movie, the audience rose to applaud what he has done with his life—his work—and what he has meant to do with it.

Not long enough ago I sat beside my wife in our Vermont living room, our children playing around us, and listened to this friend forgive me for my work as an agent of the CIA and for having informed on him and betrayed him. It had been eight years since I had seen Andrew, since he first realized—or first cared—that I was a spook, a mole, a Company Man. The years had fleshed and muscled him, added power to him, and presence, but no visible age. He is of a giving nature, and now he had dropped in on our Vermont solitude like God out of the machine, to make peace with me. Between us, he told me, the war was over. What war? Had he not been best man at my wedding? And had I not loved him? What war?

Never mind the past, he said, and he hugged me, took my shoulders in his hands, turned me this way and that, examined me, puzzled me as he had forever puzzled me. Since I had first met him, eighteen years before, he had liked to make appearances unannounced, materializing without explanation; and until this reunion there had never come a time (well, maybe once) when I had not been happy to find him filling my doorway, pausing in transit somewhere, heedless of whatever rhythm he might have disrupted. Now he was in the company of a pretty young woman, and he mumbled an introduction. He often appeared with strangers, wishing to share with friends his enthusiasm for new discoveries, and the strangers were usually female, often young, always pretty. He had the habit of mumbling introductions. Andrew is not one for the decorums, and his speech is elliptical, so that one listens to him leaning toward him, to catch the sense of what he says before it scatters like mist on the soft breeze of his voice.

This new girlfriend must have believed her smile was beatific, but it wasn't. She appeared condescending, amused by our house and situation and befuddlement, amused by us. Andrew fussed with my boys, hugged Priscilla, hooked his thumbs in his cowboy belt: "Well, well, well, hasn't time passed, isn't this more like it?" It seemed to me, as I watched Andrew's new friend listen to him reconcile himself to my crimes against him and his cause, that she valued his magnanimity but found it soft and damp, a waste of spirit. I wondered what Andrew had told her about me during their drive north from New York.

Andrew and I had met during the spring of 1958 at a Stowe ski lodge, the Round Hearth, favored by school and college kids. Andrew was a guest there, on spring vacation from Harvard, and we met in the lodge's parking lot, where I was lodging in a borrowed van. The Round Hearth wanted four dollars a night for a dormitory bunk, and these were more dollars than I could pony up. Just as I was staying at the Round Hearth (but not quite), so was I on vacation from Princeton (but not quite), having a few months earlier dropped out, to Princeton's relief, while I wrote a novel and Found Myself.

I found Andrew because he had a knockout cousin who had caught my eye, just as he had caught hers. With women this set the pattern: I hunted and he fled. Otherwise we stood as equals: he was my first hipster, I was his. Neither was the other's sidekick; he envied me because I had quit college—a rope's length ahead of the posse—while he merely threatened to. I envied him too many qualities to number, but above all what seemed to me his superior values, his sure sense of the distinction between what was authentic and what was not. His ideals, obliquely articulated without solemnity, were those of an artist (I never doubted he was *that*), derisive of team play, nice manners and commercial hurly-burly. We needled the middle class but excepted from it anyone we liked; when we spoke of revolutions, they were cultural rather than political. We liked to believe, and assured each other, that we didn't give a fiddler's fig for the good opinion of our peers.

We were young. By our precept indifferent to dress, we wore our indifference like a uniform. Our collars were frayed, but the shirts were oxford-cloth button-downs from the "346" department of Brooks Brothers. The paint- and ink-stained tweeds we wore with blue jeans and Army boots were tailored by J. Press. We looked like Tweedledee and Tweedledum.

We spent the summer after we met in Boston; we were bohemian Bauhausers, spartan dwellers in a flat empty of furniture except for mattresses on the floor, a studio couch and an Eames chair. And a state-of-the-art sound system. Gratification cut to the very bone. Except the flat was large and airy, sunny, set on the corner of Charles and Chestnut across from a Beacon Hill florist whose fragrance lifted our stoic spirits. The apartment must have cost a pile. Must have cost Andrew a pile: he paid.

His father was a Lake Forest lawyer, at the time a Cabinet officer in Eisenhower's administration. The family owned a handsome house on the beach at West Chop, and despite Andrew's aversion to getters and spenders, he was willing to cross to the Vineyard when Beacon Hill's temperature climbed above the comfort zone. There was always plenty of money around, and no little of it was wasted on me.

Andrew indulged me—floated me—for many reasons: because I was generally tits-up broke, because he was generous, because I was trying to write even as he succeeded in painting and for reasons I can now only guess at, reasons that might even have their source in shame for his bankroll. Not to make too much of this, Andrew was not attached to the sturdy Republicanism of his father's government, but neither did he—then—loathe it or wish to undo it. We did not, in the late 1950s, trouble ourselves with politics, or economics, or much of anything apart from our wishes, which we liked to ennoble as *dreams.*

Mine was to do a novel, so to Andrew—done and done—I was a novelist. And indeed, during the year I spent apart from Princeton, working at Sikorsky Aircraft in Bridgeport to support myself and my father, I did manage to complete what I fancifully called a novel, *Certain Half-Deserted Streets*; I was twenty when it was finished. It was about a boy (I called him a "young man"), Tony, already seventeen and "coming to season" in the "brutal world," a cosmopolitan world of flashy cars and flashing teeth into which Tony, poor baby, had "never asked to be born."

During the days that ran into the nights that I scribbled this thing, I worked an hour from my house in Newtown, Connecticut. I write "my house" because the rent was paid, the few times it was paid that year, by me rather than by my father. My title at Sikorsky (the helicopter division of United Aircraft Corporation) was Engineering Communications Coordinator, which meant Mail Boy. My pay was two hundred and fifty per month, and during idle moments—when I was not lugging canvas sacks, reading my employers' private communications (just like Faulkner, no?), or sleeping in the can (just like Faulkner)—I was expected to guard the blueprint cage, to assure that parts diagrams were rightly filed. So they were, except when I had stolen them. Those representations that seemed to me expendable or frivolous—diagrams, let's say, of a loading hoist or an exhaust manifold or a strut assembly—I would tuck beneath my shirt, remove to my house and boil. The drawings were on cloth and coated with gelatin, and once this laminate had been boiled off the Irish-linen backing, one

was left with glue stuck to the sides of a pot and with handkerchiefs, twelve inches square, of a most elegant texture and
tightness of weave.

Andrew was wowed by my indifference to Sikorsky's property and security. I wouldn't swear that he esteemed me as a
rebel out on the cutting edge of anarchy (we had been reading Camus's *L'Homme révolté*, in French, slowly), but the
translation of Air Force documents into linen handkerchiefs
seemed to strike him as imaginative disobedience. In fact, as
with all else of importance I then knew, the trick had been
learned from my old man.

If for Andrew my chief virtue was my poverty (as though I'd
taken a vow of bad luck), and my distinction was an ambition
to tell lies in print, then my principal attraction was my odd
association with my father. Andrew had not met dads like
mine; his was a fellow of rectitude and steady purpose, a product of Princeton and Cambridge universities. Mine was a dead-
beat and confidence man who would drink through the night
with us, listening to jazz or playing it on an upright squirreled
away in a storeroom off the garage.

Andrew at that time had cars much on his mind. His was
a '53 Austin-Healey designed for a four-cylinder motor; into
the engine compartment he had shoehorned a Corvette power
plant and transmission. The mongrel would go from place to
place with awesome noise and speed, and Andrew often fussed
with it in our Newtown garage, for soon after we met he became frugal with the hours he was willing to waste on a Harvard education.

I too was possessed by a folly, a 1937 Delahaye, just the
contraption in which fated couples plunged to their end-over-
end fiery ends from the Grande Corniche. Longer than a Cad-
illac, the machine could just seat Andrew and me. My father
had found it after volunteering to scout me up practical transportation for the commute to Sikorsky. I'd blame it on him

start (which it usually wouldn't) to finish, but fact was, the automobile satisfied me.

My father's was no less a silly automobile, fast-looking and slow, hideously expensive and utterly unpaid for. Its rightful owner sought its return, but God knows why, for it seldom worked. Neither was it registered, and when it did chance to run at such times as my Delahaye coincidentally would run, my dad and I had a problem, for we owned between us a single set of license plates, and these had belonged to yet another car, my quondam stepmother's. This set of plates my father and I shifted from car to car according to need, and Andrew found this arrangement quite miraculous, a bold and sassy strike by *us* against *them.* He thought me the luckiest fellow alive to have an outlaw father, just as I imagined him the ditto to have as his father a chap positioned to discuss affairs of state or golf after a prayer breakfast in the White House with a President, even one as unspectacular as Eisenhower. As for the license plates, my father found our deception marginally inconvenient, and I was ashamed of it.

There was about Andrew something childlike and sometimes childish. In this we were alike, and the first time I visited West Chop with him he persisted for several days in the fiction that I was a foreign-exchange student with little hold on English. We had just seen *The Young Lions*, and I liked to believe I could make myself sound like Marlon Brando playing a Tyrolean ski instructor and German officer, a curious ambition for a Jew, but I wasn't much of a hand then for behavioral subtexts, and I didn't have much of a talent for accents (how could I, with a stutter?), so we merely puzzled Martha's Vineyard summer folk.

Andrew liked to surprise people. At Harvard he fabricated from the innards of a vacuum cleaner a contrivance that could smoke to their nub a dozen cigars in half a minute and blow

their accumulated smoke through the mail slot of the Eliot
House room of any student who was in Andrew's disfavor. It
was no great trick to earn Andrew's disfavor: gravity, any af-
fectation not on the approved list of affectations, excessive care
for dress or furniture—these were just some of the ways. By
and by the entire undergraduate body of Harvard, together
with its faculty, became the object of Andrew's contumely, and
he left school—at the very time I was returning with unseemly
eagerness to Princeton.

So, less than a year after we met, we began to divide, although neither of us knew this then. We still saw much of
each other: in Boston and Princeton, in New York (where we
listened to Monk at the Five Spot, and where Andrew pronounced judgments about work hung in the Frick and the
Guggenheim and MOMA, and where I chased girls whom he
disfavored). Often I would telephone Andrew collect near
dawn, after a night of drinking with college chums, and confess
incomprehensibly that I was frightened. Of what I couldn't
have said and can only guess at now. I didn't know enough
to be gloomy about my life's limited possibilities; I guess I was
terrified by their number. It wasn't only that I didn't know
what I wished to be once I grew up—although this figured in
my fear—it was that I couldn't guess which of many parts I
was most becoming. With one set of friends I played high-
stakes poker, drank myself insensible, ran up debts and got
myself known in the Dean's office as a scapegrace. Andrew
disapproved.

My better performance was the scholar, or what passed with
me as being a scholar. On my return from Sikorsky's mail
room, I had been about my books with a will, and I began to
collect grades and the approbation of my professors (in an
earlier incarnation it had been merit badges and the approval
of scoutmasters) with fanatical calculation. In literature I preferred the classical proprieties and among critics the New. I

encouraged myself to believe I had the stamina for textual analysis and traded in the hoary anecdotes and jargon of the critical pastime; I could use with a straight face "impropriety" and "conceit" and "rigor." Another favorite was "paradox," but I failed to comprehend its application to my own case. Ask the Dean about "impropriety"! I wrote to Andrew (and to others) that I had quite decided to become Edmund Wilson rather than Scott Fitzgerald (possibilities were more limited than I knew) and would be a steady and knowing professor rather than tempest-tossed and naked to chance, a would-be artist, a mere mountebank and virtuoso. I closed this letter "Shantih." Andrew disapproved.

The disapproval stung, so I tried to keep Andrew at a distance from my motivational drift and existential turmoils. Words were never Andrew's most fluent medium, and the choices before me didn't clarify when expressed by shrugs and grunts and hand signals. I also knew Andrew well enough to know I didn't wish to be judged by him. I was evasive about my past, and this troubled Andrew. He believed that I was ashamed of my parents' chaos, of my father's brushes with the law, of our poverty—and he was right. When I met Andrew, I had not seen my mother since 1952, six years before; I hadn't heard from her, hadn't written her, didn't know where she lived. To conceal the mystery of her absence, I shrouded it in even thicker vapors, telling Andrew (with visible reluctance) when he asked about my mother that she lived abroad, hinting that her reasons were political. (How did I wish him to imagine her? A Spanish Communist exiled to Russia or a Russian princess exiled to Spain?)

I appeared to Andrew perversely elusive. What I was hiding from him—what seemed then my family's shameful and squalid mismanagement of its affairs, what seems now a merely human circumstance—I couldn't have articulated. One night at Tanglewood, listening on the grass to Mozart, Andrew

grilled me about my history, what a suitor's prospective in-
laws might call his background. As usual, I hedged and
dodged, and in sudden anger Andrew told me we couldn't
continue as friends if I kept secrets from him. Very well, I told
him, we couldn't continue as friends. He let his anger die,
stout fellow. His challenge was certainly fair, but I didn't know
how to meet it. I had been in my short time a Life Scout with
a full drape of merit badges, a duck-assed comedian of the
drive-ins, a prep-school Mister Casual, a Princeton bookworm,
a parlor snake, an Engineering Communications Coordinator,
a mail boy, a novelist, a defender of academic conventions, an
outlaw, a disciple eager to ape and please my elders. I didn't
know who I was, whence I had come, whither I meant to go.
Because I was effectively without family, I was free to choose
without interference what I might become. The world was all
before me, and Providence my guide . . . So how could I know
and share some "simple truth," as Andrew called it, about
myself? Well, he was right: I should have tried harder.

When I would share with Andrew my affection for my teachers,
he thought I was kidding. Wasn't I like him? Longing to break
out? Did I trust old farts? *Like* them? Andrew didn't. He liked
kid stuff and kids, and kids liked him back. Around Martha's
Vineyard he was a Pied Piper, drawing teens to the escapades
and art that had his enthusiasm. Young girls had immortal
longings for Andrew, giggled and blushed when he came near,
and he came near. One, who lived a few houses down the
beach from him, became a painter under his influence and
persisted in painting long after Andrew abandoned it. As a
teenager she would sit hours on the beach hoping to catch a
glimpse of him, and now, decades later, he still exercises a
powerful hold on her. She's not alone in his grip. When you
were liked by Andrew, you felt liked by *someone*; this felt good,
like election.

If Andrew favored kids, I often felt closer to the fathers of my friends than to their sons, perhaps because I was so used to my father's company, or perhaps because I sought his replacement. I looked old for my age, and took pains to seem older, yet many of my aspirations were even more childish than Andrew's. We spoke sometimes about running off with his money, taking ourselves to the Maritime Alps to open a bar–jazz club–art gallery–bookstore. It was an absurd notion, and it was Andrew who first fully understood this and let it die. For all my solemnity about the life of the mind, I was fundamentally a sensualist, hospitable to any lark that might lead to fun.

It was just this appetite for novelty that led me to Turkey to teach at Robert College and Istanbul University. To get this job I had approached a teacher at Robert College, an American who had been in the OSS with a Princeton friend's father. Perhaps I had retailed this connection to Andrew? Meantime, Andrew had got himself in a jam. Less from conviction than from carelessness, he had failed to appear for his pre-induction physical exam. He did not "believe" in the draft, to be sure, but his detachment from the appointment to present himself for inspection had nothing to do with beliefs. The draft board believed in him, however, and when Andrew's father refused to bail out his boy, Andrew was soon at Fort Dix, where they asked him his profession. He said, "Painter." They said, "Great! Paint our trucks."

Andrew was posted near Orléans just as I arrived in Paris to spend the summer of 1962 on vacation (as though I needed one) from Istanbul. By the blind luck that seems to fall to Americans in foreign places, I managed to set myself up rent-free in a big, sunny flat at 50 Rue Jacob, a couple of blocks from the Place Saint-Germain-des-Prés. Andrew came to visit weekends and whenever else he could escape his duties. I initiated Andrew to hashish, to which I had introduced myself a few months earlier. This commonplace of personal history is worth remarking only because hashish was the first novelty I had led Andrew to before he could lead me. Moreover, that summer was our only time together when he could be said to have been my sidekick. For a wonder, I had the apartment, the motorcycle and the dope.

I wore a beard and dressed in tatters; I was a veritable repertory of props by which the hip artist in exile might be recognized. Andrew's hair was cut close, in the Army way, and he was forever obliged to leave our fun and ruminations for bed check in the Orléans barracks, like a schoolboy racing to beat the bell. The Army fast soured him, and he became even more jumpy and abridged than before; he delivered muttered monologues I couldn't decipher, so I'd nod and look sage.

We had unlike attitudes toward time that summer in Paris. Andrew was stretching himself thin, giving a portion to the Army and bigger portions to pottery and photography. (He'd abandoned painting and sculpture when his taste and virtuosity could carry him no further without disciplined labor.) He was a busy dabbler, a deft tinkerer. I was idle, putting many hours into listening to the Jazz Messengers and MJQ, "No Sun in Venice," while I listlessly snapped cards off a worn deck of Bicycles, cheating at solitaire while I waited for day to close and the jazz clubs to open. Andrew could be a scold, and he didn't try hard to keep to himself his reservations regarding my character. "Where's the writing going, Geoffers?" Andrew liked exploration and explosive bursts of progress, kinesis, and there I was, all lassitude and delinquency, waste, and Andrew—more his frugal Scottish-American father's son than he understood—did not approve.

Robert College paid me eighteen hundred a year, deposited quarterly in a New York bank. These dollars I spent in two chunks: five hundred for a month in the winter in Vienna and the Tyrol, and the rest in Paris for the summer. By husbandry (cultivating a taste for pleasures that came free) and by barter (giving a bed or floor-space to friends passing through in exchange for dinner at La Coupole or a few rounds of calvados at Lipp's), I managed to live well, but Andrew couldn't imagine how. He ate and drank less and worse than I but thought nothing of buying a five-hundred-dollar lens for his backup Leica. Observing my comfort and mobility, Andrew puzzled over my means. Where, he wondered, once or twice aloud, did my money come from? He would not believe it came entirely from teaching.

In fact it didn't. I boosted my salary as opportunity allowed. I tutored the slow-witted, sometimes in literature but more often in poker. Cards and a demure trade in hashish knocked me down about a hundred a month. But I was never invited to suck at the most bountiful of Istanbul's tits, to milk the CIA. Of my colleagues on the faculty of Robert College, many—if not most—supped there.

Typically, an American would be recruited before he left home for Turkey. One colleague told me how it worked—well, there's a lie: *many* colleagues couldn't wait to explain how it worked. For a certain retainer a newly hired teacher attended a comical training course in Virginia; there the recruit was taught to memorize license-plate numbers (that's not so taxing: my dad and I knew ours by heart), how to recognize and evade a hostile tail, how to write in his pocket with a pencil one inch long. Why, exactly, one inch exactly? Because this primitive instrument could be used to calculate by elementary geometry the height of an American elm exactly one thousand feet from the calculator, and by shrewd extrapolation the height of a rocket erect on its launching pad.

The spook was sent to Turkey with one-half of a banknote (the Bulgarian lev was in vogue), the other half to be brought later to Istanbul by whoever was running him. These contacts were invariably known as "Lee," though they changed from

meeting to meeting. They would telephone the teacher at Robert College to arrange contact, and such was the transparency
of their conspiratorial manner that I once heard a man in the
faculty lounge paged to a communal telephone thus: "Mike,
for you, it's your spy." Good news, payday.

Payday never came for me. No one asked me to "keep my
eyes open" or "keep my ears cocked" or "hang around the
common room" and report the political inclinations of my
students. So far as I knew, they had none and neither did the
faculty, including the spies among us. So far as I could tell,
every American save yrs. trly. was employed to report on every
other American, and since the faculty at Robert College was
a glorious aggregation of misfits and scoundrels and layabouts
and dreamers and drunks and bards, I felt slighted by the
Agency, an Ishmael among pariahs.

The meeting with the contact was always at the Istanbul
Hilton, and I witnessed many of these, including one between
a Yugoslavian railroad agent and an English poet who had
been recruited in transit to Beirut on a Soviet freighter by the
ship's captain in the mistaken impression that the poet was
an American engineer, which is what the poet's stolen passport, bought for reasons of his own at Istanbul's Spice Bazaar,
said he was. American spies—"Lees"—invariably wore a
black hat and black trench coat. (This is difficult to take on
faith, I know.) I'd never before seen a black trench coat worn
by the wearer of a black hat indoors, except maybe in cartoons
that featured animals playing spies.

The runner (full-time spy) would slip down the bar to join
his runnee (my teaching colleague), who would show half a
Bulgarian lev to "Lee," who would show his own before slip-
ping an envelope stuffed with small bills into the professor's
jacket pocket, a transaction witnessed by no more than twenty
Turks and rival spies. My colleague would then speak, saying
within my earshot, "I may have been followed, but perhaps I

was not." To this "Lee" would reply: "Leave at once; wait for a call next month." (Oh, this is very difficult to swallow.)

Then came the Cuban Missile Crisis, and many of us in Turkey were politicized, at last, by terror—the effective way. There was speculation about reprisals (what was sauce for the Cuban goose was sauce for the Turkish gander; this made sense to us), and Americans were put on alert by the consulate, whose officers brainstormed wildly impractical plans for our evacuation. My poet friend departed for Athens, wishing (he said theatrically, at the bar of the Divan) to be where It All began when It All ended. He ran out of money and returned, resolved to quit the spy business. Not that he had ever shared intelligence with his employer, but quitting was, he said, a matter of principle, and when "Lee" next telephoned, my friend demanded an immediate meeting. In deference to the urgency of the occasion, they found each other at the bar of the Pera Palas, a now seedy hotel of preposterously romantic associations, a shrine for spies, their hall of fame. My friend, having announced his change of heart, was directed by this "Lee," whom he had never before seen, to the men's room. There, standing before the urinals, he was sworn out of service, commanded to accept an oath of silence with his hand raised. "Lee" was firm on this point, most insistent, and my friend, having sworn *omertà*, ten minutes later told me the whole story, adding that obliged as he had been to raise his gun hand, he had pissed on "Lee's" trench coat and last-a-lifetime brogans.

I chose to believe this farce, and passed it along to Andrew with no small pleasure. Andrew was by then in an Army hospital, having at the close of 1962 driven his truck into a tree not far from Verdun. His leg was smashed near the hip, and when the truck began to burn he had dragged himself and his camera from the cab and crawled across the road, pausing every few yards to shoot a picture of his bloody and ruined leg, with the truck aflame in the background. The photographs, taken with a 21-mm Super-Angulon on a Leica M3, display extreme depth of field; they were startlingly composed. Andrew is nothing if not exact in such matters, an artist with a sense—in those days—of distance from his subject.

The cause of the accident—or, more precisely, the cause of the cause—was never revealed. Had he merely fallen asleep at the wheel? Or had this been an act calculated to free him from what he no longer would bear? There had been hints when I had visited Andrew on post that haphazard contact with strangers, inevitable in the service, was becoming intolerable for him. He had come to despise the touch of people. I could throw an arm around him, brother hugging brother, if he saw it coming. But if a hand fell on his shoulder from behind and without warning, he would recoil. He was offended by the relentless carnality of his comrades, by their vulgar talk, by their roughhouse, by the food he shared with them and the drink he didn't. The Army was turning Andrew into a snob, and he hated the Army for this.

Four months before the accident we had ridden my motorcycle to Chartres on a matchless August morning, brisk for the season, through fields of cut and stacked hay, taking the sensations in our faces and marveling that we had come so far from Stowe and the Round Hearth. We had not, had we an inkling, come so far; we two-for-a-penny American sightseers had made a routine excursion. But we were carried away that day by the day, and by ourselves, and of course by Chartres. Having read Henry Adams on the place, I played guide and scholar, and Andrew played aesthetician. I wish I were back today in that day. That afternoon we rode flat out to Orléans, and walked along the Loire while Andrew skipped stones across the water and spoke, I believed, of desertion. Or maybe early discharge; we would never be so close again, but even then I couldn't fathom his meaning.

.   .   .

After his accident they tried to mend him at military hospitals in Verdun, Verona, Frankfurt and Valley Forge, and from one of these he wrote: "Geoffers—It has been too long. I have thought of what this time might have brought. And now years have passed. And more in these past few months. And yet I sit on the edge of a hospital bed with the approaching still distant. More certain and questionable though now there is known all that must be done. And this is not a mental hospital. I rise above all this but at times fall still behind these fences and guard houses. All that is without is within. And there has been great change through no change."

That's what it said. His calligraphy is exact, bold and all uppercase, but he had at best an uneasy relationship with syntax: too authoritarian, systematic. Andrew was answering the call of Eastern systems, the Wisdom of the Inscrutables, the *I Ching*, yoga, Zen archery, macrobiotic principles of nourishment, the gibberish of paradox. Simultaneously, he yielded to the pull of those cosmic hucksters Gurdjieff, Ouspensky and Orage. Meantime, the Army botched its work on his leg; the pin in his thigh bent. He visited his father in Chicago, where he went (inadvertently?) AWOL. He seemed eager to break free of the gravitational pull of this world and float free to another.

Not I; I welcomed gravity. In the chaos of Istanbul's goatish culture I had conceived a relish for order and had begun to walk, placing my feet deliberately and heavily, on carefully picked ground. I had applied for a Fulbright to study at Cambridge, and when a notice instructed me to report for an interview at the United States consulate, I considered five minutes before shaving off the beard I had so laboriously grown and come to define myself by. I wanted that Fulbright, and got it, despite the circumstance that my interviewer wore buckskins, muttonchops and a droopy Yosemite Sam mustache.

My Cambridge was a lively place, its politics expressed mostly by factional strife among faculty members, but also by earnest ideological disputation. I wrote for the radical magazine *Cambridge Forward* about the sins of white folks, the infamy of *Time*, the treachery of Jack Kennedy and the CIA. Perhaps because I celebrated the virtues of America's enemies, perhaps because I had known James Baldwin well in Istanbul, I was described by a *Cambridge Forward* editor as a "disciple of Jimmy Baldwin." This irritated me: I surely didn't object to identification with a black man or with a homosexual—the first would distinguish me at Cambridge, the latter put me one with the mob—but I wished to cast off the burden of being anyone's "disciple."

I hung out with King's College Communists, great gentlemen every one, Etonians and Harrovians who wore blue jeans under their gowns and bespoke dinner jackets to club dances. They were quick, those boys, and when we weren't joking, I liked to muse with them about the coming revolution, even as their porters made their beds, drew their baths, laid their fires, shined their shoes. If I *was* anyone's disciple those days, I was T. S. Eliot's, and I believed I had learned from his example that a writer required fuel beyond language; I was hunting for a credo, and because I had no more use for God than God had for me, Marxism, for a minute, seemed a way to vault beyond myself and pick up free a reservoir of ritual and legend, of hagiography and historical reference.

During the period of my revolutionary fervor, or appropriation—to be measured in weeks rather than months—Andrew came to Cambridge for a visit, and I attached my theatrical account of my conversion to a motor trip I had taken the previous winter through Eastern Europe. With a couple of friends, I had crossed the border into Czechoslovakia during the worst storm of the worst European winter of the century. As we made our way behind snowplows to Prague, we listened while the Voice of America broadcast news of the storm's terrible disruptions behind the Iron Curtain. We heard of fuel shortages, blocked roads, riots by angry workers and house-wives. (In fact our VW, bearing West German plates, was attacked by men coming off shift at a brewery in Pilsen. We cried out that we were Americans and devoted beer drinkers, but snowballs were thrown at us, and our windshield was spat upon by nationalists who did not approve of German auto-mobiles, German anythings.) Nothing of what we heard on the radio was true, and when we crested a hill and saw below us Prague, putatively without electricity or joy, in fact alit and on the move and the most gorgeous sight in Europe, we began to wonder about our countrymen as not even their double-dare with Khrushchev over Cuba had made us wonder.

More precisely, I had lost my patriotic cherry: my country-men lied. As the sons of preachers often turn libertine, so do the sons of libertines turn prig, and the prig in me despised propaganda, just as the would-be scholar in me despised inex-actitude. And when the *oddest* thing happened in Prague—strangers washed our car while we slept; is that a miracle or what?—I improbably concluded that I hated America. This I told Andrew during his visit to Cambridge, but not without adding that I also hated Communist tyranny: "Killing one generation to save the next just won't do." Oh my word: *won't do!* What snaky twists I showed my friend. What was he to think? His accident had turned him solemn, and time had turned me to patchwork. Even as I delivered pronouncements about the masses, so had my taste in literature become in-creasingly mandarin. (Pope was a favorite, Congreve!) Andrew was beginning to remark aloud my unresolved paradoxes; he'd cock his head when he looked at me. For my part, something about his judgments raised a bloodlust in me; I delighted in mystifying him.

.   .   .

A couple of weeks after Andrew left Cambridge for America, President Kennedy was shot. The news came at dinner, and that night I listened to America's theater of cruelty play out by shortwave at my tutor's house; George Steiner had invited fellow Americans to hear how it was at home, and how it was was distressingly distant. Later that night I took a young Louisville woman motorcycle riding, and managed to plow into the rear of a truck parked on the blind side of humpbacked Magdalene Bridge. The bike hit going seventy; she was not hurt, but I crushed the bones in my right hand, cut my head, had a concussion. I lay in the hospital watching the rain, listening to news of Oswald and then Ruby, to the funeral, to my country's trouble. I was ashamed of myself.

Maybe the rain, maybe Kennedy's death, maybe an ambition to get on with it drove me home from Cambridge at the end of the first year of a two-year fellowship. The instant I stepped off the plane in New York, where I had gone to spend the summer of '64, I knew—to my surprise—I wouldn't go back. I had fallen in love with an American. Andrew thought this was a waste of time; he had watched me fall in love times aplenty. Falling in love was my hobby. I loved to fall in love. It was difficult to go AWOL from Cambridge; I disappointed people who had been good to me there, who had trusted me to come to something—by their lights—*useful*, a critic and academic, by my lights a careerist. Andrew urged me to return to England. He wanted me to locate my mission, and to him marriage was no mission, but simply an indulgence.

I didn't listen to him. I took a job at the Washington *Post*, writing obits and night-police scare stories, and after a year, the week I was married, the paper traded me up to book editor. I was able to pay my way in the world, and this made me proud. Andrew, who had always been able to pay his way by the fruit of his ancestors' labor and wit, was puzzled by my pride. But he was my friend—wasn't he?—and he and my brother gave me away (what a gift!) in the wedding on the Rhode Island shore, at Priscilla's grandmother's, a tumble-down old house whose loss of glory was memorialized by its name, The Ruins.

The marriage had come hard for us. Priscilla's parents dis-approved; they over-our-dead-bodies disapproved, as Andrew knew, and he was cast down that I had so little self-respect as to marry someone whose parents were not enraptured to have me as a son-in-law. Andrew did a worse job than he imagined of keeping his reservations to himself, and I was irritated that he didn't seem to share our happiness. I was in love, respected my work, was fond of my colleagues, happy to have fled Cam-bridge. Perhaps I seemed smug. Perhaps I was smug.

Andrew took the wedding photographs. I sit now looking at them and recognize how gorgeously cruel they are. Beautiful: Andrew cannot make anything graceless or pedestrian. But these images! He glued them by twos to opposite sides of mounting boards, so that, flipped back and forth, they tell a story—before and after—and point a moral. The before is a portrait of me near Chartres, mounted on my black A.J.S. motorcycle, lean and scruffy, grinning, a freebooter. Flip: I'm fat and anxious, got up in wedding rig, striped trousers and rented ascot, an involuntary rictus easily mistaken for a smirk disfiguring my mug. Here is my history with my friend, in two dozen images, sent me in a case Andrew scrupulously made from rosewood, a thing better fit for dueling pistols.

Andrew went among the wedding guests like a scourge, bringing into extreme focus with his sharpest lens this lady's wrecked, eighty-year-old face and neck, that patrician patri-arch's alcoholic blear. Andrew must have hated them, maybe hated us that day. For what? I could guess: he thought them unworthy of my company, and me of his. There was a nasty scene: his outlaw dog tried, with amiable gusto, to screw an in-law's pooch, and failing, discovering it to be no bitch after all, took about half a pound out of the tame creature. Shame and scandal.

Some time later Priscilla and I visited Andrew in Putney, Vermont, where he had bought a farm. Andrew had become a despotic nutritionist, and we got lectured about organic processes, the yin of things and their yang, getting in touch with our cells. Maybe I was cynical. Certainly, as days passed, I got hungry. One night Priscilla and I, starved for junk food, crept down the farmhouse stairs after lights-out to sneak over to Brattleboro for tube steak with fries. Andrew caught us, and we all fell to laughing. Matters between us had not gone utterly to ruin.

On the contrary, he showed us the movies he was making, inventive and playful, Bergman parodies, cops-and-robbers parodies, fresh visions of common scenes. Andrew and I played Priscilla records of the jazz—Monk, Coltrane, Miles—we had heard together at the Five Spot; we were already, only seven years into our friendship, nostalgic for its past.

We decided to carry our party to Washington, where Priscilla and I lived near Dupont Circle in a perfectly precious little triplex row house, the kind of place nice mummies and daddies shared when their means were limited but their tastes refined. We had equipped it with coarse replicas of her parents' and grandparents' furniture, bought on the installment plan. Wedding-present-traditional, complete with hunting prints and ubiquitous bathroom art, cartoons of dogs queued up waiting for the hydrant. We burned pretty little birch logs—more costly by the cord than dollar bills—in our pretty little fireplace with its pretty little black marble mantel. It was Christmastime, and Andrew and his teenaged lady of the moment watched me lavish goods on Priscilla, a crazy surplus: two Pucci jackets, identical except for their dominant colors, a gold watch, I don't know what all. I wore a necktie in my own house! We ate roast beef, roast turkey, roast ham, too much of everything; during dinner we drank toasts to our well-dressed friends, appropriate wine in apropos glasses.

Andrew sneered at our furniture and clothes and friends. He was as indirect in his disapproval as in everything, but he managed—difficult trick—to offend Priscilla; he insisted on cooking for himself, untreated rice in a pressure cooker, and when he consented to eat our food, he ate it savagely with his hands, to tell us something about himself and about us. There were ugly words, and when Andrew left Washington, something had been played out for good between us. It hadn't snapped, merely stretched and lost elasticity, like the back of someone who has lifted not too great a weight but a slight weight carelessly. The flowers of friendship were fading, but I continued to think of him as my best friend. As I do now, insanely.

We saw little of each other for the next few years. One time Andrew came to visit and listened to me expatiate on the stratagems of the CIA. By the kind of coincidence that has now stung me with its tail, the fathers of three of my closest Washington friends were personages in the Agency. One father had engineered assassinations and coups, another had lied to Adlai Stevenson during the Bay of Pigs harlequinade, another was neck-deep in Indochina.

With one of these I had had some glancing professional association. During the spring of 1965, a mere boy, an inchling low in my employer's esteem, I resolved to show the newspaper my stuff with a book review and pestered the book critic till she gave me something to judge: Morris West's novel about Vietnam, *The Ambassadors*. It was thin stuff, a black hats versus white hats simplification of the overthrow and murder of Diem. The villain was the CIA's chief of station in Saigon.

A couple of hours after I had received this book, a few

minutes after I had read it, I was telephoned by one of my CIA fathers, recently retired. He wished to see me at his George-town house first thing in the morning, before breakfast. This was a command rather than an invitation, and I agreed, flattered and intimidated. I spent that night tangled in risible dreams of Istanbul and the Hilton bar and, on waking, wondered whether I should tell the man I would soon see, an OSS legend, about the pratfalls made in his institution's name.

Seeing him at his door, dressed in his robe, exceedingly agitated, I knew I would tell that man nothing. He was not used to being told but to telling, and even then I reflected that such overbearing impatience was not the model temperamental equipment for a collector of intelligence. This man, mighty and consequential, revered by others mighty and consequential, astonished me by saying with immoderate anger that the book I had under review was a masterpiece of falsehood and treachery, that it posed a fundamental threat to the welfare of the United States and its allies, and that it *must* be denounced, that I must do "the right thing." He then took inventory of the book's few factual errors, none momentous, and sent me away. He seemed satisfied that I would do the right thing, when in fact he had enhanced West's stature in my eyes.

How had he learned that I was *The Ambassador*'s reviewer? Why had he bothered—at what risk of my gossip?—trying to manipulate the critical judgment of a cub reporter? I shared these questions with Andrew, who took the episode (I now know) as evidence that I was myself an agent, a secret-sharer in a plot against truth and fair play, taking instruction from my superiors.

Soon thereafter I wrote an exposé of the USIA and the CIA, both of which were subsidizing and commissioning works of propaganda put forth by trade publishers, without reference to their origins, as disinterested works of scholarship. I knew

I had caught the USIA with its britches down (its scheme was memorialized by the *Congressional Record*), but I had no documentary evidence of the CIA's witchwork. So one night at a Georgetown dinner party, in violation of decorum and common sense, I asked my host, an Agency personage, whether the CIA paid for books and bought writers.

"Sure," my friend's dad said. "Many publishers are our pals. Don't say I told you or I'll be *very* cross."

I was stunned. He was so courtly, so sympathetic to my piece and to my career, so amused, so indifferent to having poisoned wells. With his help I went forward with the story, which exposed a practice I now guess he found distasteful (and costly). The report attracted publicity and did me no harm.

Andrew read it: "How did you nail down those CIA details?"

I smiled a deep smile, the smile of an insider protecting a secret. I said nothing. Andrew cocked his head, squinted, tried to read me. Now I know that he believed my information came from the best place of all, from within my own company.

I saw Andrew only once again before he broke in on us in Vermont years later, on his mission of acquittal and repair. He passed through Washington after filming black Mississippi farm workers who had struck rather than starve on wretched wages. They had built a commune, Strike City, where they gathered in tents to decide what to do. They proposed to organize a brickmaking factory, but there were squabbles, and too little money, and it rained and it rained and it rained, and Andrew's documentary had no happy ending.

He was driving home to Putney when he decided to show us the rough cut, and also there that night were my brother Toby and the I. F. Stones. Toby was about to leave for Vietnam as an officer in the Special Forces, and he was more mindful than I what a mixed audience we made. My brother was for me my brother, no imperial running dog, no kid-murderer. Izzy Stone didn't make him feel on top of the world about his forthcoming trip, but by the standards of the day Stone was gentle that night, more eager to teach than to hector. He was grimmer in response to Andrew's movie, finding it beautiful, lovely, exquisite, delicate—but somehow beside some important point. I was disappointed that he and Andrew didn't warm to each other. Andrew was making radical noises, but he and Stone didn't seem to recognize each other as allies. Maybe Stone had already seen a beautiful documentary or two about the oppressed.

It was difficult those days to sort friendships and beliefs. What a mess, the late sixties.

Following a fancy dinner party one night, Nick von Hoffman and I pledged to quit our jobs at the *Post* the next morning if the paper didn't immediately and publicly repudiate its editorial support of the Vietnam War. We were to meet at ten sharp in the office of J. R. Wiggins, to force on him our ultimatum. But when the telephone woke me at ten I was a sick and wretched fellow. "Well?" von Hoffman said. "Maybe tomorrow," I said. "Jesus, it's a big move. Let's discuss it." Von Hoffman laughed an odd laugh, and I crawled back into bed, and a couple of years later he confessed he'd phoned me from his own rack.

All good people hated the war, of course, but there were elegant and clumsy variations on this rancor. I remember another dinner, at our place, with several *Post* reporters and an editor. It was an easy, bright occasion, what we'd come to expect with journalists, quick laughers and late-nighters. One of the reporters had brought along a knockout date, eighteen, maybe younger. She was sullen and mute, picking at her food; thinking to draw her out, I remarked on her ornate ring, and paid it a compliment. "This is a poison ring," she told the table, with no smile, "and unless that bastard McNamara has stopped bombing by Tuesday, I will poison myself with it." (I

checked: on Tuesday, and two weeks from Tuesday, Mc-
Namara had not ceased bombing. I forgot to ask my reporter
friend where they buried his date.)

Sometimes, after too much drink on such a night, after the
guests left, I'd turn morose, decide I'd lost my chance at something. Then, near dawn, I'd phone Andrew and wake him from
his sleep in Putney to bang his ears with my beefs, or to orate
against the war, or to knit a tangled narrative of the CIA's real
and imagined intrigues. I'd ask Andrew what did he make of
the Company, that snake ranch of knotted motives and inter-
locking plots? I couldn't understand his response—surprise,
surprise—because he was too drowsy to speak other than gibberish, or I was too crocked to interpret him. So then I'd ask
the commonplace questions. Where have you been? What
have you been up to?

He'd tell me, with some reluctance (as I now recall), that
he'd organized a filmmakers' cooperative called Newsreel, and
someone else told me that its short movies, shown at com-
munes and on campuses, were introduced by a logo spelled
out with machine-gun bullets. I heard that Andrew had been
in North Vietnam and had made a movie there and that some
of his undeveloped footage, shot on Chinese stock, had been
seized by customs officers, opened and destroyed. And that the
rest had been saved because Andrew had had the cunning to
suggest that the customs officer telephone the CIA, and tell
the Agency what they were destroying.

Later, he would blame me for having informed on him, and
would remember a question I had asked—"What's coming up
next?"—and his reply: "A trip to Hanoi."

I heard that he was teargassed at the 1968 Democratic Convention and that he returned to Chicago to film the Days of
Rage. The year before that, he had broken with me. The occasion was the levitation of the Pentagon by the Fugs, attended
by many a thousand but principally by Norman Mailer. I heard

Mailer do his Southern-sheriff number at an abandoned movie theater; there was a light show, and Robert Lowell did a drunk act, and the following day kids burned their draft cards and driver's licenses and stuffed flowers into the rifles of perplexed soldiers.

While this theater was in progress, I was in my study at home, winding up an essay for *The New Leader* about Ezra Pound, trying to explain why a writer, by design subversive of the common interest, must nevertheless function as a social animal. Two-thirds through this piece I got a demonstration of its conundrum: Andrew phoned to announce that he required the use of my house the following few days, beginning *tout de suite*. He was in Washington with forty or so protesters; they would need a place to crash and food within the hour. I told my best friend that he would not be welcome with his mob, that my baby boy was teething and wailing, that there were other complicated reasons, that I was busy, that I had no choice.

I didn't see or hear from Andrew again for eight years.

Andrew's Putney farm became a commune, and its communards were often rousted by the state police or the FBI during dragnets and manhunts for Weatherpeople or for Angela Davis or for lesser, more local public enemies. I heard tales of a lack of comity on the farm, that while Andrew assailed the values of the middle class, so did his collective brothers and sisters assail his own. One friendly neighbor—there were unfriendly neighbors in abundance—believed Andrew was a patsy, but that he knew he was being used. The tribal women struck and accused the men of treating them like chattels. Then communards of both sexes faced Andrew down and demanded that he share his fortune with them, all of it. They wanted clear title to his farm, and he refused to yield it. Hearing this, I recollected a hoary political fable: a man of high ideals applies

for membership in the Communist Party, and during an admission interview he is asked questions. If he had two houses,
would he give one to the Party? "Of course," he responds.
And two cars, would one go to the Party? "Naturally," he says.
How about two shirts, what if he had two shirts? "No way,"
he says. Why? "Because I got two shirts." Assuredly, the brave
new world bristled with paradox.

Andrew never told me how he had found us in Vermont, or
why he wanted to. At dinner he spoke of his new movie, described by its blurb as a "vast, sprawling fresco whose subject
is birth and rebirth in these United States in the mid-1970s."
Andrew said it was about the Movement and its "survivors,"
about loose ends, truces, navigational checks, interregnum,
pardon. It had, he said, "done well at Cannes." I was surprised
by the show-biz locution, as later I would be by his familiarity
with the ins and outs of hype, his accurate sense of "key"
reviews and promotional timing; the film was about to open
at the New York Film Festival at Lincoln Center. Andrew was
warm to us, sweet and condescending. I suspected that for
Andrew I was a loose end, to be forgiven, a figure for the New
Peace. I began to think, as I drank my wine, that mine was a
role I did wish to play, and I asked Andrew why he had abandoned our friendship.
    The question made him squirm, as though it were a social
climber's gaffe at a formal dinner. His friend cleared her
throat, and Priscilla cleared the table. No one spoke.
    "What happened, Andrew? Where did you *go?*"
    "That's done, Geoffers. Forget it."
    "No, I don't want to. Why did you give up on us?"
    "Well, on you. I gave up on the side you chose."
    "What are you talking about?"
    "During my friends' march on the Pentagon, you said you
didn't want to see Washington burn."

"I didn't."

"I did."

"You were wrong."

"You were wrong."

Then he explained that he couldn't afford to trust me. He told me of the Movement's betrayals, of drugs planted by brothers on brothers to rig charges. He told of COINTELPRO, informers, seditions. I was sympathetic, asked what all this had to do with our friendship.

"Look," he said, "I know what you were and what you still are, I guess."

"And what is that?"

And he told me: I was a spook, a mole, a Company Man. I had been recruited at Princeton, perhaps even before I met him. I had been an agent in Istanbul and in Paris. My Fulbright had been arranged by the Agency so I could infiltrate the radical movement at Cambridge. The Washington *Post* was notoriously a collaborator of the Company and so was *Newsweek*, where I'd worked. Andrew's friend nodded vigorous agreement with these judgments.

"How about Princeton? I taught there. Is Princeton wired in?"

"Are you kidding? Of course. My *father* went to Princeton."

"And my Guggenheim?"

"Howard Hunt had one."

"And now. Here? Perched on the edge of a meadow beyond the back of the goddamned beyond? What am I doing here?"

Andrew shrugged. "I don't know. Hey, Geoffers, I don't care! Deep cover, who knows how you guys work? This isn't why I came, to dredge up these things."

"And my books. My life?"

Andrew shrugged again, made a wig-wag gesture of dismissal, shooing flies. Two of my novels had minor characters in the CIA. Had I been trying to warn him? Anyway, the books were a side issue, not important, of a piece with my strategy of cover and deception. He told me this cheerfully, and I tried to remember that I had loved this man.

His companion spoke, from some deep well of contemplation: "Hey, Andrew? Guys like this [and here she made her own sweeping hand gesture, taking in pets, bric-a-brac, my wife, my sons, my furniture—I mean the furnishings of my life, our tangibles—as well as my countenance] weren't the kinda guys who ratted us out. The pricks who sold us out didn't wear neckties."

"I'm not wearing a necktie," I said.

"Yeah," she said, "but you look like a guy in a necktie. The worst finks were the coolest dudes."

Doubt creased Andrew's brow. Could she be right? And then an odd feeling swept me. I didn't want to be a fellow in a necktie, some square who was no other thing, neither less nor more, than he seemed. I welcomed Andrew's faith that I was deep, a mole-like creature of secretly held codes, a masked man, underground man, slant deceiver. So when my friend, suddenly again a hanging judge, inquired how I had managed to afford my house, to quit *Newsweek* and Princeton, I could have told him. Instead I shrugged: "That's my business, Andrew."

He recapitulated his doubts about me, my preoccupation with spies and their plots, my friends in the Agency, my freedom from conventional responsibilities (in contrast, say, to his bondage?), my questions about his own wartime comings and goings.

"I was your friend, Andrew. Friends ask friends questions."

He shook his head from side to side. Studied his fingers. "I don't know."

And then I was furious. The error was gross: he thought of me as the lowest of things, capable of betraying him and doing him hurt. In my anger I defended myself on the narrowest grounds. Had I not excoriated the CIA in print? (Andrew smirked: what better way to burrow deeper? Anyway, who cared? He was right: who cared?) Had I not . . . had I not . . . had I not *what?* Well, hadn't I many times taken the hide right off America in my essays and reviews?

Andrew said: "What did that cost you? Just words. Did you help? Name someone you helped. By name. What did you change? What did it *cost* you?"

Andrew had no right to this. I owed him nothing now. Once, but not now. Now my debts were to others—Priscilla, my boys. I would justify myself no more to this old friend. I wanted to go to bed. Andrew and I grabbed each other's arms from reflex or learned habit—"Good to see you again, pal," I said; "Good to see you again, my friend," he said—and we parted, he downstairs to bed and I upstairs, where I would lie till sunup staring at my ceiling.

A few days later I wrote Andrew a letter, told him he was crazy: "I know not without reason. I know that you have had reason to suspect people, many people of many things. I can't worry about that: you chose a risky life, and I respect you for that. But I have never done anything, ever, not once, to betray you, hurt you. Imagine if you will, try to imagine, what it means if you have been utterly wrong about me all these years. Imagine that I am *not* an agent of the CIA, FBI, Amerika, of anything except myself and what I believe in. That what I have said to you over the years has had no subtext. Jaysus, I'm stunned, just bowled over. I feel as though I've been McCarthyed, Stalined, Pintered. But I think you know all this. And that you weary of judging people so harshly. But we won't get anywhere until you know that you have been wrong, wrong, wrong about me, who and what I have been, and why I have done what I have done. What I seem is what I am. [!] I hope that's enough for you."

I received a reply, friendly enough, ignoring what was between us. A postcard showing a war scene busy with soldiers, dive-bombers, trenches, red flags. The painting is hung in the Imperial War Museum and shows Lenin and Stalin looking down, as though—improbably—from heaven. It is captioned: "Under the banner of Lenin and Stalin onward to the west!"

I went to New York to see Andrew's movie. Alice Tully Hall at Lincoln Center was filled, and before the lights went down Andrew came onstage to read a plea that we cease murdering our brothers and sisters in Indochina. He read without evident passion, mumbling; the audience was bewildered by his purpose, for America had at last left the field to its enemies. There were a couple of intermissions, and at the first more than half the house took off for good. By the end only a few remained.

The New York Times liked the movie, and I wanted to, but it was a mess. It had radiant sea- and landscapes, shots of sunsets and snowfalls, mountains and coastlines. It got the grubby look of American cities; the photography was professionally—let's say, slickly—executed. But the movie ran past three hours, of which forty minutes showed a natural childbirth that will go far to rouse sexual partners to the banner of contraception. Andrew was co-director, co-screenwriter, co-photographer and co-editor. He also played a blind homosexual potter and saxophonist, the best acting in the movie. There was my old friend: he had somehow learned, during moments stolen from the Revolution, to play tenor sax, and he was good, doing a fair imitation of Coltrane's sheets of sound. What gifts! He still relished playacting, showing off, clowning. *There* was his curiosity: what's it like to be blind? Let's pretend, stumble here and there, roll back the eyes, sniff the air for clues, cock an ear to whispers. What a ham! How proud I was of my old friend, those few minutes he was on screen.

The rest was cant and jargon, mindless, humorless crap:

"You kids have a better relationship to your feelings than I did," a character characteristically verbalizes. The movie was a prolonged complaint by "society's victims" against the crummy cards they had been dealt. What a parade: nudists, acupuncturists, Maoists, Trotskyites, dopers, middle-class hoboes on the lam from the burbs, gorp eaters, crybabies.

I wanted the movie to fail; I didn't want it to fail. And then, as I saw Andrew's face—still boyish, no meanness in it—looking over the almost empty auditorium when the lights at last came up, I thought I understood him. For a moment he had come aboveground. He was himself a mole, but for the moment he was a movie hustler up from underground to walk among us, looking to put his finger on our systems, wishing for his movie success and a long run. Had he powwowed with his comrades about a "media blitz" even as they discussed how to raze our corrupt society and its office buildings? Did they speak communally of "points" and "net of net" and "turnaround"? Had they "shopped" their "property" at the studios? They had.

Well: there would be none of that, as the empty theater foretold, and Andrew looked relieved, a slave emancipated from success and his secret vice, a longing to be well loved and loved by many. There are worse vices; there are few better.

I saw Andrew the next afternoon. I was staying at the apartment of a friend who was in Europe. I telephoned Andrew at his Greene Street loft and was answered by a PhoneMate. Think of it: taps on tape! What revolutionaries these were! I left a number, name and title: "Wolff, from the Company." Andrew returned my call, and we agreed to meet where I was staying, not at all Andrew's turf; I gave him an address on Central Park South.

"Whose apartment?"

"Ask for Joe Fox," I told him.

I heard him sigh, a kind of whistle of admiration. Joe (Geoffers) Fox (Wolff): the network spread wide. Double blinds, safe houses.

When he came over, I talked of his movie, and I was more cruel than candor licensed. (There's repayment for your indifference to *my* work. Shame on me.) Andrew was itchy to leave, looked this way and that at Fox's estimable antiques and paintings, things such as Andrew's father cherished.

"I like pretty things," I said. Perhaps Andrew thought the sideboard had been liberated from Allende's drawing room by some of the boys in my command.

What had undone us? Bad times, the cruel, silly melodramas of the 1960s. Marriage unbinds friends, surely, but I don't believe mine had. It would be easy enough to conclude that we had never approved of each other; Samuel Johnson described the pathetic circumstance whereby "dislike hourly increased by causes too slender for complaint and too numerous for removal." That wasn't us: I remember how it felt to laugh together, and to share—what wasn't too costly to share. Perhaps we never understood each other's interiors; surely we were preoccupied, as the young are, with surfaces, style, affects, manners and short-term consequences. For me art was play—and singular. For Andrew art showed itself as play, but its purpose was to disrupt the conventions he had received; it was political, always had been for him. Because no resistance was raised against either of us, we were not revealed to each other by tests. I would hate to believe that we merely drifted away from what we had loved in each other without even noticing. Such ignorance would be indifference, bad character. I would prefer to believe that we were casualties of that damned war, but I know better. Time, simple time, did us in.

I glanced at my watch, and Andrew asked me for the time. We spoke listlessly of another meeting later in the year. There came a knock on the door, someone to see me on business.

He wore sturdy brogans and a black raincoat. We were not friends, merely professional associates. I introduced him to Andrew, who shook his head sadly. My associate was anxious—perhaps he had interrupted . . . perhaps he should return later? No: Andrew said he was late, had to dummy up an ad for the *Times*.

The movie had a short run in the Village. I have not seen my friend again. But I think about him. Not so much anymore of the wrongs we did each other. I think that whatever friends may be, that's what we were for a while. I think that he taught me, and I taught him. I think, given the odds, that we were lucky to have had as much as we had. And I miss him. Not enough to try to win him again, or to try to be what he would have me be. But enough to have written this.

Drinking

I'm looking at a bookshelf lined with spiral notebooks, my journals. Writers keep journals; I was an apprentice writer so I kept journals, daybooks, night books. I kept them current obsessively, you might say addictively. If I read it, saw it, thought it, ate it, overheard it—in it went. If I drank it, into the record. I began this solipsistic account when I graduated from college, on the theory that my life had just begun; what I did and was done to me thereafter counted. Thereafter was *material*; as writers sometimes say, it's all material.

The thing of it was, inventories were a drag: one meal got to sound much like the couple of dozen that came before in my journal. My sustained narratives were protracted whines: the torts varied in their particulars, but pared to essentials my journal entries tell of lackwits who failed to appreciate my virtue, warmth, tact, candor, generosity. Bad actors who made me mad or sad. I could have written "October 3, 1961—Istanbul: Screwed again" and saved time and ink. Woe was me. My journalistic tic was pathos—pathetic!—and seeing this when I read what I had written made me unhappy with myself. But I reasoned that we're stuck with ourselves; we're our prisoners, no? Back then I was a *que será será* kind of guy; if my privately revealed posture was put-upon, so be it—character was destiny.

As time passed, my journals relentlessly multiplied one pastime or hobby or pursuit, or what should I call it? My journals
came to read like cocktail menus and wine lists written with
a hungover shaky hand. They told so persistently and similarly
of excess, loss of control and morning miseries that their accumulated burden cast me down, finally spooked me so alarmingly that I quit. Keeping a journal.

I wonder, if I can articulate how I got to be a drinker, might
I understand why I wanted to be a writer? At seventeen, sixteen, fifteen, I haunted New York jazz clubs, Jimmy Ryan's
on West Fifty-second and especially Eddie Condon's down in
the Village. Cranked by music and an atmosphere of the illicit
(the places where my school pals and I liked to drink were
said to have been speakeasies: this seemed interesting), I drank
rye-and-ginger by the yard. I was charmed by the ruined faces
of Condon's house band: the awful pallor and florid noses
("grog blossoms," we called them) on Cutty Cutshall and Pee
Wee Russell and Wild Bill Davison and Eddie Condon himself, virtuoso and entrepreneur of ill-spent nights. Believe an
adolescent envying a bad complexion and you might credit
the high times we enjoyed later at college, making an institution of dissipation. Our campus well was a garbage can filled
with fruit juice, a fifty-pound block of ice and gallons of vodka;
we drank from it, dipped our heads in it, were known to puke
in it. This was fun. Heavy drinking in the 1950s was what we
did; not to drink heavily was provocative, off the reservation.

My Silent Generation prized moderation in schoolwork and
career ambitions but practiced passionate excess at the Nassau
Tavern and Spring Houseparties blowouts. Our syllabus sang
of Achilles' armor but our own epics were tales told of horror
shows, blackouts, cars wrinkled or misplaced. Monday's sagas
were of dates ditched and dates who ditched. We behaved as
though we were monarchs, beyond the laws of physics and
physiology; we behaved as though we were monarchs' jesters,

with a sacred duty to distort the tame proportions and decorums of the Eisenhower years. We saw ourselves, upside down
and bottoms up, as mockers and mocked, as childish fools sent
to liberate our post-adolescent old selves too wise for our own
good.

I'm not here to tug my forelock, scuff my toe, put on a long
face and tut-tut-tut who I was and what I did. If I can't remember why it was a ball to stumble headfirst into a garbage
can brimming with grape 'n' grain, I remember very well why
it was agreeable to hang around men who had known the
mighty Bix, horn players in worn double-breasted worsted suits
who slept till sundown and smoked Camels or Luckys and
drank and jammed till sunup. Oh, I miss those nights! I'd sit
again at a small table below the bandstand, eye-level with
Ralph Sutton's feet pumping the piano pedals, squeezed next
to a honey whose complexion wasn't in the least pallid, whose
silk stockings rubbed against my flannels, who smelled of per-
fume and tobacco, who knew better than to tap her swizzle
stick against her highball glass, who drew a nod of appreciation
from Peanuts Hucko while he noodled "Someday You'll Be
Sorry." How can I be sorry, how can I pull my beard and say
I wish I'd spent my nights more profitably, in better company?
I want to shut down this recollection now, and crank up the
turntable and listen to "Just Friends" and "Yellow Dog Blues"
and "Davenport Blues" and "What-cha-Call-'Em Blues" and
"Indiana" and "Minor Drag" and "That's A-Plenty" and
"Someday You'll Be Sorry."

I'm back, and I'm sorry. I couldn't play the cornet like Wild
Bill or the clarinet like Peanuts or even the four-string guitar
like Eddie, but I could stay up all night making a kind of
music, and I think staying up all night and sleeping all day
was half why I came to write; the other half, I hope, was the
music. The drinking was incidental.

. . .

Many writers drink. Maybe it's the irregular habits, the off-the-clock hours—many writers are drunks. Maybe some ultrahigh frequency in writing's music screws up the liver's works, queers the kidneys, but many writers are alcoholics. Correction: many American writers are alcoholics. How many? Too many. The dead cannot sue, so I'll name the dead: F. Scott Fitzgerald, Jack London, Hart Crane, Conrad Aiken, Edna St. Vincent Millay, Thomas Wolfe, Dashiell Hammett, Truman Capote, Tennessee Williams, John Berryman, Ring Lardner, Dorothy Parker, John O'Hara, James Agee, Robert Lowell, John Cheever, Raymond Carver. I think I neglected to mention Jack Kerouac, Edgar Allan Poe, Edward Arlington Robinson, Ambrose Bierce, J. P. Marquand, James Thurber, Robert Benchley, Theodore Roethke. Oh, and five of seven Americans who won the Nobel Prize: Eugene O'Neill, William Faulkner, John Steinbeck, Ernest Hemingway and Sinclair Lewis, who once in conversation asked, "Can you name five American writers since Poe who did *not* die of alcoholism?"

The vocation sounds as perilous as stripping asbestos, mining coal. So who'd wish to be an American writer? Incredible question. A credible question: who wouldn't wish to be an American writer? But why? For the art of it? (Eventually, if the aspirant hangs in there, for the art of it, maybe.) For the fame of it? (Seven and a half minutes of experience added to seven and a half of reflection will teach the densest careerist that Warhol was wrong; everyone doesn't get fifteen minutes of street recognition.) For the money? (Get serious.) For what, then? Why did I want to write?

For the romance. At eighteen I traveled back and forth across Spain for the spring season of *corridas*, carrying *Death in the Afternoon*. Central to this experience—you might say its ruling purpose—was squirting wine from a *bota* approximately into my mouth. I can taste it now on my tongue, a coppery bitterness, the nasty rotgut *roja* in no way improved by having been decanted into an unseasoned goatskin sack. This was glamorous. Lady Brett was glamorous. Jake Barnes was glamorous, although, in fairness to my generation's general good sense, I'll concede that no one I knew got himself emasculated in order to be glamorous in just the way Jake was glamorous.

Does this sound mannered? Farfetched? After the stock market crash, after Zelda's crash, after the crash of his reputation, F. Scott Fitzgerald took account of his wrecked health and cracked-plate spirit and wrote in his notebook: "Then I was drunk for many years and then I died." Trying without much luck to dry out, jittery and bone-tired, he was roused from shaky sleep in the Great Depression gloom of 3 a.m. by a mighty banging on his door. There he found a stranger, a young college boy, drunk: " 'Here I am at last,' the young scholar said, teetering triumphantly. 'I had to see you. I feel I owe you more than I can say. I feel that you formed my life.' "

That's an old story about Fitzgerald. I read it in *The Crack-Up* when I was a schoolboy. I thought it was a funny story then. I saw the brash kid, understood his quixotic mission. I knew what he meant, too: I already had a hunch I wanted my idea of Fitzgerald to form my life. I wanted to ride up a great New York avenue on the roof of a taxi, maybe even steal a dip in the Plaza's fountain. Was that inspired or what?

Now of course I see another scene on Fitzgerald's stoop, 3 a.m. Now I see a man with the shakes, in a seedy bathrobe, his hairless paper-white stick-legs scuffling a pair of slippers to the door. Now I see Fitzgerald in the pre-dawn sick and scared and bewildered by the ruckus. But if I had seen then what I see now, would I have ever begun? Writing, I mean. (Drinking I would have begun.) Sure, because it was all wonderland back then. Dissolution was romantic. Death by consumption was Keatsian, fervidly true and beautiful. Self-destruction was visionary. Baudelaire had written: "Always be drunk. That is all: it is *the* question . . . How? Use wine, poetry, or virtue, use your imagination. Just get drunk." No religion could have been as unyielding in its commandment: Go Too Far. Appetite and carelessness seemed to me in the fifties and sixties to be indispensable properties of literary writing. Getting drunk did. How? We used wine, tequila, Pernod, Hudson Bay rum, dimies, whatever.

Why did self-ruin seem such a fine idea? You might say self-sacrifice was at the root of it, the notion of the writer so feverishly called to his art that he burned himself on the altar of its exactions. You might say this if you're full of crap. You might say the writer is fundamentally an outsider, outlaw, outcast, outlandish, out of bounds, out of phase, out-and-out outrageously out of his mind. This gives excess an audacious air of derring-do, a refusal to be bound. This would be a glamorous explanation of drunkenness, were it not for the reality of William Faulkner passing out on his toilet in the Algonquin, falling back against a steam pipe, so drunk the pain didn't stir him, cooking the flesh from his back, suffering a profound third-degree burn, getting skin grafts, feeling the pain for the rest of his life, telling a friend who asked why Faulkner did it, why he drank himself insensible, "Because I like to!"

A place to divide here is on the question of whether you find Faulkner's reply heroic or flip. I can hear a previous incarnation of myself reading "Because I like to," nodding approval concurrent with feeling an uncomfortable frisson of recognition. My father liked to.

My father was not a glamorous drunk. Sober he could enchant, charm, bewitch, con; Duke was a stutterer with a gift of gab. Drunk he was a stumblebum. Late at night as a kid, I'd hear the front door open, listen for the step. If his step was deliberate, we were in for it. After my mother had enough, and then my stepmother, I was in for it. We lived many places low and some high, but when he was high, high was worse.

The stairs: he'd pull himself up a step at a time, muttering. There'd be a failure midway: he'd knock a picture off the wall, or lean too hard against the rail and break a baluster, or trip. Then he'd be on my bed reminding me what a miserable pismire I was, how I'd failed him, betrayed him, held him back, kicked him in the ass: *Old Lyme . . . Sarasota . . . Seattle . . . New York . . . Wilton . . . La Jolla: Screwed again.* Then he'd be on his knees, driving the porcelain bus, heaving up his Dutch courage; then, next morning, he'd be on his knees, begging forgiveness for words he claimed he couldn't recall, words he maybe couldn't recall. I could recall them pitch-perfect, and what I wondered then: Is *veritas* in *vino?* If so, the truth had been said last night: I was a miserable pismire; he'd been sapped by me. Come morning, my dad wasn't interested in my metaphysical inquiry, but in his: "Why do I do it?" he'd ask me.

Maybe he liked it. Maybe he had a disease. Who cares? I'm sorry: *now* who cares? What I care to ask is why—knowing what I knew—did I do it? I could say genetics. I could read my journals and hear his melodramatic keening and explain: DNA dunnit. Raising a glass black with Wild Turkey, I'd cry cheers, to your health, bottoms up . . . just like Dad. Like him, I'd drink myself sick and call it a toot. I'd be *overtaken*, or say, like Duke, "It got drunk out last night and a little fell on me."

But I know—I mean I *know*—genes didn't dunnit. I'll forever be the prisoner of my memory of him, and sometimes that memory is as sweet as sometimes it is foul. But I'm not him. He drank from leaden despair, and I drank revved from excitement, elation. He got potted (again) the night he got canned (again); I got lit on Publication Day. He'd scowl; I'd sing. He'd insult his best friend among a rapidly diminishing store of friends; any stranger on any stool beside me was my best friend.

As an apprentice writer, I had a drinking buddy, an apprentice writer. Now we're friends the way people are friends, but then we got together to drink together. We'd meet in the city at dinner parties and together drink up the hosts' spirits and patience, and then we'd go back to his place and keep his wife awake all night, or my place and keep my wife awake all night. We'd put jazz on the turntable and talk above Billie Holiday or Ben Webster or Fats Navarro. We'd talk about the things closest to our hearts; no one else could understand. We'd talk about art, vision, restlessness, recklessness, sacrifice, a sacred calling. Scotch for him, for me bourbon. One would confess his highest hopes, deepest fears; the other would listen, nodding. Unless of course the confessor's or the confessee's drink went dry mid-confession, in which case so much for highest hope and deepest fear: to the kitchen mid-sentence, to the ice bucket, to the bottle.

Boozing was ever a matter of timing. Time came when cities were too ruinous for me, when I took to the hills and did my serious drinking solo. I'd put the jazz on the turntable, gather my mixings close to hand. Earphones were available; my wife could pretend to sleep after midnight, two, four . . . you know. What was the harm? I was never never never never never mean. I was sweet as pie: fat, dumb and happy. I'd fill my glass at two in the a.m., and play Side A, Track 1, John Coltrane's "Cattin'." By the time the needle got to the end of Side A, I'd still have an inch in my glass. I needed music to wash down the drink, so I'd flip to Side B, "Anatomy." Before the needle reached Track 2, "Vodka," I'd run out of bourbon. I needed bourbon to appreciate Coltrane's "Vodka," so I'd reload. The timing was a bitch. At four I'd laboriously dial my brother in San Francisco—shank of the evening out there—and get the wrong number, and dial again, all thumbs, till I got him awake, and bring him the Good News, he was about to hear John Coltrane play "Lush Life," long distance, just for him, this was going out to my brother in California, "Lush

Life," a long, long track. This was before fiber optics, before
you could hear a pin drop over the phone line. It was difficult
to get high fidelity out of the earphones into the telephone
mouthpiece, so my loudspeakers were rumbling "Lush Life,"
and my wife wasn't pretending to sleep anymore, and she
thought it was time to end the last set. That was always a tricky
moment, the Jiggs & Maggie confrontation. "That's enough,
now. Come to bed."

Standing on my dignity, I'd weave; I'd squint, maybe think,
Who's she to talk to *me* that way? But I'd obey. And next
morning, wrung out and sick and of no use, I'd apologize for
stealing sleep from my family, but for sure I wasn't my father.
Of course once upon a time my father wasn't my father. Once
upon a time he drank to loosen up, giggle, tap a toe to a tune,
tell a tale. Once upon a time he didn't brood out loud.

The day came when I felt ready to brood out loud. It came
over me like a low-grade fever. Well into a fifth of Mount Gay,
I'd been laughing with my wife; abruptly, the effect of no
knowable cause, I felt aggrieved, began to simmer. I was on
the edge of giving words to my grievance, looking for just those
words that might most forcefully deplore the bad cards I'd
been dealt, been dealt *by her, by God!* And on the edge of
finding those words (in *vino* is for sure not *veritas*) I put a sock
in it, corked the bottle, shut up, turned in.

That was years ago. The plural makes for a nicely vague
personal history, suggesting a then too far gone to locate now.
Fact is, that was several years ago. I drink a little; I don't get
drunk. Whether I am or ain't is not a question I want anymore
to ask, not a question I can answer. I met a few times with a
counselor expert in these matters and I was eager to attest to
the malady, but he kept raising the stakes on me. Our meetings
declined into disputes about semasiology, diagnosis, inference,
exegetics, veiled subplots, the meanings of meanings. There
were the Ten Danger Signs (I scored a mere nine, never having

had a yen on waking for what put me to sleep) and AA's Twelve Steps. I quit for a summer, drank nonalcoholic beer unfortunately called Moussey, pronounced not like Mighty's surname but like the diminutive of a great antlered creature, but still. My counselor was alarmed about the nonalcoholic beer, said it was confirming evidence of my addictive personality, that if I didn't stop drinking near beer I'd soon be a slave to cocaine. Really and truly. He was most anxious about my future with cocaine. I was eager to give him confessions as lurid as those I had heard at my AA meeting (one meeting only: its narratives were so extravagantly squalid—and so polished from repeated tellings by out-of-town ringers imported to the basement of a pretty little church in our pretty little village—that they humbled me, held me at arm's length, made me ashamed to pretend to belong in the same room with maestros of misery), but cocaine was beneath my interest and beyond my means. *Just wait*, the counselor warned. If I continued to drink nonalcoholic beer, *just wait and see*. He had a point. I was going through twelve and fifteen bottles a day, and this bewildered me until I studied the label and discovered that Moussey was *almost* nonalcoholic. After all, Beck's was a simpler solution. For me.

Still, whatever I was, I'm not it now. This wasn't jogging or throttling back on spareribs or eating oat cakes; this was a turnabout. But I wonder still why so many writers drink? I think some drinkers, from solid self-knowledge, knowing what will come of them working nine-to-five in the company of others, choose to write, to keep their own counsel, hours, company. But it can be a drag, keeping your own company. Samuel Johnson, asked by his friend Spottiswoode why he chose wine for his companion, answered for me: "To get rid of myself, to send myself away." Writing is hard. I don't mean it's harder than everything, because it's not; I mean only that it's uphill work to write. And what's toughest is the din that echoes in a

writer's ears after day's work is done. A writer can't shut down
the damned noise, his characters' voices, their competing complications. You walk from the desk rubber-legged and sit picking at dinner like a zombie, coming awake to scribble a note
on a napkin or on the palm of your little boy's hand. Day's
work's done, but you can't keep your fiddling hands off the
pages; the book's machinery diesels on long after you've turned
the key to shut it down. It won't shut down, won't shut up.

And this is why I write? To hear those insistent, nattering
voices? To lie on my back, staring at the dark ceiling, imag-
ining disasters for make-believe characters? To turn on the
reading light, scribble a note at 3 a.m., edit it at four-thirty?
To race the mind into sleeplessness? To see a dim unfocused
light and then to focus it on the back of your mind and turn
it up so bright it stabs your eyes and clamps a vice on your
head? Malcolm Lowry, who wrote himself to glory and drank
himself to miserable death, said he felt as though he had been
born without a skin. Indeed. I write to take off my skin, lay
my nerves bare. I write to hear unwelcome voices. Booze will
send me to never-never land, dress me in thick wool, earmuff
me against the voices, blink off the light, give rest and sleep
and peace. Just what I must have wanted. Just what I don't
want.

At the Fair: Dairyness
and Human Sacrifice

From the Ferris wheel it's possible to experience the fair's schitzy character, bucolic and menacing. The seat's slats have been cracked and many times painted over, bright blue, bright red, bright green—what's the use?—bright blue again. Grease has congealed at the joints where the seat swings on its groaning axle, and light rain leaks from a dismal sky that presses like an iron lid on the rusty mud below. The air is cold today, Saturday, nearly two weeks past Labor Day. The wheel has stopped, and from this prominence the Vermont hills cupping the fairground at Tunbridge seem almost companionable. To the west, the sun—were there a sun to see—would be setting, and the trotting races have just ended, and the sheep and swine and oxen have been returned to their stalls from the judging runs.

A few children ride the Ferris wheel, and their earthbound parents are anxious to scoot them home; night brings mischance to the "World's Fair" (people have come from the known world's far corners, from Canada and Connecticut even) here in Orange County. The wheel has not moved, and the rawboned operator wearing a greasy duck-ass hairdo is busy scouting the mud with a metal detector—hoping, I guess, it will buzz with the discovery of coins fallen from the riders' pockets. The contraption's mute, and the young operator re-

turns to his levers and spins the shaky wheel a half-turn. I've
been riding long enough and I'd like to dismount, but the kid's
mind is elsewhere, not on my wishes. Others have been re-
volving longer than I, and some are visibly uneasy. There's no
government here, and I'm spinning on a huge and complicated
contrivance casually knocked down and reassembled by people
indifferent to me. The young man cocking his eye for windfall
from our pockets is no airline pilot. Now he lets the shuddering
wheel rotate untended, leaving his controls to bullshit with a
buddy who pulls on a smoke from the pack he's unrolled from
his T-shirt sleeve. Our operator drinks from a half-pint of
something. Aren't there rules outlawing this kind of thing? No
one shouts at him to stop the damned wheel. I feel, grinding
round and round, like an organ-grinder tethered to a monkey.

Lights have been winking on along the midway, and the
noise is reaching higher. Motorcycle engines, barkers, customers working their damnedest to fill the night with laughter. I
hear the sad falling note of bells rung in the heavy air. To the
left down there, strong farmers from hereabouts and workers
from the marble quarries up in Barre are trying to ring the
bell. They pay four bits for three swipes with a sledge, driving
a weight up a column; the weight may or may not strike a
bell; if the bell rings, a guy who never looks at anything except
the cash—in his fist—hands over a nickel stogie. The challenge is to ring the bell with one arm, and then with the other,
weaker arm. But these strong men are too drunk on beer to
drive the weight high, and when the bell doesn't ring, they
shrug, pretending not to care. They care.

The wheel on its rounds passes the loading platform, and I
let the operator know I've had enough. What does he care? I
spin away from him, feeling as silly as a tot in a swing-set, go
through an almost full revolution, slow, fumble with my safety
catch; he grins and pushes the lever to full throttle and up I
go again, *knowing* it's dumb to give this jerk the finger, giving

him the finger. This wheel and my vantage are creaky fabrications: I'm riding it to establish a point of view *du haut en bas*. I don't so much want to grasp what I'm about to tell as poke at it with a long stick, which I'd like to hold in a gloved hand. Now I'm on high again, looking down at a concession called GIRLS that has brought me to this place. The year before, I was on this wheel with my kids, one on each side, looking down at three or four near-naked women taking a full shot of noon sun on the Lord's Day. One of my boys was looking at farm animals, or daredevil drivers, and the other was looking with me, at GIRLS, listening to the barker's cry.

Calling all the men—girlie-girlie show time for the men! Red-hot and ginger, spice is nice. Hootchy-kootchy, carnival-style, get your tickets, we're starting right now, get right down there in front, right down there in the baldheaded row. Right down there in the finger-lickin' good row where you can look up and see the hole, I mean the WHOLE damned show. Show time for the men, no ladies and no babies, people as wears pants and looks like men, calling all the men . . .

The year before, like now, there had been two girlie shows. One had big girls, the other had young girls, and the "bally call"—the name carnies give their pitch—was for one much as for the other, same phrases, with kindred internal rhymes and singsong rolling cadences. Last year I had left my kids with my wife and bought a ticket to the show featuring big girls. I entered the tent with a couple of pals, smirking, recollecting burly-que I had seen as a teenager in Florida and Tennessee, all come-on behind feathers and fans, as innocent as the unveiling of Little Egypt. Inside the tent were cops, sheriff's deputies armed with maximum flashlights and billies but no revolvers, and my friends and I smiled at the police like accomplices; we meant to have the law understand we were here to look at the lookers rather than the girls. We kept our hands out of our pockets and stood near the deputies, who didn't smile back, who moved from us as though plague bells hung from our necks.

Beneath the canvas, men pressed as close as they could, chest-level to a makeshift stage. These men, mostly past middle years, made up the baldheaded row, and behind them, far enough apart to announce themselves as a different class of being altogether, lounged younger men, lady-killers. And behind these I stood with my friends. And behind us the cops. There were no women in the tent except the three whose business it was to show us whatever we had come to look at. For a wonder there were no teenagers, with their hands in their pockets, clamping down on their boners while the performers' gauze and boas swirled. The show lasted less than ten minutes, and before it ended it wiped the smirk off my face. My friends and I didn't look at one another when we left, stooping to exit under a flap at the rear of the tent into bright sun. Our wives asked for a rundown, teasing us, mock-scolding with playful libby jargon about chauvinist boys and their sex objects. My friends and I didn't want to talk about what we'd seen, less to laugh about it. An old guy, drunk and witless, without teeth, had tried to pull himself up on the stage and the cops had chucked him out like a spadeful of manure, tenderly lifting the tent flap so he wouldn't soil it. He was wearing a red sombrero with cotton tassels, a prize from the dart-throwing booth, and I told Priscilla much about the sombrero. She must have wondered what about the sombrero so amused and interested me. I couldn't say to my wife *I don't want to talk about it*, as though I'd been traumatized in war, but I *really* didn't want to talk about it.

For months I thought about what happened under that tent, and then began to talk about it, and then talked too much about it. So I came back alone to look again, and try to make sense of this pipsqueak World's Fair. So here I am, orbiting back to earth on this Ferris wheel, whose operator sets me free. I stare at him; this is meant to be a baleful look, a terrifying squint. He looks right through me; if I didn't know better, I'd swear I haven't terrified him. I loiter with the crowd in mud while the rain falls, looking up at two women moving more or less in time to distorted rhythm and blues amplified way past the capacity of an overloaded loudspeaker. A third woman, half her body backstage, licks her lips and humps a curtain, conventional striptease moves, garden variety. Meantime a barker with patient eyes paces leisurely back and forth giving the bally call.

Don't hesitate and don't be late, they're gonna shimmer, shake and vi-bo-rate. The big one the bad one the long one the strong one the red-hot one. Red-hot ramble, shake it up, shake it down, shake it all the way to town. Charge your battery, wind your clock, they're gonna put pepper in your pepper pot. You know what you wanna see, they know what you wanna see, that's what you're gonna see. That's exactly what you're gonna see. Shake it loose like a bucket of juice—they're gonna do it. Have no fear, these girls are here. Racy, spicy, horny and red-hot. Hootchy-kootch, a red-hot ramble waiting for you. They're gonna shake it to the east, they're gonna shake it to the west, they're gonna shake it down the middle where you boys like it best. Come on, boys, when the line breaks, the show will start. When you walk out of this one, boys, your hands are way down deep in your pockets, you have a smile on your face and a brand-new grip on your life. It's raining, boys, come in out of the rain . . .

Carnival is fundamentally case-hardened conservative, a process of repetitions lockstepped into the condition of ritual. Surprises: rain, a police bust, gear breaking down, a dancer angry or in tears—these are not welcome. Actions slip into grooves and polish themselves slippery with use. Thus bally calls vary only subtly from barker to barker and are said by carny legend to have evolved from a black man, the Ur-ballyhooer, a genius of insinuation. Carny legend tells too of the first girl—Georgette—who decided in the middle of strip-tease to hell with the tease part; they say she was nothing to look at, pop-eyed and skinny, the daughter of a girl-show impresario; they say that one night in the way-back time she quit dancing, stripped, and shoved her crotch into a man's face and said, "Here it is, jerks, this is what you want, this is what you got." The better mousetrap.

So now a huge woman, her pale flesh lapping like seas, re-moves a patron's eyeglasses, hearing aid attached, and wipes them between her legs. There is music, but she pays its beat no mind. She straddles another consumer's face and coos, "Ooooh, baby, don't bite." Another customer fingers her; she doesn't seem to notice; the man feeling her wears an abstracted expression, as though he's wondering whether his left front tire might be losing air. Men throw their hats on the stage, and their pocket watches, to have them touched to the magic place. The performer is good-natured. The next dancer is not. She of the erstwhile come-hither look, so recently doing it outside with a beaded curtain, is not pleased to be here. She concentrates on the music, counterfeits something like a dance, scowls when the clients shout at her to be friendly, be nice, come close. Even the women who'll be touched don't like to be held. The story goes that not so long ago a performer removed the eye of a customer with her spiked heel when the sorry joker grabbed her ankle and wouldn't turn loose. The sullen dancer splits and the third hootchy-kootchy comes on stage, and about a dozen men, who seem to know her, call her a pig, and then eat her out. She seems not to take their abuse seriously. Boys will be boys, nothing personal. She grins. Hey, it's a hard dollar, but who said a job was all strawberries and cream?

What am I doing here? Well, at this time I live in Vermont, near the Mad River, a couple of valleys over; I might say I have come the better to understand my neighbors. Nah. I've come to reckon some puzzles about myself. Even before I was a Boy Scout, I'd thought of sex as black comedy, the carnal as carnival. Throughout my adolescence, and the prolonged adolescence of college and bachelor years, I'd regarded women as angels or whores, as tricks to be mastered. To "get in," to get "it," to "grab" it, to "bang" it had been my boss preoccupation. During a lecture on *The Faerie Queene*, I'd make a list of girls I had known, ranking them on which base I'd been allowed to reach. According to this calculus, I'd regarded progress as manifest destiny, base to base, a kiss today followed by two tomorrow, covered tit by bare. This was a campaign, but fundamentally farcical: the would-be loverboy prayed in the back seat for three hands and composed himself with the lexicon of "lover's nuts" and "huge huggers" and "hand jobs" and "rubbers" and "boners"; on the battlefield we suffered geographical confusion (here? there? is it in?). As in any combat, we soldiers armed ourselves with bluster: to the besieged's archetypal question—"How can it be fun if you know I don't want it?"—came the besieger's archetypal response—"You supply the pussy, I'll supply the fun."

Now I'm here at the fair investigating my complicity in a grotesque, Bosch-like model of men and women together. Am I, after all, like these troglodytes, merely less drunk and more discreet? I plan to explore as though I am a disinterested reporter this straw man of a question, this scarecrow I have fabricated. I show a press card: I interview the performers.

The girls don't class themselves with hookers or even bar girls. This is show biz, they're dancers. One lucky break and next week it's "Tony Orlando and Dawn." Hoofers. "It's freaky," one said. "The men are better performers than the women, honest to God, the men are the performers, the women are the audience. It's not like I'm doing it, it's their show that I'm going to see, it's not mine. The guys are getting into it, the guys are pulling each other's pants off."

With an occasional time-out for war or hurricane, the Tunbridge Fair has been held since 1847. Its purpose is to give folks an occasion to let themselves go after a summer of hard work, after the crops have been brought in, before winter screws down on them. Tunbridge is a handsome little town in central Vermont with a couple of Federal brick houses—sure sign of bygone wealth thereabouts—and a covered bridge contiguous to the fairground. Shirley Jackson could have set "The Lottery" in Tunbridge. Ask a local woman about the fair in her town and she'll tell how it brings a nice wage to the locals to provide services. Ask her when's the best time to bring children and she says, "Almost any day, never at night, never on Saturday at any time." Ask her what goes on at night, on Saturday at any time, and she shrugs, and tries to grin. "You know."

No one can know—can guess—without seeing. What happens inside the tents of the girlie shows has no bearing on sex and everything to do with violence, with ritual sacrifice. "It's really scary," a dancer said. "You don't know whether they're going to laugh at you . . . you're afraid they're going to laugh at you, or else the men're going to leave, or else they're going to demand their money back, or else they're just going to stare and look at you, or else they're going to—I don't know what all."

Inside Whitey's girlie show the tent is cold and damp. Two black performers and a white, basic routine. Young men stick out their tongues at the stage, give war whoops and laugh, "Come here goddammit, let's see them tits, my hands are cold, bring on them muffs!"

It costs three dollars this year. The young bravos shoulder

aside the old coots who come down once a year from the hills for a peek and a taste. Two days ago the girls got off easy; Friday was raw and Saturday—today—is unspeakable. The men are pinching the women, biting them, pulling their pussy hair. Sometimes it seems they'll eat them alive, truly eat them. Dionysian rites called for such orgiastic feasting, the tearing apart and consumption of sacrificial animals. This bacchanal connects with some such primitive free-for-all. License is the purpose. Chaos makes these men feel great. What's happening here in this pretty New England town is fundamental, ancient, base. The law watches disgusted—that much is clear—and stands motionless, fingering his billy. The performers look confused, unsure what is expected of them. Nothing can satisfy these men. The more forthcoming the women, the more savage the men, snapping at them. I mean it: wanting to bite. The men are farmers, druggists, salesmen, motorcycle hoods, construction workers, accountants . . . I see a farmer from my valley, one of my town's selectmen; when he wears a jacket and tie to Town Meeting, he looks like an ambassador to the Court of St. James. Now he's not wearing a jacket and tie, and he's here in the tent. Together with a policeman. And by the way: me. No, whatever else I may have been, I am not and never was these men's accomplice. These men scream: "One, two, three, four, we don't want your fuckin' whores!" What *is* this?

Remember "The Lottery"? In just such a pretty town, the narrator tells in a rational voice, a citizen is selected by lot, in an annual ritual, to be stoned to death. It's possible, I guess, to press this too far: cannibalism, rites of expiation and sublimation, Bacchic festivals, low-down barbarism. It's possible to argue that this is no more than a gamey county fair, the boys a little too far gone on beer. Old-timers refer to the Tunbridge Fair as the "drunkards' reunion" and tell apocryphal yarns of years past when any man found sober after 3 p.m.

was ejected from the grounds. A newspaper from 1901 reports that "there was liquor on the grounds and several arrests were made late in the afternoon of both the hilarious and the stupid."

The men come to booze and fight. There's a beer hall beneath the grandstand of the stadium where Chipwood Brothers Daredevil and Hell Riders do their thing. It's brightly lit, with a cement slab floor and long tables covered with oilskin. There's an entrance and an exit, where the police cluster, ready. The windows are protected by wire mesh, and from the outside looking in you have a vision of bedlam, of the bear pit. Ditto from the inside looking out, at the midway. Sots sit jammed together on benches, puking and pissing in place from time to time, swilling beer as fast as they can grab it. Mostly they have come to fight, with one another or with the cops. The game is to try to enter through the exit or exit through the entrance, provoking hard words and a billy upside the head. An arrest. Loud cheers. Victory sign. Blood.

A Vermont bard, Mark Whalon, wrote some lines titled "The Saddest Sound at the Fair." (He had in mind "the last toot of the merry-go-round.") His second stanza catches an idealized vision of such a festival as the Tunbridge Fair:

> *The youngsters are tired and whine and fret*
> *With the stomach-ache from all they've et.*
> *Your woman starts in a-jawin' you*
> *Because you took a "swaller" or two.*
> *She's mad clear through because you went*
> *Into that Hawaiian hula tent.*
> *What makes her maddest is just because*
> *You didn't come out when you seen what it was.*

The fair is sweet, too. Sheep and poultry are shown, usually by kids. The best plate of eight plums, any variety, wins a premium of a silver dollar. Exhibitors show their rutabagas and kohlrabi and Swiss chard. The biggest sunflower, grandest pumpkin and most distinguished display of gourds do not go unremarked or unrewarded. In Floral Hall one will admire embroidery and needlework, handmade dolls, doilies, crewelwork. In these exhibit halls people are easy with one another, admiring, chipper. Little kids wander here and there, munching cotton candy and fried dough. Chelsea High School sponsors a monster barbecue, and the students work hard to make it nice. Out behind the barbecue tent animals are being judged; this is serious business, the improvement of the breed, class tells. Four teens, two girls and two boys, lead fawn-colored Guernsey cows before the judge. He studies them, hefts their full sacs, praises one especially for her "dairyness," for her "useful kind of udder," for her "impressive teats."

"Swing those tits, you fucking sow! Give me a feel, goddammit."

A baldheaded man in the girlie tent yells at his friend: "Luther, looky that nooky. Ain't them titties too much?"

"No such of a thing as too much, Curly." Luther's motorcycle jacket commends him as a member of the Happy Swallows. He and Curly each fastens himself to a tit, Romulus and Remus. Curly's tattoo says "Born to Lose," of course. Another man, like Luther and Curly middle-aged, watches the performers with a critical eye, periodically muttering *sheee-it*. His jacket displays a dragon, for some reason upside down, above the legend "Born at Sea, Baptized in Blood, Crowned in Glory."

Many of the bumper stickers read "I'm Proud To Be A Farmer." This pride is palpable. The migrations from the farms of Vermont have been devastating, but those who have stayed and held the line are as tough and serious as the people

who improbably settled this state, removing tons of rocks for
every acre of mean clay they managed to put into cultivation,
settling here when land was open to the west, facing this
damned climate—"eleven months of winter and a month of
hard sledding," as the playful saying goes. Future Farmers of
America, teenagers who present their beasts for judgment, are
expected to wear khaki or white clothes, and they'd better be
clean. They are judged not only by their animals but by mim-
eographed standards nailed to every barn door at the Tunbridge Fair. These include "proper manure disposal; pails and
tools—neat, adequate, practical; cooperation; willingness to
cooperate with rules and regulations; assist with other exhibitors and have a good attitude toward management."

Ed Larkin's Old Time Contra-Dancers draw a decent crowd.
Local people from Tunbridge and Chelsea get themselves up
in antique costumes—beaver toppers, swallowtail coats, bon-
nets and shawls—and dance to a fiddle and piano. The calls
are as intricate as the steps. The dancers dance up near the
old schoolhouse on the Green. Preservation is the purpose,
instruction, community. They dance to "The Moon Is Shining Bright on Pretty Redwing" while urban runaways and
communards—of whom there are a surplus in these parts—
clap their hands gravely, or photograph them. Farther up the
Green, antique buggies are aligned, and antique farm machinery, and antique steam engines puff, lovingly preserved.
There's a museum of antique crafts. A blacksmith shows how
to beat horseshoes into shape, and Vermont's recent pilgrims
from the big and bad cities sigh in wonder. Blacksmithing—
what a folkway! Someone is blowing glass, another hammering
silver, another weaving cloth. The weaver and the blacksmith
wear costumes maintained with unimaginable care and
handed down through generations of Green Mountain Boys
and Green Mountain Girls. The people from the cities look

at these exhibits as though they were pressed between the leaves of an anthropology textbook, or behind glass, or displayed on a stage.

Back in 1958 a local minister harangued and scolded, and managed to get the girlie shows shut down. Next year the shows were back, as raw as ever, and the preacher had been run out of town. (After a decent interval of eight years, a special service of worship was instituted at the fair; it is well attended.) This year the Orange County state's attorney shut down the gambling concessions—a minority of them, fifteen. Most games of chance are dice games that pay two-to-one against three-to-one odds. There are also variations on roulette, played for a quarter or dollar a spin, the money flying from the pockets of shrewd, squint-eyed farmers and horse traders to the pockets of edgy, baffled-eyed carnies, the money moving in huge amounts. The losers know they're being jobbed and don't give a damn. The Tunbridge Fair comes once a year.

The state's attorney shut down some gambling concessions because he had had complaints of flimflam, would you believe it? Not about the dice and roulette games but about the pick-a-duck, knock-over-the-milk-bottles, pop-a-balloon cons. They're nominally played for small coins, for fun, to win a stuffed animal or a plastic statuette of Jack Kennedy. Someone lost more than a hundred dollars. He picked a duck, won a prize. Picked another, won another. Again. The operator said, "Okay, let's cut the crap. You've got me boiling. I'll play you for a sawbuck." The operator lost to the player. Again. Up went the ante. There went a hundred dollars. Great was the hubbub when the state's attorney shut down these enterprises. The carnies cried foul, the lawman was playing politics with a way of life, with their livelihoods. Not even political ambition would mislead him to interfere with the girlie shows. The girlie shows "disgust me," he says. He gets "occasional complaints," he says—say, from a mom who feels bad to have had her little girl have to watch a stripper hump a beaded curtain on the way from the parking lot to the Contra-Dancers. But what happens inside the tent: that's First Amendment stuff, sacred.

The menfolk of Vermont will not abide dictation. An acquaintance from my valley, a veteran of a quarter-century of Tunbridge Fairs, says it's not like it was. "Cops here, cops there. What the hell's going on these days? I come to do what I want, drink as much as I want to drink, have fun. Now someone tells me I can't sit here, can't piss away my money on a bet. Why?" He weighs maybe three hundred pounds, and has the touch of a pianist with his backhoe and bulldozer, and when I saw him at the fair his face was badly cut. I asked him what had happened. "A little scrap with my wife," he said, and winked. "What do you think of the girlie shows?" I asked him. He was stunned by the question, visibly insulted. "Do you think I'd watch that crap?"

He comes mostly to watch the oxen- and horse-pulling. A yoke of oxen must pull its load—up to eleven thousand pounds—six feet forward, on a sled called a "boat." The concrete weights are added in slabs weighing half a ton each until all the teams except one have been eliminated, and the winner takes home seventy-five dollars, not enough to pay for feed and transportation. The men driving these teams spend maybe a thousand dollars, sometimes three thousand, for one animal, and they beat them with their fists to encourage them to pull. The teams used to skid logs through the woods, or pull plows, but now they pull metaphorical loads for their owners' diversion and metaphorical pride. This is a brutal attempt to hold to old ways, and what impresses a spectator is the near-hysteria, the killing rage of the drivers. Beating those animals to pull those weights has no comprehensible end except noise and violence. It is a rite played out within earshot of Ed Larkin and the Old Time Dancers, within sight of the schoolhouse preserved with its antique map, globe, potbellied stove, *McGuffey's Reader*. But my God what a distance is one rite from another; you can't avoid the connection—the performing girls and their consumers, the ox drivers, the pointless beatings, the queer humanish look of inhumanity.

Across a footbridge from the main fairground, guarded by a couple of police now armed with shotguns, is a huge parking lot. Bonfires smoke and smolder in the drizzle. The license plates on the campers and motorcycles are mostly from Massachusetts and New York. Here are the hard guys, Billy Bad-Ass and his gang, pissing on someone's fire, showing the ladies his pecker, offering to whip anyone's ass. These boys fight, of course, mostly with their friends; they listen to Hank Williams, Merle Haggard, Johnny Cash. It isn't fair: the music's too good for assholes. Their bellies are acts of aggression. They swallow beer in a gulp and crush the cans, naturally, worth a nickel in Vermont. They make noises: roosters, bulls, wolves, swine. One of them gives me the finger as I walk past looking straight ahead, and his friend throws him on the fire. This interests me, which is my mistake; I look at the drunk man lying on the fire, and he says to his friend, "Be nice, Jesus, be nice." His friend stares at me: "What the fuck are you looking at, fuck?" I say, "Nothing, nothing." I thought I'd been in bad parking lots before, tailgating at the Yale-Princeton game, the Maryland Hunt Cup. I'd never been in a bad parking lot before.

The girls are outside now, Larry and Whitey have brought their girls outside. Something weird is happening. The rain is driving hard now. Guys search in the mud for money they think they just dropped, money they lost hours earlier, maybe when the gambling joints mysteriously reopened. There are women among these men standing in mud, being rained on. Regular women, amateurs, hooting at the performers: "ONE, TWO, THREE, FOUR, WE DON'T WANT NO FUCKIN' WHORES!" The chant grows louder, even meaner. Whitey looks at Larry. Larry shrugs. Whitey shrugs. One of the performers makes to a young buck a plea I just heard elsewhere: "Be nice." No dice. This is a mob, near midnight, ready to tear the place apart. "What do you guys want, anyway? What are you guys after?" But no one answers the stripper, and Larry and Whitey shut down their shows and the mob melts away.

Next day the sun struggles back. It's Sunday, family day, cold and clear. The carnival is being torn down, but Whitey's still hawking his show. His call is fundamental. He sounds like a plumbing contractor quoting an estimate for a job he knows he won't win: "Buy your tickets. It's a good show. It's a girl show. It's a sex show." This he follows with a sentence oddly beside the point of a sex show, precisely to the point of some other existential axiom: "The strong walk over the weak, they've always done it, that's how it is." Inside the tent, one of the girls has connected with a customer who is, as she says, "oh so sweet!" He tucks his head between her legs for five minutes, climbs right up on stage with her, you might even say performs for her. That seems fine by her; she says, "Bring on another girl, I'm done now, I'm not moving from here," and her newfound friend keeps at her. Partnership, a grace note to close with, a gentle valediction.

A Day at the Beach

I'd be the last one to brag up my vacation, show slides of Mustique's Cotton Club, Curtain Bluff you, Bitter End you, call Petit St. Vincent by its initials (PSV). As for chit-chatting my physiological bona fides, my regime, pulse rate at rest, systolic upper (let's talk through the roof), and diastolic lower (shoot the moon), my SGOT abnormalities, the uric acid settled in gouty crystals at my extremities—would I impose the particulars?

But to reveal both beach and body: here reticence yields to candor. All too soon you'll know of Sint Maarten and cardiac catheterization, of La Samana and acute aortic valvular stenosis, of the Wolff Family Christmas, of surgical procedures, of the very heart of me.

Not long ago I flew with my family from New York to Antigua. The jumbo jet was full, and occupied principally (my two teenage sons noticed) by people old enough to drive but young enough not to know what is an IRA. These travelers smiled and had good teeth. I was old enough (then) to have all the friends I wanted, but my sons had another perspective, and they smiled back. Until we descended to Sint Maarten, our stopover, ten flying minutes from Antigua. The airplane unloaded every person with perfect white teeth, leaving us to

fellow passengers plenty old enough to know their 401(k) retirement strategies. Golfers, hatched from madras eggs.

Oh, my poor boys! They pressed their noses to the Boeing's
windows and watched the smiling young people skip toward
Sint Maarten's terminal.

"We'll visit Sint Maarten someday," their mummy promised, calling it "Saynt Martin."

Not so fast! By June, all seats had been booked to that island
for that Christmas vacation. I tried to pull strings, making my
way up a chain of command to an executive of one of our most
venerable international airlines. He wished to serve, but I
heard in his voice a quality I couldn't then put a name to; I
think I could now, if only I knew the exact antonym for "bal-
lyhoo": would it be "demotion"? Perhaps "derision"? He suggested Jamaica. How about Barbados? Why not try Trinidad?
He boosted other islands, to which his airline did not fly. For
a fellow with almost as much experience living well as I had
of living, I wasn't hearing the music.

We would go to Sint Maarten, by God, and so, with a sigh,
the airline executive accommodated us.

An alarm bell rang a few days before takeoff during a phone
talk with my mother, who had on some dreamy caprice visited
during a single journey every Caribbean island with an airport,
and some without, returning thereafter to none.

"Saint Martin?" my mother said, "or Sint Maarten?"

"What's the difference?"

"Sint Maarten is the Dutch part. Saint Martin is French.
The French have fun, and eat good food."

"Our destination is Sint Maarten," I said.

"Oh," my mother said. "Huh."

"What do you mean, 'huh,' " I asked.

"Well," my mother said.

"Did you not care for the island?" I asked.

"Well," my mother said, "it has beaches. The French part. Or it did when I was there."

"Why would the beaches not be there now?"

"Oh, the construction. There were buildings going up all along the beaches."

"Pretty buildings?"

"I think I liked San Juan a little more than Saint Martin," my mother said.

"Did you like San Juan?"

"Not at all," my mother said. "It was tacky."

I concluded that Sint Maarten might be just the place for my sons, and I felt virtuous thinking this, the way St. Sebastian must have felt when the arrows came.

Travelogues and medical logs first intersect at Theodore Francis Green Airport, Providence, Rhode Island, 6:15 a.m., Saturday, mid-December. I am famously efficient, dependable. I use the old noodle, pack early, remember to bring tickets, passports, extra eyeglasses, maps to be studied en route, the novel by Dostoyevski I have still not read, medication—*all* the necessaries. These I arrange in a canvas briefcase, and leave it in our driveway. Priscilla, for a wonder, had taken upon herself responsibility for the tickets and passports, so we were not grounded. But I was destined to fly away without my drugs. This was the conventional pharmacopoeia of a fellow of late-middle years: Benemid and colchicine (gout), Vasotec (hypertension), Inderal (heart rate). I didn't like flying to an island, at the beginning of a weekend, without these medicines: a general practitioner in our little town had a few days before, during my first visit with him, expressed quiet alarm at my blood pressure. I had visited him because, seized by a fitness fit, I had labored several months to row nowhere fast, and the more often I pulled on the handle of that Concept II Ergometer, the very machine favored by Olympic oarsmen, the less my stamina. My older son, Nicholas, can row the unmoved contraption more than twenty miles, and take a telephone call, and talk. I'd row three and double over. This didn't seem fair; it wasn't fair, my new doctor agreed, asking by the way did I know I had a heart murmur. I told him I had been told this since childhood, but it was nothing, it had been checked out.

"Checked out how?"

I explained, perhaps condescendingly, that in the metropolis of Providence I had not three years before been tested hi-tech with an echocardiogram, and the results had shown I had the heart of a baby. Those were my city doctor's very words, I explained, "heart of a baby." My new doctor said very well, but my blood pressure must be diminished medically and, by the way, might he send away for those echocardiogram test results, just to see them, satisfy his curiosity about the clamorous mutter he had heard listening to my heart?

Just before and after this physical examination I had been preoccupied with photographs, arranging the slides and prints of twenty-one years of marriage and nineteen years of daddydom in albums, to give as Christmas gifts to my kin. I am obsessive, but in the process of finding and sorting these pictures of a life, likenesses of my father and mother, their fathers and mothers, this innocent labor radiated out and became even by my tolerant lights weird, alarming. I dropped business and pleasure to sort, hunting through trunks and cartons in the attic several nights till dawn. Priscilla, whom I had meant to surprise pleasantly with photographs of herself, asked what I thought I was doing. Meaning to answer truthfully, I said I didn't really know.

"I'm arranging things," I said. "It's as though I think I'm about to die," I said.

"I don't find that amusing," she said.

"I don't either," I said.

In truth, I think I thought no such thing. I didn't imagine dying, or didn't imagine dying any more often than I usually do, which isn't that often. But I'd felt *something*, and it had sent me to trunks in my attic and to a doctor, who urged me to take my medicine.

Flying to Sint Maarten I considered Vasotec. Landing at Sint Maarten, Saturday afternoon, I brooded on Benemid. I am not famously even-tempered; our bags, minus the carry-on of essentials snowed under in our driveway, were delayed. It seemed to me, elbowing through throngs to the baggage carousel, that I was being elbowed back. Irritable, I felt a bellicose rush of blood to my face; I was showing my fighting colors.

Our taxi was no jitney daubed pastel but a businessman's sedan; the driver was all business, no *Welcome to de Islands, mon*, but "Where to?"

We told him where. He seemed amused. Leaving the airport, he turned left and drove beside a chain-link fence bordering the runway. Left again, beside a fence bordering the end of the runway. Left again, along a rutted mud road, deeply puddled, with mosquitoes skimming the puddles, beside a fence bordering the runway. The fifteen-minute ride had brought us thirty yards from the place our jet's wheels had touched down.

More to the point, as we soon learned, it had brought us thirty yards from the place wheels would lift off at that moment when the pilot shouts "Rotate!" above the din, and mighty engines go to full power.

(We had noticed during this journey a large hotel set near our own lodgings, behind a stucco wall, the "Caravanserai," let's call it. A friend who had stayed there during a business convention later told me of his terror his first afternoon, having shed his New York clothes down to his boxers, standing in those thunderbags looking seaward from his ninth-floor picture window, seeing fly, right toward his window, a widebody, sliding into its landing path. On approach, aviators say, "Pan Am heavy." No amount of time, my friend said, would delete from his mind's eye his first sight of a jumbo at eye-level, coming at the conversation pit of his suite, at *him*. Not that there weren't other experiences to share with me later, like his first dip in the pool, an announcement coming over the hotel's public-address system: "Please, peoples. We have many complaints about pee-pee and doo-doo in swimming pool. Please don't forget to sign up for tonight's barbecue and salad bar on the beach.") But I'm making Sint Maarten sound like Iwo Jima, Bataan. I'm not writing *Guadalcanal Diary*; mine is a story of a heart murmur during a tropical vacation.

That first late afternoon we had a few unpleasant surprises in our seaside condominium, nothing acute: low water pressure from the taps and high voltage from the refrigerator door (we learned to pry it open using a mop handle). Otherwise, subtracting huge, lurid oil paintings of black-and-Day-Glo swans, the lodgings were dandy: slide the front door and there, fifteen yards dead ahead, was the sea.

Our view across the bay was dominated by a rusted dredger moored offshore from a monumental and immoderate time-sharing project, a mausoleum of doomed real-estate specu-lation, the Pyramids of our time and that place. The half-baked and half-finished concrete resort and casino had been erected on land called Billy Folly, and was named Pelican Resort. Pelican because pelicans fished our common water, flying in threes, throttling back to stall speed, diving in a wings-back free-fall, gobbling the catch. We learned to watch this process hours at a whack. That's what a Caribbean vacation is for, in my book, to zone out, narrow the concentration to what is least my own business. To buy a breather.

The pelicans' swooning fall and frantic takeoff reminded us of the enterprise at our backs, as though we could possibly have forgotten. The din began before breakfast, and quit during dinner. It was a stunning racket. What you hear at an airport isn't a patch on that uproar, because at an airport you don't pass your time in the open air a few feet from the runway. The blast shook the condo, shook us. It was not a Caribbean noise.

There was also a suspicion, vaguely perceived as a slickness to the epidermis, of oil finely sprayed at each takeoff. This was not Coppertone. Afterburners would cut in at full power, and those three or four great GEs or Pratt & Whitneys would go pedal to the metal, and we would cover our ears, and a fine mist of jet fuel would settle in the planes' wake, skim-coating my expensively vacationing family. Call it a "vapor trail" if you prefer; I call it kerosene.

The folks next door were untroubled by this phenomenon. They hailed from Queens, within easy earshot of JFK, and the takeoffs and landings made them feel at home. Our condominiums appeared to my untrained judgment identical, two-bedroom "units," but there seemed no end to this neighboring family. Each morning, as with passengers piling from a circus car, the cry was still "*they come!*" As many as they were, so were they similar, one big happy family.

Big! Here in Rhode Island there was a restaurant of legend, Custy's, all-you-can-eat. A few years ago it changed management, and on his first Sunday the new owner saw an out-of-state charter bus swing into his parking lot. As the bus unloaded its freight, anxiety turned to horror: a banner stuck to the bus's side proclaimed its origin and mission: THE BUFFET BUSTERS OF NEW JERSEY! (Custy's is out of business.)

Our neighbors were buffet busters, and we were at first stand-offish when they approached us to share Sint Maarten dining lore. They had in their generous company a dog; his collar named him Butch, and he wouldn't be stood off. He would come to the *terraza* of our unit to scratch his ass against a chaise longue while we watched the rusty dredger and listened to planes take off. Butch would curl up, a hint of a smile baring his canines, and languidly masturbate, until we left him to his self-absorption and took our piña coladas indoors, where the swans hung motelly.

It didn't take long to notice that our Buffet Busters were having better fun than we. They laughed, and when they weren't laughing they smiled, like Butch. They seemed to love one another (but less ardently than Butch loved himself). Every morning they took a group picture, one member of the dozen or so grams and moms and in-laws darting out of the great assembly to memorialize the rest. Even their sunburns seemed to amuse them, and these were *sunburns*, the kind to be got only by spending hours without moving, floating belly-down staring at sand through a fogged face mask, or lying belly-up staring at the sky.

While these good and happy people took their ease, I was about my business. To protect myself against the consequences of hypertension, I boiled my blood driving crowded potholed roads searching for a doctor to give me a prescription. Failing, I wandered from town to town to town (there are three: two French, one Dutch) to entreat pharmacists for drugs, and to be insulted by them. At length, sweating and shaking like an addict from my frustrated mission, I found a worldly French druggist, all shrugs and tropical sophistication, dressed like Bogey in *Casablanca*, a coffin nail dangling from his lower lip. He was willing to sell me anything that wasn't what I had been instructed to use. I settled on reserpine, from *Rauwolfia serpentina*, Indian snakeroot. Potent.

After looking for The Man, finally making my connection, shopping in a supermarket whose linoleum floor, slick with spilled daiquiri mix, gave me a tumble amusing to other shoppers, I paused at one of the island's thousand or so casinos to lose my folding money to the wheel and my coins to the slots.

At "home," going for a Heineken to wash down my drugs, I forgot what I had urged those in my care to remember, and got a hundred-plus volts, and this caused me, more in anger than in sorrow, to sweep my prescription Vuarnets violently from my brow to the floor, where a lens broke. That was my second full day in Sint Maarten.

The following days we fended off the friendly approaches of the Buffet Busters and the amorous urgencies of Butch. We swam. Mostly we spent money. We spent at casinos, with workaday stupidity. We could as easily have blown a wad at Nice, or Baden-Baden, or in Venice; I'm not even saying the company would have been classier in Europe. But the Sint Maarten casino crowd was very Atlantic City, *muy* San Juan.

We spent money eating. I mean *money*. We hadn't flown to the Islands to eat. We'd eaten in the Islands. We knew about Island cuisine. We'd tried veal birds at Bequia, "rack of jambon au mustard" in Antigua. We wished to eat and run, snack, go the simple route. So it was pizza for four at a fast-food place in Philipsburg, $83. American dollars. Dinner in Marigot, the French port, $200, plus tip (*sans vin*), not an unwholesome piece of local fish, *très nouvelle*, teensy.

The most pleasing restaurant in town we were told but did not, alas, believe, is *at* the airport, soundproofed against the din. Instead we chose a place set at the far end of the runway, very *intime*, popular with return visitors (who could they be, and what could they be thinking?), called Mary's Boon. It has evident charms: old wicker, a macaw in a cage (or maybe it was a fish in a bowl), guests got up in natural fibers, a single menu served take-it-or-leave-it at long, communal tables, an "honor bar," which means guests pour their own drinks, whose number they are honorbound to report, and for which they are charged several dollars apiece, which imposed, to be honest, a heavy burden on my sense of honor.

We ate at Mary's Boon with friends who knew the owners.

Let's say the bill was $300. (We ate some shrimp was why.) When it came time to pay, we asked—discreetly I thought, so the other guests didn't have to see the ugly transaction—if we might pay $150 a couple. It was a matter of American Express traveler's checks, you see, because credit cards—nasty plastic things—were not . . . honored.

"I don't want to get into this," said the owner. "One bill, one person pays."

"Well, it's quite simple," I said. "We aren't asking for a mathematical computation, just that you take half in checks from me, half in checks from my friend."

"Must I speak more slowly?" the owner said. "What you do to each other with your 'traveler's checks' is quite your own business. I wish to have three hundred dollars, and I wish it from *one* of you."

Cross my heart.

Two days later, Christmas, my wife and I stopped for a couple of drinks at La Samana ("untypical," the brochure says, "uncompromised") where movie stars stay, but weren't staying that day. Our check was $16. I offered a $50 traveler's check.

"Haven't you got something smaller?" asked the waitress at the least compromised al fresco resort in the Caribbean, $520 a night double, no meals, plus service.

But I run before my story. Back to Mary's Boon, or the hours following our honestly drunk drinks and $6-per-shrimp seafood at the runway's end, so complexly paid for. Sometime that night someone broke into our unit, patrolled our bedroom while we slept, and stole what was worth stealing, and much that was not. Now we were deep in it: no keys, identification, credit cards, cash, or traveler's checks.

The Buffet Busters, worldly old hands, were resigned to our bad luck.

"See the plywood screwed over our slider?" (Indeed, we had remarked to ourselves the oddness of this use of a sliding-glass door fronting the ocean.) "Only thing to keep the fuckers out. And I keep a loaded hogleg on the night table."

But of course! How silly of us not to have thought of it.

"They come in boats. Swim ashore, grab the loot, they're gone. Did they get your medication?" (My medical adventures were not unknown to our immediate community: the single phone nearby worked according to the volume put into it, like a tin can connected to a tin can by string.) "They love drugs. One drug looks like another to those fellows."

We were told how lucky we were: it was Christmas Eve morn; another day, and the Island would be shut tight till after New Year's. Many a red-letter day in the Lesser Antilles.

Karl Malden was on the money. We had the providence of having had stolen from us not just any traveler's checks but the right kind, and sure enough, American Express has a Philipsburg office, and I found my way to it. I stood in line to tell my grim tale, behind half a dozen or so other desolates, similarly deprived at poolside, on the beach, asleep in their hotels. I asked an agency employee if it was always like this, and was told, runically, that where there are casinos, tourists lose money.

Perhaps experience had educated the traveler's-check-refund people in their brisk manner, their refusal to say, as I might have liked to have heard: *This is tragic. Let us sit upon the ground and tell sad stories of the theft of cash.*

Or, at least: *Gee, downer, you must be bummed.*

Let *me* say it: I felt awful. Angry, hot, panicked. (I saw for the first time the glimmer of an improbable possibility: that a fellow might come to this island, get picked clean and never leave; such a fellow would wind down drinking Jamaican Red Cap beer, wearing white clothes that weren't white anymore and not caring that they weren't.)

I was also short of breath, as though a barber were wrapping a steaming towel around my face. I had felt this several times the past few days, and mentioned it to Priscilla, who took it more seriously than I took it. I wrote it off to heat, and stress, all those double sawbucks flying pell-mell from my pockets into the pockets of strangers.

When I at last got to the head of the line of wronged ones, I learned that American Express would have no business with me until I filed a police report, which a policeman must sign. The American Express agent looked meaningfully at her watch, and explained that I had wasted much time in line, and the office closed, for Christmas and other holidays, in two hours, and I had better move with dispatch to the office of detectives, at the other end of Philipsburg's main drag.

Oh my! A speedy walk past the duty-free boom boxes and porcelain kitty-cats to another long line. As this crept, winding indoors from the hot alley where we miserables stood gnawing our lower lips, it dawned on me that to get a signature on a piece of paper was not so casually done as demanded.

"We hab no crime on dis island," I heard a detective explain. "Mainland peoples bring de trouble. And Dominicans." (As Turks are to Swiss, and Koreans to Japanese, the people of Dominica, who labor with their hands, are to the entrepreneurs of Sint Maarten. It is a time-worn story.)

Lacking criminals, the detectives made do with victims. The victim immediately ahead of me was an Islander. His story was sadder and more complicated than mine. It seems that the night before, a person or persons unknown had invaded his property, taking advantage of the peculiarity that it was without a cyclone fence ringed with razor wire, and made away with the man's dog. The detective stopped writing, and looked up. The dog could be identified, the victim explained, and began to give an account of an animal I could have sworn was our neighbor Butch, until I heard a final detail: "My dog got three legs." (Butch had five, always.)

My interview was not successful. The detective, studying my lack of composure, the red-faced urgency of my manner, concluded that I was a confidence man, and he was no stranger to "devices," as he assured me. We were soon on the subject of signatures. I wanted his, in any form, on anything. I had an easier time getting the Splendid Splinter's when I was a boy. I believed I might weep. The detective saw something in me that made him wish I would go away, as the former master of a three-legged dog had gone away, and I explained that I *would* go away, but only with a detective's signature. And that is how I got a name written on my airline ticket, which the cat burglar(s) had neglected to steal. This signature I rushed to the outskirts of Philipsburg, a town composed of outskirts, to a Dutch bank. Here, American Express had sort of suggested, the detective's signature would be exchanged for traveler's checks. Waiting in line, I was offered a fruit punch—rum-and-cherry Slurpee, with a custard garnish. These were served by a Dutch bank officer who was busy drinking most of those portions of the concoction she was pouring for her puzzled customers; I thought I saw a pathway to her sympathy if not her heart, and invited her to enjoy the cup she extended toward me. In turn she invited me to sit at her desk. Her fingernails were too long to make it possible for her to open ledgers, but she invited me to her cabin after the close of business to "happify Yuletime." I promised that that cabin was the only place I longed to be, and got new traveler's checks, and the residue of her lurid lipstick on my nose. (She had removed her bifocals to cuddle me.)

The rest of our holiday was less fun.

Well, let me be fair. Putting aside an episode with our rented automobile in Marigot—where it was sideswiped while parked and while we ate a hundred dollars' worth of sandwiches on Christmas night, a mischance that would cost me two (maybe three) hundred, and resulted in a fight so terrible between

Priscilla (who parked the car) and her husband (who signed the rental contract that left us nakedly exposed to the driving skills and honor of other people) that my children preferred to hike to their runway-side villa, from France to Holland, by shank's mare so they wouldn't be obliged to listen to a Mr. & Mrs. that ended only because I ran out of breath to prolong it—Christmas was mezzo-mezzo.

During our holiday disagreement, I asked speculatively: "Will we ever get off this miserable island?"

The next day I found a way.

For a consideration a catamaran, the *Bluebeard*, chartered on a head-boat basis (charging per passenger to all comers), would sail us from Marigot to Sandy Island, a reef-girt sandspit two hundred by fifty yards, a couple of miles northwest of Anguilla. Anguilla, under British colonial rule, is the place to which people flee when the pressure of Sint Maarten screws too tight on them; Sandy Island is where they go when the bustle of Anguilla mills them down.

The arrangements were businesslike. In the shadow of a casino I bought three tickets (Priscilla was left to guard the few remaining dollars and, especially, the plane tickets), and we were to surrender these dockside next day to the crew of *Bluebeard*. We were up early; I felt hinky, wanted to leave time aplenty for the untoward to waylay us before boarding. I believed two hours would be adequate for the seven-mile journey to Marigot by sideswiped car, time enough surely to find a bulletproof parking place. I wanted this to go smoothly.

It did not; we were rained out.

We took it well. Yachtsmen we were, sports. There was always tomorrow, our last full day. And tomorrow, in fact, came without intervening tragedy. We never left home, and remembered to open the refrigerator with a long wooden stick, and took baths instead of showers, so we wouldn't fall down and injure ourselves, and kept our doors and windows shut and locked, all day, even after the rain stopped, so our tickets and passports would not be stolen by foreigners who come from the sea. No pelicans fell on us while we swam.

Come next morning, I got Nicholas and Justin up with the sun, and packed, and found we were just that little bit short of suntan lotion. We stopped at a convenience store along the imperfectly executed "road" to Marigot, and bought Sea & Ski, for only fifteen dollars. I rummaged for the money at the bottom of a canvas bag holding our *Bluebeard* tickets. I had examined these tickets several times that morning, had held them in my hands, had stared at them and read their promises: the bracing sail, the "dazzling white beach, the coral reefs that teem with bright, colorful tropical fish set in incredibly blue waters." I had not failed to note that after "complimentary beverages" the "magical sound of a conch horn announces the readiness of a plentiful barbecue" on the beach.

So: we parked the sideswiped vehicle in Marigot and walked briskly toward the yacht basin, and then—half an hour before we were to sail—I felt an inkling that we and our tickets were no longer together. A cursory look in my canvas bag revealed this horribly to be so. Throwing the bag to a son, yelling over my shoulder "Beg them to wait," I ran to the car, and drove it, in violation of sense and law, careening around curves, ignoring a red light at a drawbridge, *fast*, to the "convenience" store. Breathless, I broke in ahead of other customers.

"I left my tickets."

"What you talking about?"

"Hey, we were in line."

"Tickets. Suntan lotion. Counter."

And then it dawned on me. To black people, white people look alike. I am bald, and wear a white beard, and stutter, but the woman who twenty minutes earlier had instructed me to have a nice day did not know me. I tell you: it hurt.

"Could my tickets be in your wastebasket?"

And then I was behind the counter, rummaging through trash, while her husband or co-worker or brother or son or father came toward me with a look that would have frightened me had I had the composure to feel fear.

"You stole our tickets," I reasoned. "I will never shop here again," I promised. "Fifteen dollars for Sea & Ski is not right. I will tell about this. I am," I explained, "a *writer!*"

And then I drove back to Marigot, weeping. There would be for us no "magical sound of a conch horn," no "plentiful barbecue." I may weep again, maybe ten minutes from now. But I had not wept for many years until then, and have not wept since, and while I wept, I drove as recklessly as a teenager, with the difference that by then I knew as I had not known when I was sixteen that I could die, or kill, driving like that.

Parked and ran, and again found it difficult to breathe, but now there was an iron band under my arms, cinching my chest.

The boat was preparing to sail.

"She stole the tickets."

"Chill out," Nicholas said.

"Take it easy," a crew member suggested. "Have you looked in your pockets? Checked that ice bag?"

"Of course I have!" Now I was yelling, while Justin dug his hands deep into the bag and found, where I had put them for safekeeping, the tickets.

It was as promised. Free drinks, sunshine, cool breezes, grilled fish. I apologized to everyone, blushing, my heart pounding with shame, I thought. The passengers were not boors. The crew were not cynical beach bums. They forgave me. I put aside a twenty-dollar bill to tip them generously for the trouble I had put them to. I wanted them to know I was not as I seemed. I began to relax. I could be a good guy. Tomorrow we'd be gone. My tip would go far to set things right. As we approached Marigot at day's end, I lay on deck, rolled to my left, and watched a twenty-dollar bill, the only money any Wolff had aboard, blow from my pocket, and bob in our wake. Justin saw it all, and looked away:

"Wow," he said.

Our flight was to leave at four. We had been forewarned of chaos at the airport, long lines at the ticket counter, passport control, customs. We agreed to arrive at two. We packed. At noon my wife prepared to take a shower. My sons and I decided on a final swim. In the sea, for a reason I cannot fathom, I decided I wanted a water-fight; I wanted the kind of water-fight *they* fight once a year, the real McCoy, not just splashing, but dunking, wrestling, slick violence. Me versus them. They played horse, and wrestled me down, and I remember my head going under, and coming up trying to catch a breath, and not getting a full load in my lungs, and then running toward them in deeper water, my legs heavy against the surge, feeling not right, turning toward shore, walking deliberately toward a beach chair set at the sea's edge, understanding that to reach that chair not thirty feet away would be to get somewhere I *had* to reach, not as though my life depended on reaching that aluminum-and-plastic chaise longue, but as though it were an important goal, in the sense that one might run to board a slow-moving train that was not the last train ever to roll to one's destination, but what the hell, one had not come so far to miss trains.

I got there, sort of. I was trying hard to breathe. I managed to say to my older son, "I can't breathe."

But I couldn't find the posture to inhale what I wanted so badly. Upright, dignified: not enough air, something pinched off. Slump-shouldered, sagging: the diaphragm wouldn't deliver.

I tried to lie down.

"Lower this chair for me, Nick."

What happened then, I didn't witness. As far as I know, I

asked my son a favor, and the next thing, just a blink out of my life, there were people standing above me, and I heard a little girl crying, and asking, "Is he dead?"

What bad manners, I remember thinking. Much later I was told that was no little girl, but my wife. I had no trouble recognizing the voices of my sons, who were saying, not in unison but at the same time, two incantations, a fugue: "Be all right. Don't give up. Come back." And much else.

It was embarrassing, all those strangers.

A Buffet Buster was holding my wrist. "He's got a pulse again."

She knew her apples.

I tried to reassure them. I wanted to walk away from all this, and even then I knew it was important to escape that island. I didn't try to stand, but when I spoke I made my voice purposeful: "I'm okay."

No one seemed interested in my opinion of myself, because they had seen what I hadn't: gray skin, eyes rolled back under my lids, convulsions—to the untrained eyes of my wife and sons, death.

Now—soon—came a doctor, Dutch, running. I mistook him for a jogger.

Then the ambulance, a wild ride to Philipsburg, just wild; what a trip, lying on my back below the scream of the siren and seeing, blurred beyond the distracted nurse, palm trees shoot by.

"Where are my glasses?"

"Just calm down, Dad. We'll be there. Please be quiet. Don't worry."

But, my God, Nicholas was edgy, the laid-back one, a grace-under-pressure boy. What was going on? I was, as they say, beside myself, trying without success to share a secret: *I was okay.*

.   .   .

The Dutch physician from the beach was met at the emergency room by a Dutch cardiologist, and they laid me down and hooked me up and asked questions. Was I in pain? (No.) Where had the pain come? Shoulders? Arms?

Now this called for a more complicated reply than seems invited by such simple questions. My situation with the doctors was a bit like the situation of someone guessing which hand holds a coin. If the tempting obvious guess is *right hand*, a simpleminded guesser will say *left*, a more subtle mind *right*, subtler still *left* . . . I knew what story was told by pain radiating from the shoulders, and the doctors guessed I knew this and would deny it, and I denied it because I had not felt it, but the doctors had to decide whether I denied it because I had not felt it or because I didn't want to have had a heart attack.

The vocabulary of pain is discriminating. I aimed to illuminate rather than disguise my difficulty, but the emergency room of a Caribbean hospital is not precisely the site of choice for precise lexical delicacy. A patient's diction can express, and it can delude. Words, we do not tire of reminding ourselves, count. There is "sharp," "dull," "throbbing," "hot," "unbearable," "steady." I had experienced none of these sensations; instead, hurried, I chose an approximate locution, inaccurate in fact, but in the spirit of my experience: "It felt like a heavy person kneeling on my chest."

Oh, how vigorously I would later try to retract those words, to delete them from my transcript, to change my grade. But they were my words, and I said them close to the moment, and they went from English to Dutch back out to English, and they added up to the single conclusion I least believed or wanted to believe: *heart attack*.

Now the EKG. I lay in the emergency room, watching the terror on Priscilla's face and Justin's; I couldn't imagine what they were thinking. My attention was in the present tense; now a nurse was exclaiming impatiently that the monitor cups wouldn't adhere to my white-haired chest; now she was shaving my chest; now I felt the cold shock of jelly rubbed on me to hold the cups. I listened to doctors discuss, in a language I could not have understood had it been English, what it was with me. I knew I was just fine, that once this rigmarole was finished, I'd fly home and put paid to this fiasco of a holiday.

The diagnosis was heart disease. Syncopes here and abnormal repolarizations there. I tried to argue them out of it, explaining that I had been using reserpine, a drug new to me. That must have keeled me over, the reserpine. My instinctive distrust of that drug was not, I later learned, as desperately farfetched as you might believe. Reserpine is potent, can provoke suicidal depressions that hang on for months. More to my point, it so slows the heartbeat as sometimes to cause fainting, not to mention rashes, weight increase, lethargy, troubled dreams, blurred vision, nosebleeds, premature ejaculation: let's conclude that depression is a side effect of these side effects.

I explained about my medications: they were in my driveway, all could be traced to that ill beginning. The Dutch doctors were curious as to how I managed to prescribe for myself a drug so potent as reserpine, and I mentioned Marigot, a pharmacy there, and they looked at each other, illuminated.

"Ah, the French." The doctors shrugged, so predictably that I laughed, but I found myself laughing alone.

It was decided, without interest in my opinion, that I would be checked into the hospital and observed until more was known. The stethoscope, the charts, did not suggest the side effects of reserpine.

I gave in. Tame as a puppy. Fact was, I wanted to be in a room alone, with the door shut. I was done now searching for better words, wondering *what next*, reckoning how we would escape that botched island. I wanted to nap.

I was wheeled into an air-conditioned room, with a window

fronting the harbor. I was getting my hand held by one and then another of my family, and that was nice, but—I thought—theatrical, uncustomary. More familiar was the nature of Priscilla's question to my sons after I was hooked up to a monitor by wires leading from my breasts, ankles; the monitor, just like the television monitors you've seen (I mean the ones *on* television, "St. Elsewhere," say), clicked busily but irregularly, sketched peaks and valleys, jagged yellow lines.

My wife asked my boys, the cardiologists: "Does that look right to you? It doesn't look right to me."

And then they left me to rest.

Immediately came a nutritionist, asking was I hungry; I said no, not a bit hungry. So she produced for me to eat—half an hour after the emergency room, an hour beyond the ambulance, an hour and fifteen minutes after the water fight—chicken creole. There were French fries, and butterscotch pudding, and a huge breast of chicken with tomato sauce and okra. There were thick slabs of white bread. A bottle of Orange Crush. If I had asked for a St. Pauli Girl, I could have had it, and a squash racquet too. When the food was removed, I thought I might rest.

I remembered a story a friend told me about his adventure in Jamaica thirty years ago during spring vacation from boarding school. Shy around girls, he was quite a diver, so he had put in hour upon hour diving from cliffs to amaze them but was then unable to hear their amazement. Water had collected in his ears, and he did what we do: shook his head violently, jumped on the left foot, jumped on the right, whacked the sides of his head with his palms. He bought Jamaican Q-tips, cotton swabs just the wrong size, and they seemed to drive the water deeper in his ears and to cause some small pain.

His roommate knew a remedy, was surprised it was not a remedy familiar to all divers: "Pour bourbon in your ears. Melts the wax, and flushes out the salt water."

In Jamaica, thirty years ago, bourbon was scarce, but there

was 151-proof rum, and my friend poured this in one ear and then, despite the sensation you may guess at, poured some in the other ear. He spent time in a Caribbean hospital. The hospital stay made an impression on him—changed him even.

"Do you believe in Our Lord Jesus *Christ!*"

She was immense, a figure only Flannery O'Connor could have imagined, breasts like shoats squirming to escape from a croaker sack. Black she wore, and a florid hat, and plum lipstick. Rouged, bearing a Bible.

"I say, do you *believe* in Him!"

For a moment, I almost thought of thinking whether I believed in anything the way she needed to know whether I believed in Him. Instead I thought, I don't need this.

"No."

"I say, will you *declare* your belief in the Son of God!"

"Please go away."

She was astounded. She was rattling off a rap from memory, let's call it a litany. This was not in the script, getting shown the door, on *Sunday*.

"I do this by the commandment of the Lord Jesus Christ! This is my day off work."

"Take a load off," I said. "Enjoy a day of rest. I'm a bad customer."

"I'll tell you, mister, you are sick! They told me."

"Go away."

The apostle dropped to her knees. Her hat was ornate, almost interesting.

"There ain't no hospital beds in Hell, mister. Pray with me!"

I rolled over, away from the missionary's hat, and looked out at the harbor. A cruise ship was coming in. My eyes without my glasses saw it all blurred. I was infirm, unwell. But I could hear the clanking anchor chain and a bustle below my window on the beach, the excitement of people near a place where money will soon be redistributed. I never heard the proselyte leave, but I knew she was gone, and with her the Good News.

Later that night, Priscilla came back with the boys. Justin thought it might be interesting to touch together the two electric paddles, those things you see in television emergency rooms, when the intern yells "clear!" and gives some luckless sod the juice, and the patient's chest heaves, and his legs buck like a bronc's, and his monitor line goes wavy ("We've got a pulse; his blood pressure's coming back!") and everyone smiles, or it goes flat ("I need a drink. Sometimes I hate this job! Anyone coming?"). Anyway, Justin was bringing the resurrection paddles together, Priscilla yelled at him, I jerked, my own life-sign line went kind of jagged, and Priscilla and I argued. Was what I might have had on the beach properly called a "myocardial infarction" (my choice), or "myocardial infraction" (Priscilla's and, once they heard the two side by side, the boys' choice). I was right, but let's concede "infraction" makes a world more sense.

Then Priscilla, just before they left me for the night, said, "I'll never be mean to you again."

She meant it, too. It made me laugh.

"Don't say such a thing. It makes me sad to hear it. I can't do without."

"I mean it. I'll never be mean to you again."

Well.

Near midnight, finished with a junk novel I was reading to keep my mind off my worries, which were worrying me less than they should, I got to my window, stretching to their farthest reach the wires connecting me to the heart monitor. I was drawn by lights in the harbor, and friendly shouts from the beach. I leaned my nose against the pane and tried to focus. Below on the beach I could see what looked like fireflies, wavy flickers seeming to signal to the sparkling cruise ship offshore, dressed with lights; to my blear vision the vessel seemed afire. My attention was drawn to a noise below, and I realized what I must seem to anyone looking in my window, an old geezer with cups stuck to his tits, wires leading out. The fireflies came closer, and I thought someone was waving sparklers at me in a friendly way, and then I saw the orange trail of a comet arc toward me, and then felt an awful concussion, full explosion, and I heard glass break, and by the time the nurses were there, in response to that monitor honking like a French flic's car, I realized someone had lobbed a cherry bomb at me, and the outer of the two windows had been shattered by it.

So I lay awake waiting for the blood test whose results would tell me whether I had had a myocardial in*far*ction, killing a region of my heart, or whether something else had made me eat sand. I lay tense, looking toward the open door where the evangelist in black might appear again with her Holy Book and Glad Tidings, and then toward the window, waiting for another bang. Staring out the window, I saw the nimbus of the sun rise, and had blood drawn, and heard a doctor tell me the blood test revealed none of those enzymes that accompany a death of heart muscle; I had probably not had the experience called heart attack.

"How soon can I get off this dangerous island?"

"Next week, five or six days, after we observe you."

"Today," I said.

I was warned not on any account to show signs of malaise at the airport, or the airlines would never carry me off that unspeakable place for fear I'd make trouble for them: die, say, or—worse—litigate them. It was an odd sensation, but not at all unpleasant, to be coddled by my family, to have my bags toted by Justin while Nicholas checked us in, to have Priscilla deal with the wrecked rent-a-car, and gesticulate, and argue, and by sweet advocacy save a buck or two. (I would have fought to win a moral judgment, which is one reason, I guess, I have high blood pressure. Priscilla just wanted to get the damage payment down a little, bless her.)

In fact, I felt fine, okay, not so bad. Tired, distracted, but I managed to watch the sappy holiday movie, a colorized *It's a Wonderful Life*. I began to notice, as Jimmy Stewart finally noticed, the decencies manifest around me. Flying north, into the teeth of a winter whose forthright sharpness I welcomed, I thought how kind the Buffet Busters had been, how quick to help, how competent. Even Butch, watching me heave back to life on my beach chaise, cocked his head, concerned more about me, it seemed, than about his pecker. I didn't like the news the Dutch doctors gave me, but they gave it, on a Sunday. The appraiser at the car rental—LUCKY (!) CAR RENTALS —had been just. As our stay at the condo was necessarily lengthened, instead of bills we got checks, refunds to atone for the nastiness of the refrigerator; the extra night was on them, they insisted cheerfully.

I was learning lessons. Not the kind that is taught with a club that knocks you down: that kind of lesson I had always expected to have forced on me, and in fact it taught me nothing, except to remind me, around my family, of something Priscilla had read, that the one thing nobody says on his death-bed is "I wish I'd worked harder."

I was looking ahead to complicated news, though on New Year's Day I didn't guess how complicated. The messages coming in were about ratio, proportion; everywhere I turned people tried to smooth things for me. Near-strangers would write. Friends with whom I had nursed antique grievances— feuds blossoming black from disputes over how many port-holes in a 1951 Buick Special, or why didn't you like my book better, or pick up that dinner check, or phone earlier when you knew you couldn't come for the weekend, or help with the dishes when you came? These people were kind, wise, on call.

Snow fell with us on Kennedy. In the customs shed the boys fought for luggage, and Priscilla tried to learn whether Providence was snowed in, whether flights would leave for that place, whether the parking lot there had been plowed. I telephoned doctors. I telephoned my father-in-law, a surgeon. For many years he had wisely dismissed as beneath serious discussion his family's anxious questions about sore throats and aching feet. To this story he listened. His interest did not reassure me. Neither did the product of a late-night conversation with my new doctor. He wanted me in his office tomorrow, no kidding.

I got a crash course in cardiology. While I was keeling over in Sint Maarten, my doctor at home had been studying pictures and numbers from that echocardiogram administered three years earlier; these had not shown him "the heart of a baby"; these had sufficiently alarmed him that he was telephoning our house while I was snorkeling off the *Bluebeard*, losing money at roulette, all the rest. He was not surprised, alas, by what I told him, and brought forth cutaway pictures of the heart, and especially of the heart's valves, and especially of the aortic region.

Priscilla and Nicholas sat through his patient explanation. I had found books about prescription drugs, and had photocopied—let's say obsessively—the dire, possible (improbable) side effects of reserpine. Surely this explained everything. A reflex had evolved: at the end of every test I expected to hear: *Go home, you silly goose! There's nothing wrong with you. Reserpine tossed you a curveball, is all.*

The doctor listened. The doctor said, "Anything's possible." The doctor got me an emergency appointment with a cardiologist.

The cardiologist was laconic, self-assured. He resembled Hal Holbrook, and gave off that same aura of prematurely gray-haired competence. This was not the man on whom I wished to exercise my reserpine theory of fainting. The cardiologist didn't at first seem to have, as Priscilla put it, "a heart as big as all outdoors." (We were compiling an omnium-gatherum of clichés; I didn't resist the temptation to call friends on their expressions: "You'd die to see her," "My heart's with you," "I feel heartsick for you"; my favorite, after a chest X-ray revealed my abnormally enlarged pump—"You're all heart.")

The cardiologist listened, and listened harder where other doctors had listened hard, and listened there some more. He was brisk; his hands were delicate; as he finished with me, he patted me on the head. I could have wept with gratitude for that gentle touch; Priscilla, watching, said it was like a man patting a dog. She was right; I was right. The pat was perhaps condescending, but if ever I wanted to be touched from above, from Olympus by a god, it was that day. I didn't want a cardiologist who was my equal; I knew what I was and was not. I knew how inaccurately I could parse a paragraph, or misdiagnose a meaning. I wanted to be in the hands of a master.

This master didn't like to answer questions. He especially winced at *what-if* questions; they made him less terse than silent as a tomb. He knew what he knew, would tell when it came time to tell. He knew what he *thought*. He thought I had acute aortic valvular stenosis, which meant my aortic valve was defective, narrow, failing properly to open, which meant I was not pumping sufficient oxygen-rich blood up my ascending aorta, the great artery, to my body—to my brain, for example. (Thus one faints, falls down, and the head—if all goes according to the inventor's plan—lies below the heart, and is fed by gravity.) But I learned what aortic valvular stenosis meant from *The Book of Knowledge*, later. In that office then, I learned only that the cardiologist wanted me to get a chest X-ray and have another echocardiogram, immediately. I had been warned that I might have to undergo a procedure called "cardiac catheterization," which I loosely understood to be the threading of a long tube up an artery and into the heart, where pressures could be read, and dye injected and photographed as it snaked through tributaries.

An echocardiogram, by high contrast, is performed in Rhode Island Hospital's cardiac "non-invasive" wing. Oh, I liked "non-invasive." Give me "non-invasive" any day. It uses Doppler, a radar that can translate sound waves into pictures and numbers. The snowy Saturday morning Nicholas drove me to the hospital to have my heart televised, we found in the waiting room an aged couple. It was no trick to know which of them was there to be tested: her face was gray, and she trembled from stone terror. Later, I would think that to have seen her was to look into a mirror, but now it seemed I was on one side of a high fence, and she on the other.

Nicholas talked to her. The weather. The Patriots. How 'bout those Celtics! His college courses and summer jobs. Smart boy: she was forgetting here and now; forgetting herself, almost. This was life, talking this way.

"Does it hurt?" her husband asked me.

I wondered whether he thought I was a doctor. I wondered what they had been told, whether they too had thumbed an encyclopedia. I thought how needless *this* terror was.

"Not a bit."

In fact it did hurt, a bit. Not me, as it turned out, but the nurse who made her way by microphones up and down and across me. The examining room, all electronics and monitors, was dark, so only the green light of the monitor lit us dimly, as murky pale as the floor of a shoal sea.

I heard the murmur, a surfy snuffle, a wet whisper, like this: *be at peace, be at peace, be at peace.* Say it fast, honest. That's what my heart, amplified and sounded, said.

The nurse working me over was teaching the procedure to a nurse from another hospital. The student was bored and distracted; she chewed gum loudly enough to have the noise picked up by the echocardiogram mike, and was asked to give her jaws a rest.

"Where do you get these handiwipes?" she asked her teacher. "I love these; they're pre-moistened. I wish I had some at home," she said. "They sure are handy."

My nurse was annoyed. She wasn't seeing the pictures she was told to shoot.

"Aortic stenosis has terrible mike angles. It kills, really hurts my hand to have to hold the mike this way. What a hassle!"

"For me, too," I said.

"Quiet," she said, but the gum-chewer didn't obey.

"One thing for sure," I had told Priscilla that morning. "No one, *no way*, is threading anything up my arteries into my heart. Go to the bank on it."

In fact, walking a short distance from a Newport parking lot to my bank, less than two blocks, I had felt a catch in my lungs, a want of something. Breathe as I would, I couldn't get a full shot. (I popped a nitroglycerine tablet under my tongue, the time-honored remedy for victims of angina, but because angina wasn't my problem, the "nitro"—as it's known to its friends—was no remedy.) Two days later, two weeks after my felling in the Islands, I tried to drag a garbage can fifteen yards up my driveway, and I couldn't. I stood in the cold that day, alone in the small town where we live, and put a hand under my jacket and under my shirt, and tried to feel my heart, as though it were willing to tell me what it wanted, what I had done to it.

As soon as the chest X-ray was in the cardiologist's hands (confirming that my heart was abnormally enlarged, from laboring to pump blood through a bum valve), together with the echocardiogram, I was told the next step was to thread a wire up my arteries into my heart.

"How soon?" I asked.

"Beginning of next week," he said.

My cardiologist would not discuss what lay beyond cardiac catheterization, which would confirm his suspicions, or—lots of luck—confound them. I knew. The encyclopedia explained it all under *Cardiac Abnormalities*. Next they "crack your chest," and the knife goes to work.

But, for now, we weren't to discuss sharp knives. Our topic was catheterization. This we discussed in the cardiologist's office, examining a model of a heart, organs cleverly fit within organs, a contraption of hinges and lurid colors. I watched him manipulate it, and pretended to understand what I was being told, much of it in Latin.

But about the procedure he couldn't have been clearer. He told me everything, because this was not speculative; this would happen. He explained hospital admission, and what and when I would eat, and when I would begin my fast, and when and where they would wheel me down to the catheterization ("Cardiac Invasive Unit," presumably) room, and what would run through my IV, tranquilizing me, and who would do what, and for how long, and what I would feel.

"It will hurt when you get the local anesthesia. We'll give you a shot right next to the groin. Then the pain will dull. We'll insinuate a tube up your femoral artery; it is about the diameter of linguini; no nerves there, so it won't hurt. Then we'll thread another into your coronary arteries, to look into heart disease." (Blocked coronary arteries; insufficient blood *to* the heart; bypass country.)

Before I could ask, he told me: "We have problems a few times for a hundred procedures. These can vary: heart attack, stroke. It is possible to puncture a vital artery."

My cardiologist is known both vulgarly and respectfully as

a "cath jockey." If there was anyone in the neighborhood I was prepared to trust with wires the size of pasta, and with my vital stuff, there he sat. He smiled; I melted with gratitude.

What he said would happen, happened. It was an operating room, with a jungle of wires and screens. Many technicians, two cardiologists. The IVs had been run into me, thinning my blood, or thickening it, tranquilizing me. I got the shot, and never felt the deep incision about two inches from the jewel box (*my* jewel box), where they cut into the artery. I felt pressure. I was awake, and was to remain awake, eyes wide open, so I could issue reports, and "cooperate," holding my breath, exhaling.

Meantime, the team talked. They were all business, looking, judging what they saw. A time came when I knew the wire was at my aortic valve (such as it was), because they told me, and because I felt something I didn't like, a crazy quickening of the beat. This called for a shot, right into an open vein, and mechanisms calmed again, and I heard the subtlest change of pitch and attention in the cardiologist's running commentary into a tape recorder. I had been all smiles, believed I was getting a good report card. Then someone whistled and said, "*That's* tight!"

That was the valve.

Then they warned me they were about to inject dye, to get pictures, an angiogram, to see whether my coronary arteries were silted with fat, whether maybe they needed to be bypassed with a length of vein from my leg, *my* leg.

I had been warned the dye ("contrast medium") would give discomfort, a few-second hot shot through my body. Precisely as foretold: discomfort rather than pain, and great heat, which soon passed.

"Let's get the stuff out now."

And bingo, after an hour's work, about noon, they were done with looking.

In the hall outside, while they did another customer inside (we were parked like cars on a full lot), an intern leaned for twenty minutes with his full weight on my groin's bleeding artery. He explained I'd have a sandbag on it the following twenty-four hours, and if there were no complications, I could go home tomorrow.

My cardiologist told me I'd be thirsty when it was over. I'd fasted twelve hours—neither food nor water—so the dye could do its thing without making me puke, and the dry surgical theater . . . I was thirsty. And just as my cardiologist had promised in his office last week, he appeared with a root-beer popsicle. I hadn't eaten a root-beer twin-stick popsicle since I was a kid. Had they been out there all this time? Oh boy! It was sweet, and on the instant I was hooked.

"Where do you get these?" I asked.

The cardiologist looked at me as though he had something else on his mind. Why so closemouthed? Why not share his connection? Who needed him: if Chasen's flew chili to Rome during the filming of *Cleopatra*, I could get root-beer popsicles sent to Rhode Island.

Not twenty-four hours earlier I had told Priscilla: "One thing for *damned sure*. No way, José, are they 'cracking' this chest." I had banged my breast for emphasis. "I'll go to the dye and linguini, but beyond the pasta, count me out." I knew a thing or two myself: how a local cardiologist, Dr. Belasco, had got himself in the steel château the year before for putting pacemakers in people whose hearts needed no pacing. I had just seen a report on "20/20" about the failure of mechanical mitral valves, with consequences you don't want even to imagine, and you haven't got one in you. And I had read a letter to *The New York Times* on the subject of heroic rescue of heart-diseased patients, from a Florida woman who wanted next time her heart played tricks on her to wake up dead. Called "Don't Save Me Again," the letter said, in part:

I had open-heart surgery after two years in bed with congestive heart failure. I was a pioneer in valve replacement. This was followed by hepatitis (bad blood transfusion), coronary (valvular clot), hysterectomy (bleeding from anticoagulants), loss of vision (cerebrovascular accident), loss of ability to read (stroke), open-heart surgery (replacement of first mitral valve), more open-heart surgery (bleeding in chest cavity), cranial and internal bleeding (anticoagulants).

Call me a stubborn fool, but I thought I'd take a pass on the chest cracking.

The cardiologist spoke: "Your aortic valve is badly stenosed."

"A mess?"

He nodded.

"How soon can we get someone to cut it out?"

It was a genetic botch. It would be tidy to believe that the defect was a patrimony, given my persistent labors to memorialize in written and oral history my father's peculiar legacy to his sons. I had thought that his estate—twenty-five dollars—shared equally with my brother, was the last of him.

Save for memories, it was. If my poor excuse for an aortic valve can be blamed on either parent's genes, I'd have to choose my mother's; her own unlucky mother died at forty-one of mitral stenosis and regurgitation, the failure of the other principal heart valve. In fact, even that sad end probably had nothing to do with my state, inasmuch as my grandmother was known to have had rheumatic fever, a common cause of heart-valve disorders.

No, this was no one's fault. Not my father's, not my mother's, not even mine. The *"why me?"* mechanism never kicked in. It made all the sense in the world that my aortic valve was stupid. It was just a thing that happens sometimes to some people. The night before my operation, the surgeon was very clear about things. To have my chest sawed and cut open, to be put on a heart-lung machine, to cut into the aorta to remove something, and replace it with something else—man-made—this was not without risks.

Maybe five of a hundred patients don't come out of the operating room alive. Improving these pretty good odds were my otherwise good health, his celebrated skill, his faith in the valve he meant to sew in me. He was serene, a late-night reader, *very* late-night, after a day of scheduled heart surgery, followed by the unforeseen: shotgunned chests, ice-picked pumps. He was too busy for a bedside manner, but he admired good writing. I hoped he liked my prose. I thought if maybe he admired my writing, maybe I'd have an edge, maybe even get what a friend in a similar fix got from his heart surgeon, a written guarantee that my friend would *never* die. That kind of edge. On the other hand, maybe I'd do without the edge, and the cutting. What then, I asked the man who was next morning to hold my heart in his hands.

Oh, for sure, without a valve replacement, I could expect to live maybe another year, probably less than half that.

What was to decide?

The morning Nicholas drove me to the hospital, I sat at my desk in what an in-law had called our "Terminal House" (because it is commodious enough to store a lifetime collection of junk), paying bills, working on—can you believe it?—taxes. Deposited (I know, I wouldn't believe it either) a "kill-fee" for a failed commissioned essay that was—as editors sometimes say—lifeless.

The night before the dawn cutting-in, considerate nurses and counselors said what they needed to say, clarified, explained, explained again. While they were "in," as they said, "there," they might do that bypass, but probably would not. Time, I was told, is precious on a heart-lung machine. I feigned comprehension.

Priscilla and Justin and Nicholas had come and gone and come and gone. They were great. Justin saved the occasion from sobersidedness. I mentioned that I needed bifocals.

"Dad," he said, "did it occur to you that you were twenty-what—thirty, maybe—when Nick was born . . ."

"Twenty-nine . . ."

"Twenty-nine. *Old.* Too late to have kids. Irresponsible. You can't even throw a ball to your tykes. Now from four-eyes to six-eyes. Lousy foresight."

To them, I had something that was bust, and could merely be fixed. I took peace from them. They wanted to see me as soon as it was over, in the intensive care unit, seemed to look forward to it, as to a happy ceremony. The surgeon had not exactly discouraged them, but I could tell, and Priscilla could tell, he'd sooner they waited. He suggested that I would make an alarming sight to people unused to seeing a person fresh from open-heart surgery. (Later, when I was thought well enough to be told such stories, I heard about a woman who came to see her husband—immediately post-op, as they say —minutes after a valve replacement. The shocking sight of him—his color, facial slackness, less man than junction box for wires and tubes—blew her heart, killed her dead.)

Alone, I willed myself to think *de profundis* about what was about to be done to me, to happen after. It has been a point of dispute between me and people I love that I suffer from a failure of gravity. I excuse myself by believing it wrong to confuse seriousness with solemnity, to pull a long face when I believe, believe right in my heart, that most things are funny. I do not exclude death, entirely. I know (but have had little experience) of deaths that were not approximately funny, but I won't dishonor them with easy pieties.

My own imagination, for worse or better, inclines toward absurd ends. I was once in a near-collision at sea, aboard a famous Mediterranean steamship, flagship of the fleet, in the Straits of Gibraltar on a clear and moonlit night, when she altered course to draw close and salute her sister ship. It was a very close escape, and I knew in that moment that had it happened, my friends would learn of it and feel awful, but that part of the story, an important part, would be difficult to resist as comic narrative.

Or difficult for me. I'm sorry.

Now, though, I wasn't laughing. On the other hand, I wasn't frightened. (I put this down to consoling ignorance, but I also put it down to a temperamental abhorrence of theatricality.) What *would* have frightened me was root canal. I don't have any notion what root canal is, and I don't want to know.

Lying alone that night, I thought ruefully that I might miss by more than a little my ambition to check out debt-free and penniless. Let me just say that as difficult as it would have been for pals and kin to walk this planet without me, it would have been catastrophic for Visa and Diners' Club. Sears, had it known my situation, would have sent specialists from Mass General. American Express would have demanded a second opinion.

On the telephone, my mother reminded me, perversely, how frightened I had been of the needle. Not just as a baby, but in sixth and seventh grade, when I needed a tetanus booster, how I'd had to be dragged from beneath the examining table. My sons—stitched up, down and sideways from bike accidents, rock fights, skiing accidents, falls from heights—had put some steel in me. Time had.

And, finally, with sleep coming down fast, near midnight, I made myself think *what-if*. And I told myself, without tricking myself (I think), that I was ready for whatever, truly. It came down to a simple question. Did the people I love know I loved them, and were they apt to remember who had loved them? I thought so. If Justin were nine instead of seventeen, oh how I would have bawled that night! I would have known that he'd try and try to recall me, that my likeness would dim, and this would make him feel as though he'd betrayed me, or I'd betrayed him. And then I'd be merely an idea to him.

But Justin knew me, Nicholas did, Priscilla in and out. They'd float without me, and if I died they wouldn't have to live with the strangest story ever told, but with a story that could be told, and explained, and accommodated in a sane scheme. The terrifying part, seeing a standing man tip over, seeing their father fall, and quiver, and drool: they'd seen it, and come through it. That night I was kind of the same, but they were not. Whatever happened next would be better than that day at the beach.

After all, here I am, down the road from my valve job. I don't remember the morning hours before they did what they did. Such amnesia, induced chemically or physiologically, is commonplace. I remember waking, and that my wife and boys were there, and that I couldn't talk past the tubes down my throat, and that I wanted to talk. I remember a nurse in intensive care who fed me chips of ice through a whole night, a chip at a time, like a kid feeding an abandoned bird.

They sent my miserable excuse for a valve to pathology. Rhode Island is a teaching hospital, so they will show off what was meant to be paper-thin fluttering valves and was in fact a chunk of calcium with a pinhole. *What do you think* this *is?* Students will scratch their heads. *Knuckle? Pig's foot?* This way students will learn just how bad it can get before it can get no worse.

I got an easy ride. It was not more fun than a day at the beach—let me be frank—but it was supportable. No nurse

addressed me in the first person plural. Morphine rubbed the
edge off for a couple of days, and then I went for a week to
industrial-strength Tylenol, and then household strength, and
within a few weeks nothing. For quite some time Priscilla leapt
to my croaking pleas for ice water, crossword-puzzle assis-
tance, a little help changing channels, or plumping my pillows.
Pretty soon it was "Get it yourself."

Of the get-well cards, I liked best the generic: elephants in
doctors' offices, and puppies in baskets. Trust Hallmark.

My breastbone is wired and stapled like a packing crate,
and they say I'll set off metal detectors in airports. My scar is
a beaut. Purple, visible at a good distance. It's not like that
show-off LBJ's gall-bladder scar, a twisty chaos, map of Southeast Asia; mine is reasonable, straight as Park Avenue, the
cross streets running at right angles—to Madison one way,
Lex the other. When I remove my "Life's a Beach" T-shirt,
the scar should make an electric impression on suntanners
with a few days off from mortality, dreaming of weiners and
fried onion rings. Me? I've got a *bad* root-beer twin-stick jones.

I wear a Medic Alert bracelet, engraved with dire warnings.
It jangles cheaply, and I can hear my valve tripping seventy-
to-the-minute, ticking over like a Baby Ben, or a tuned '56
Chevy, idling. My aorta is carbon and Dacron, simplicity itself,
and it's called a St. Jude, after the saint of the impossible,
patron of hopeless cases. When I asked my cardiologist how
valve manufacturers handle recalls, he said (was that with a
smile?) he hadn't really given the matter much thought. ("I'll
tell you this," he told me; "I worship at St. Jude's in Pawtucket,
and I haven't noticed any dead people manning a picket line
in front of the church.") The valve was made not in Korea (or
knocked off in Southern Italy, where craftsmen would have
mis-stamped it "arctic value"), or worse luck by the Heart
Valve Division of General Motors (I'd want to shun models
built on Mondays and Fridays). It was fabricated in St. Paul,

Minnesota, where they haven't even heard rumors of recreational drugs, and people wash their hands after using the lavatory, and quality control (*I don't like the look of that weld, Sven*) is top-of-the-line. It comes with a lifetime warranty, I'm quite sure.

I think of what happened on the beach and after as training for the future. But some questions I didn't ask. While I was in the land of Nod (they use curare, the stuff little people put on their blow darts), my heart was chilled (frozen?). Okay, where *was* it? What's your hunch? Was it in me, or was it *on another table?* Would that not be a prudent way to work on a pump, as a mechanic might repair a carburetor, on a bench, handy to the tools? What's your best line on this? I could straight-out ask, but I won't. I could ask how much time I bought, but I won't. I've got a more urgent question. Do I ever again have to go to Sint Maarten?

Matterhorn

There came a moment when I needed to climb a mountain. Not just a mountain, a *mountain*. My notion incited some friends to unbecomingly undisguised incredulity. This I expected. I did not expect the response of other friends, and some kin: my ambition seemed to insult them. They either disbelieved or mocked me, sometimes to my face. Others close to me, wishing to seem gentler, fretted in that avuncular way that can end friendships: *What's up with Geoffrey? I wonder, Does he know it's difficult to climb a mountain? Who does he think he is?* They "worried" that I didn't remember I had passed fifty, and they "worried" that I had forgotten my open-heart surgery the year before, a new aortic valve, the contingencies.

Well, exactly: downslope of middle age, bionic heart, narrow escape—what better provocation to stir things up? I'd never climbed before or dreamed of climbing; I was quite sure I would not climb again after this once (just as young Nick Adams, of Hemingway's "Indian Camp," having witnessed a suicide, was "quite sure" he would never die).

But what about duty, responsibility to others, to my wife and little ones? Well, the little ones are growing older than their old man (or, at least, less childish). They thought to climb was a high idea, and if they hadn't thought this, so what? Priscilla knew I wanted to do this, and she understood why mine was a solitary rather than a family ambition, and while laissez-faire would not customarily describe her policy, she had no wish to stand between me and the uphill path to the summit of a high mountain. Well, not just any high mountain, the best high mountain, the Matterhorn.

Some very few sights are self-evidently what they are: New York's skyline and the Eiffel Tower require no elaboration. The Matterhorn is of this tight family of marvels, recognized in the blink of an eye. It's not the highest mountain in the world, or in the Alps, or in Switzerland, or in the Valaisian canton, or within view of Zermatt. So why is the Amai Dablang, higher by six thousand feet, called the "Matterhorn of the Himalayas"? And why do likenesses of the Matterhorn dress up wrappers of chocolate bars and Jamaican cigarettes? Why did Walt Disney erect a 360-foot model of the Matterhorn in Anaheim for Disneyland's roller coaster? Why would Baskin-Robbins name its grandest ice-cream sundae a Matterhorn? Why is it the logo for Paramount's motion pictures? Because the Matterhorn *is* paramount is why.

To think mountain is to see Matterhorn. Unshouldered by nearby mountains, it diminishes higher peaks. I mean it stands *alone*. The Matterhorn has been likened to a ruined tower, a sphinx upon a pedestal of ice, the bust of a giant, an obelisk, a rearing horse, a masterpiece of Art rather than a blind accident of nature.

Guido Rey, Italian mountaineer, author of *The Matterhorn* (1907), understood the limits of language in the face of that formidable thing: "Every time the Matterhorn appears upon the landscape it is wise for the writer to cease his description, and to refer the reader to—the Matterhorn."

Well, I could tell you that the Matterhorn is 14,691 feet high. A great rock pyramid with sheer faces, razor-ridged, saved from an illusion of artificiality by a hunched, off-true peak. In clear light, with feathery billows pluming like vapor trail from its bent crest, the Matterhorn appears unearthly. In hard weather—the summit disappearing in furious black clouds, then, stabbed by lightning, abruptly materializing— the Matterhorn seems ungodly, and to climb it unimaginable.

What the spicy Indies were to Columbus and the North Pole to Peary, the Matterhorn was to mountain climbers of the nineteenth century. A local Italian guide, Jean-Antoine Carrel, attacked the heap of stone as if by ambush, shrewdly advancing, year after year, always higher. Otherwise the assaults were mostly by the British, who elevated the climbing of mountains from the arduous necessity of high-altitude travel (in the service of religious missions, warfare, smuggling, scientific curiosity) into an immoderate passion.

Al Alvarez, a poet and mountaineer, uses Jeremy Bentham's phrase "deep play" to describe the enterprise of climbing. Bentham, celebrator of utility, despised deep play, in which "the stakes are so high that . . . it is irrational for anyone to engage in it at all, since the marginal utility of what you stand to win is grossly outweighed by the disutility of what you stand to lose."

During Victoria's toplofty decades of Empire, improbable conquest was useful and quotidian. Young British athletes, who regarded discomfort as a virtue almost as fine as understatement, challenged summit upon summit, cutting notches on alpenstocks at higher and higher altitudes, climbing from rough, isolated valleys where travelers seemed to have no reasonable business, where hospitality—let alone the concept of Swiss innkeeping—was uninvented.

London's Alpine Club, founded in 1857 with members drawn from the professions and peerage, from universities and the clergy, was joined by a wood-engraving son of a wood engraver, Edward Whymper; Whymper was commissioned by a London publisher to prepare illustrations for a record of Alpine explorations. The issue of this enterprise is Whymper's *Scrambles Amongst the Alps*, perhaps the best account of mountain climbing ever written.

Whymper has been called a "hard goer in an age of hard goers." Indeed. During eighteen days early in the summer of 1865, he ascended almost 100,000 feet. Fifty-five hundred feet of vertical a day—*up*—every day! And then down; some say down is harder. Whymper was known to have walked eighty-six miles in twenty-four hours.

Precise, imaginative, he had ingenuity, knew languages, invented many climbing devices. But above all, above even his stamina, Whymper had will. Oh, did he have will. Beginning in 1861, Whymper made seven assaults on the Matterhorn's Italian side; four years later it remained the last major Alpine mountain still unclimbed. Whymper was adding to his reputation for courage a quality more dangerous than courage: reckless compulsion. In 1862, during his fourth of five attempts that summer, he fell two hundred feet in seven or eight mighty, destructive bounces and still he flung himself at the thing's implacable stone face.

As Whymper well imagined, there was hubris in any contest with the Matterhorn. He wrote that "there seemed to be a *cordon* drawn around it, up to which one might go, but no farther. Within that invisible line djinns and efreets were supposed to out of sight exist. . . . The superstitious natives . . . spoke of a ruined city on its summit wherein the spirits dwelt; and if you laughed, they gravely shook their heads." (And hurled down rocks.)

Mid-July of 1865, Whymper's urgency was fueled by envy. He learned that an Italian party was readying an attack from their side of what they know as Monte Cervino, with a high probability of success. He made pell-mell for Zermatt and checked into the Monte Rosa, where he happened on two other

British climbers: Lord Francis Douglas and the Reverend Charles Hudson, the latter accompanied by a nineteen-year-old friend, Douglas Hadow. Whymper's favorite guide, the Frenchman Michel Croz, was in the service of Hudson, and Lord Douglas had arranged to be assisted in his try at the Matterhorn by a couple of Zermatt guides, the now infamous Peter Taugwalders, father and son.

Whymper liked to climb alone, or with a single guide, but the pressure of the Italian venture tempted him to join forces with his countrymen. So after dinner at the Monte Rosa an *ad hoc* and ill-considered alliance was struck, casually, as British gentlemen liked to agree to grave matters. Nevertheless, Whymper was uncomfortable with the inclusion of young Hadow, who was inexperienced in high-risk climbs. He took Hudson aside after dinner to inquire about the boy. An artisan, Whymper wasn't the Reverend Mr. Hudson's and Lord Douglas's social peer, so it may be imagined with what deference his questions were asked, and how they were answered: by arched eyebrows, with nods and grunts between pulls on the cigar, sips of the Madeira, "Fine chap," Hudson would have assured; "game, a gentleman." "Oh quite," Whymper would agree; "*rather!*" And thus was born a catastrophe.

The ungainly party set out on July 13 from the Monte Rosa in perfect weather to attack the Swiss (Hörnli) Ridge. Conventional wisdom had held this route to be unassailable: viewed head-on from Zermatt the ridge seems knife-blade-sharp, and sheer. Whymper, as an illustrator so well trained in observation, came to see this as an optical illusion caused by foreshortening. The climb began with gorgeous ease, as though to mock the trials of Whymper's earlier attempts: the lightning storms that had pinned him, battered and exhausted, to some toehold crevice; the cannonades of rocks and boulders falling randomly as the mountain, freezing and thawing, came relentlessly apart.

The group bivouacked at eleven thousand feet, and the next morning, Bastille Day, as though climbing a natural staircase, they gained the summit—piece of cake!—and, spying the rival Italians twelve hundred feet below, Whymper heaved "a torrent of stones" down toward them. This uncharacteristic meanness of spirit, a belligerent mix of war-rush and spite, marked the beginning of Whymper's awful descent.

A month later, writing to a stranger, Whymper told his sad progress after conquering the world's most spellbinding mountain: "For five years I have dreamt of the Matterhorn; I have spent much labour and time upon it and I have done it. And now the very name of it is hateful to me. Congratulations on its achievement are bitterness and ashes and that which I hoped would yield pleasure produces alone the severest pain."

The plunge was morbidly portrayed at the time by a Gustave Doré drawing showing four men tumbling toward space at the onset of a half-mile free-fall. What went wrong is in dispute, but Hudson, Douglas, Hadow and the revered guide Michel Croz fell, and died. A postmortem and any number of amateur investigations agree that the proximate cause of the accident was the inexperienced Hadow, who was so unsure of his feet that Croz was obliged to place them properly with his hands. Still near the summit, Hadow, roped together with the other three, stumbled at an easy place, for no evident reason, and took his fellows with him. Old Peter Taugwalder, tied to the luckless four, took the weight of the fall, and the rope parted. (The rope that broke is on display in Zermatt's Alpine Museum; it's fit to tie a package, but not to hold the weight of a climber, let alone two, three, *four*.)

Taugwalder fled Zermatt in infamy; many Zermatters suspected him, forever after, of having cut his fellows loose. Whymper, who judged both Taugwalders to be swinish cowards, denied that any such crime was possible. The tragedy

put Zermatt on the map, and confirmed the Matterhorn's sinister magic.

My corner room at the Monte Rosa looked to the south at the
Matterhorn's Hörnli Ridge and east across the main drag,
the Bahnhofstrasse, to the boneyard. No sooner unpacked than
I was down there, walking the rows of graves where more
than eighty climbers were buried, marked by headstones em-
bellished with bronze coils of climbing rope, or ice axes.
Some of the stones were mountain-shaped, Matterhorn-
shaped.

Jonathan Henry Convelle, 27: ". . . fell from the North Face
of the Matterhorn on 29th December, 1979."

Donald Stephen Williams, 17: "I chose to climb." (Breithorn, 1975)

French: four young men on the Breithorn, "*morts acciden-
tellement dans l'ascension . . .*"

A couple of Spaniards: "*desaparecidos en el Monte Cervino . . .*"

A young man from Stuttgart: "*Gefallen am Matterhorn.*"

But mostly the dead there (and in the graveyard of the English Chapel, a little glacier garden of granite set on a hill behind
the Alpine Museum) were Whymper's countrymen, Oxford
and Cambridge boys and their chums memorialized in Latin
(*Per Ardua Ad Alta*) or plain English, telling of this one "killed
in a crevasse" in 1925, or by "falling stones" in 1895, or
"during a terrible snowstorm 18 August, 1886."

I meant, I have said, to climb the Matterhorn. Why? Let's
say because *I* was there. No: I'm being flip. I meant to climb
the Matterhorn because to climb it was for me so improbable.
For too many years now I had failed to surprise myself, to
reach beyond my grasp.

Not that the Matterhorn was Everest, or the Eiger. No less
an authority than the Alpine Club of London's official guidebook, the *Pennine Alps Central*, calling the Matterhorn "the

most sought-after [mountain] among climbers in the world," told that it has been climbed by "cats, dogs, monkeys and a bear, and by children (one of seven reached the top in two hours)." Of the Hörnli Ridge, which turned the honey to ash in Whymper's mouth, the Alpine Club remarks casually that it is "monotonous, especially in descent." After a summary of stunts on the Matterhorn—speed climbs, successful attempts to girdle the summit, winter climbs, the ascent of all four ridges in a single day—the guidebook concludes its patronizing theme by quoting a remark of Guido Rey: "Its slopes are still considered unsuitable for skiing." (Not so: the Japanese fellow who skied down Everest has also skied from the summit to the base of the Matterhorn, incidentally causing the escapade to be filmed.)

Guido Rey had also written that despite the commonplace conquests of the mountain, "the Matterhorn will never be a vulgar mountain." My first afternoon in Zermatt I was given cause to wonder about that. Put aside the Disneyish knick-knacks, disregard the Japanese wonders-of-the-world collectors photographing the knickknacks; regard Zermatt's goats, bells jangling cutely at their necks as they are driven along the Bahnhofstrasse by a bucolically tricked-out goatherd. The goats work on commission—farmers are *paid* to drive their bewildered beasts through town, a round-trip promenade without destination, with no end other than quaint photographability. And the goaty mess they drop? Not to worry: the streets of Zermatt are cleaned—I mean *cleaned*—every six minutes or so.

During a visit to the town tourist office to learn the telephone number of my guide, I found a young Swiss woman being assailed from across the counter by a countryman of mine, a primitive with a smoker's rasp and a blended-whisky-drinker's nose. This fellow held in his left hand a tourist brochure, which he smacked emphatically with his right fingers.

"Look here, missy! It says, 'See the Matterhorn up close,

from the comfort of your air-conditioned bus.' Now where does the bus *leave* from?''

"As you see, sir, we have no cars or buses on our streets . . .''

"I want to ride in a *bus* to the *top* of your darned Matterhorn!''

He was invited to dart out on the Bahnhofstrasse to examine the elevation at issue, and judge for himself whether it seemed suitable for assault by (air-conditioned) bus. He waved his brochure. The patient lady explained that while it was possible to rise by cable car to the flanks of the mountain's steep summit, the only way to the top was to climb the thing, one circumspect step after another.

"No way! Iris will never sit still for that!''

Iris, wise lady, nodded her vigorous assent.

So the Matterhorn's ubiquity may breed a kind of offhand contempt, and the would-be climber is torn between the scorn of well-wishers who deride an old hubby/daddy's audacity and mountaineers' derision for a well-worn path, overtramped by amateurs clinging to fixed ropes.

Josie Furrer, my guide, put the matter in fit perspective. The Furrers have farmed the valley since the Middle Ages; the past century or so they have climbed, and some Furrers have died climbing, and two Furrer guides have died on the Matterhorn. The Alpine Club's dismissal of the mountain as "monotonous" was not my guide's view.

Josie is tall and ropy thin, with a cowpoke's easy lope. He once made a long visit in the States, coming like many Swiss mountain men to ski-instruct; some deeper instinct drew him to a Durango, Colorado, ranch to herd cattle. As a kid, he was a shepherd (the kind who later goes to college), tending sheep and goats in the mountain pastures above Zermatt and Winkelmatten. To ease the boredom, he and his young pals—on dares and double-dares—would climb whatever was handy, and up there above the tree line, rocks were handy.

Like many Swiss and most mountain men, Josie is taciturn, his energy and irony radiating from his eyes rather than his words. Taciturnity is a luxury, the fruit of Zermatt's prosperity. In older times, during the pioneer days of climbing, Zermatt's guides (many of them smugglers and mule drivers) gathered along a wall facing the Monte Rosa, touting their strength and valor, showing off books of testimonials from previous climbers. In not-so-old days, most of a Zermatter's family income came from guiding, and every able-bodied young man and boy set up outside the Monte Rosa with his book. (Josie has his, a keepsake rather than an advertising medium.) For decades Swiss guides have been stringently examined and licensed; a dozen people, more or less, die every year on the Matterhorn, but none in the company of a guide these past thirty years.

In the bar of the Monte Rosa, Josie inquired, delicately but directly, into my fitness. I made no vainglorious claims: I do what the doctors order, and a little more; I walk, row, ride a bicycle, play squash. He knew my mountain-climbing biography: *tabula rasa*. We did not discuss a certain medication I must take to thin my blood, a remedy for clots on an artificial aortic valve at the heart of me. Coumadin makes me an abundant bleeder, an easy bruiser. Some informed medical opinion holds that Coumadin users should avoid hammers and screwdrivers, let alone ice axes, crampons and sharp stones.

"I'd like to climb the Matterhorn," I said.

"Yes," he said. "So you said."

"What do you think?"

"There's ice on the rocks. The guides aren't climbing it."

"But if there weren't ice, what do you think?"

"Tomorrow morning we'll climb some rocks, try the Riffelhorn. We'll see."

We caught the earliest morning cog train to Gornergrat, as far as Rotboden. (At the end of the nineteenth century porters carted well-fed tourists up here and higher in sedan chairs. Four francs! I know, a franc then was a franc, but this is a forty-five-minute train ride.) Along the gorgeous way, through forests of ancient larch, past waterfalls and sheer drops, Josie seemed stimulated by the scenery as though he'd never seen it before; he pointed out glaciers and peaks, but always our eyes returned to the Matterhorn. (It's odd, the relentless pull of that mountain. First thing every morning, last every evening, I glanced out my window to verify it was still there.)

We swung down at a little station and walked a path to the base of a rock cliff, and at the base Josie helped me fix a harness to my chest, and to this he connected one end of a long coil of rope; then he began to climb, and told me to follow, and that was that. (Oh, he also exhorted me to "trust my boots.")

The Riffelhorn is a serious hunk of rock, used by Zermatt guides to judge their clients' upper-body strength, dexterity and, above all, their tolerance for "exposure," that great emptiness below and to the sides through which one would fall should one fall. Climbing the Matterhorn's Hörnli Ridge, one looks a foot or so to the right to a half-mile drop, and to the left a ditto to a ditto. Some people don't enjoy this. Some, climbing the Riffelhorn, looking beneath their toes jammed in smooth and minuscule dimples in the rock, looking down a couple of hundred feet and more, know they won't enjoy what they see on the Hörnli Ridge, and there's an end to that: home we go.

The exposure didn't trouble me; my eyes were fixed near, on the handholds and toeholds inches away; concentration effaced imagination. Not that I wasn't frightened by the here and now: to climb that face seemed at first out of the question. I found myself spread-eagled, a fly on the wall, always fixed (as Josie insisted) at three points. I would have preferred four, but such a system makes progress difficult.

"A few inches to the left and up, there's a *nice* grip."

How, above me, looking up, did he know? He beheld the way as intimately as a person comes to know the route from bedroom to bathroom. His voice was patient, serene.

We began to climb faster; the progress seemed easier—but Josie said later the line became more difficult, modeling the Matterhorn's demands. I felt exhilarated, and then we were up there, the summit. Josie shook my hand, and I felt like a million Swiss francs. Looking toward the Matterhorn, Josie said, "I have to tell you, you didn't do badly."

I slipped out of my harness. "Can I climb the Matterhorn?"

"First we'll climb the Breithorn, and then we'll see."

"Are the guides climbing the Matterhorn yet?" The weather had been clear and warm the previous five days, and it was difficult to imagine the Matterhorn's upper rocks varnished with ice.

"No. Others have tried. Two Belgians fell yesterday."

"Hurt?"

"Dead. Coming down, it is thought. The trouble usually comes on the descent. They set out too late, become tired, light-headed. Now, we must descend."

Coming down you face out, like having a ladder's rungs at your back, and it is impossible not to regard your miserable possibilities; you are *meant* to look down. Josie was above me, and noticed I had failed to put my harness in place, and I paused to secure it, then began to lead down fast, showing off. Just as he suggested I slow the pace, my rucksack jammed between my back and the cliff face; using my heels as a fulcrum, I felt the rucksack wedge me forward, and I was already beyond the point of recovery when I observed (if that isn't too incredible an understatement), "I'm falling," and Josie snugged down the rope. I was trapped (his rope pulled what the rucksack tried to push), and Josie had to pay out line till I was facing down, secured by the rope and my heels, better educated than a few minutes before in the physics of this pastime. Then my rucksack fell back where it belonged, and I knew why Josie's was secured at his waist.

At the depot we made an appointment for the Breithorn climb two days later. Josie said he would like to observe my stamina.

Climbing the Riffelhorn, I had not felt spent; rock-climbing is deliberate, requiring many pauses to calculate the route, enforcing rest. The Breithorn is a snow-and-ice climb to almost the same altitude as the Matterhorn.

Dawn was midsummer temperate in Zermatt, and I felt preposterous in my long johns, wool socks and knickers, with mittens and cap in my rucksack, to which were strapped crampons and an ice ax. (I also carried glacier cream, glacier glasses to prevent snow blindness, a chocolate bar, water, medicine for altitude sickness.) Thus burdened, I clomped in heavy leather climbing boots to the cable car that would lift me by stages a half hour from Winkelmatten to the base of the Breithorn.

By its simplest route, in good conditions, the Breithorn is said to be the easiest four-thousander (4,000 meters plus) in the Alps. I met Josie at the staging area for our ascent and without small talk or delay—to assure that this would be a climb in good conditions (the snow's crust too hard to break through)—he roped us together, walked ahead ten or fifteen yards and commanded me to follow.

The first hour or so—descending gradually to a valley between two peaks, leveling off, walking on firm snow—was effortless. (In warm, soft snow a Breithorn climber can sink with every step to his crotch, and that can very quickly get to be a very old story.) The view was stunning: the Breithorn has a rounded vanilla crown, massive, toward which I moved freshly, feeling frisky on my leash, wondering why Josie walked with such slow, considered steps. The rope, I knew, was to save me from the consequence of crevasses, which were, with whiteouts (and lost routes), the mountain's principal peril.

After an hour, at the foot of an ascent, Josie directed me to strap crampons to my boots, and the following hour offered a full curriculum of my middle-aged limits. By now the wind had come up, and at our altitude it was cold in the bright sun, and still I was sweating from the labor of a steep climb up a narrow ice path. The crampons' teeth, extending forward from the toes as well as down, made for clumsy going, and occasionally my right boot tangled in my left, and then Josie, climbing relentlessly above me, would unintentionally tug my leash, bringing to mind a conceit altogether different from master and pup; now I was on a chain gang, and I began to wonder, for the first time since I had hatched this plan a year ago, what in the world was I doing in that place, tied to that young man, being towed uphill?

Swiss guides climb taking dainty steps; the rule has it that however strenuous the ascent, a climber should be able to talk in a normal voice, and continue up without pause, and in that way those wee steps cover great distances. We went up mutely, saving our breath; what we were doing was difficult. I was determined not to complain, to be a stand-up guy at 13,666 feet, but soon I was pausing every thirty seconds or so. My calf muscles burned, and the air was thin, thin, thin. I watched climbers strung out below, gaining a little on us. Gray clouds were sweeping up from Italy, and the light had gone flat.

Josie looked unhappily at the sky. I thought he might suggest we go back down. He blew warm air into his mittens, and said, "We should move on. We can't stay long at the summit."

Looking where he pointed, I saw we were there, almost. And seeing this I breathed easy, and felt a rush of unwarranted pride. And just short of the summit I heard footfalls behind me. Let me say these were rapid footfalls, and someone, not at all short of breath, said in several languages "Excuse me," and a young man passed us as though he were walking a city street, late for a romantic appointment, grinning, all bounce and cheer. He was carrying *skis* on his shoulder, and through his eyes I saw myself—an antique person.

But I got my handshake, and ate my chocolate bar; the sun punched a hole in Italy's smoggy clouds, and there was the Matterhorn.

"Do you think I'm fit to climb it?"

"Maybe," Josie said. "But not yet. It's still iced. Crampons go badly on rocks."

Indeed. That afternoon a young American died on the Matterhorn.

Two weeks in Zermatt, two weeks of perfect weather, and up there on the mountain that mattered the snow clung to sheer faces and ice glazed the rocks. After the American died, I asked Josie why they didn't close the mountain, and he looked at me with wonder, as though he had just then learned more about me than he wanted to know, that I was a sea-level flatlander through and through. *Close the mountain?* What could I mean? To climb was to risk, a personal choice, deep play.

My final day, I wearied of looking at the Matterhorn from a middle distance, preparing for it, reading about it, studying the tombstones it had sowed. From its base at Schwarzsee I hiked two thousand feet to the Hörnli Hut, where climbers spend the night before taking the thing on in the cold dark hours before dawn, setting off with headlamps to get up there early enough to get down again alive.

It was a hard walk up to the hut, but the way was well traveled, and I was not alone. Below the sheer cliffs I saw the glacier gardens fan out; great crows climbed and fell on the thermals, and then I made my studied, solitary way along iced patches, and through new-fallen snow. The Matterhorn makes its own weather, and last night it had made bad weather.

At the hut the sun drilled down, and young climbers fiddled with their equipment, preparing for the morning. Some were jittery, laughing too often and loud; others were grave, like bullfighters waiting for it to begin. I sat on the terrace of the simple hut, trying to strike up talk, but I didn't belong there, and so I moved along, climbing, till the hut had disappeared. I was looking for a hand-lettered sign Josie had told me about. It had been erected a year or two ago—maybe three, Josie said—by the mother of a young American who had died on the Matterhorn. The sign was a warning to take the mountain seriously. I never found the warning. Maybe it was set higher than I wished to climb, or maybe someone had removed it, spooked by the bad vibes it gave off, or maybe time wore it down, as it wears down mountains, and us.

I cranked my head back and back, looked up. No. This was not to be. I turned my back on the summit, and moved out, down. My feelings were complex: I had dragged myself to the bottom of that wonderful mountain, just this once. I drew cards, once. I was dealt a low hand, and now I'll stand pat with it, at sea level.

Waterway

The Deal

One May afternoon, end of Nicholas Wolff's junior year at college, drinking beer so cold we needed mittens to hold the cans, aboard our boat reaching rail-down into the sun and toward the beach at Mackerel Cove on the island where we live, himself at the helm giving orders (ease that sheet a tad, you might want to tighten the luff line on the main), we struck a deal. Or I dictated a deal, simplicity itself: on graduating from Bowdoin he would take this boat, the *Blackwing*, to the Bahamas, with one or two chums. There was nothing to it—other than taking full responsibility for our boat, which *I* pay for, and teaching his friends to sail, navigate, cook on a galley stove without blowing up the unfortunate boat; other than maintaining the sails and gear and engine and electronics, and troubling that the dinghy wasn't stolen, and earning enough money before he sailed from home to keep himself afloat without work for six months, and making certain the anchor didn't drag when autumn and winter gales blasted him, and learning first aid, and keeping his friends out of the ocean and clear of the boom . . . why, there was nothing to the venture but a nod, a wink, another beer and a faraway look on Nicholas's face that I took to be gratitude for my trust, but was in truth cogitation. During the following year, when friends would remark what a generous fellow I was and how trusting (how could I bank on a mere boy with so much boat? wasn't he grateful?), that circumspect countenance would steal on Nicholas's face, and he'd catch my eye, and I'd shrug. In fact, I had every reason to trust him: he was handy; he didn't get seasick; he knew (as I didn't and don't) celestial navigation; he'd been trained to strip down and repair a diesel engine; he'd sailed offshore weeks at a time on a tall ship; he'd been aloft in great seas and screaming winds; his instincts on the water seemed flawless. We'd been together on the water since he was ten, and in trouble he had never failed to come through.

Besides, *Blackwing* would either winter over in my back yard (while I paid the bank and watched her cradled in blocks, swathed in tarps and crusted with snow a few yards from a blue spruce) or in the Bahamas. Which would she prefer?

Also besides, any trouble Nicholas could get into was the same trouble his father could get into. That the 30-foot cutter would suffer battle scars I had no doubt. There was no end of things to go wrong. So what? An anchor could hook an obstruction and be twisted or lost, a winch could freeze up, a mainsail rip; Nicholas and his friends would fix or replace what ingenuity and their thin wallets could make right. While Nicholas seemed to consider it was not his boat to be philosophic about, I was philosophic. *Que será* and all that.

And besides, I had an interest. Of course I had an interest. A couple, in fact. Although I prefer to believe it's not my vice to nurse bygone grievances against my father, although you won't catch me at fifty-three bawling from the rostrum at Children of Alcoholics and although I assure myself that I'm a good sport and a good son, there is one grudge I bear, and now I'll bare it.

A week after my graduation from college I was aboard a 50-foot ketch in Buzzard's Bay with a classmate whose father owned the boat. My father, from whom I had not heard in more than two years, reached me by radiotelephone and supplicated, implored, demanded, begged, nagged that I come immediately to California to spend the summer with him. In September I was going to Istanbul to teach, and I had plans for that summer, which were to spend it aboard my friend's father's ketch, sailing from resort to resort, up and down the East Coast, earning my keep by the application to expensive wood of sandpaper, tack rag and varnish brush. My friend's father had lent us his boat for the summer, and by God we meant to put some water under her keel and a débutante or two in her bunks. Instead I hopped a hound to California, seduced there by a chance to see my brother, who had been similarly lured a great distance from his summer plans by my father's improbable promise of a family at last (if incompletely) fused.

It was all fission, as I have told in another tale. The day my brother arrived, my father sailed his little land dinghy of an unpaid-for sports car into the Nevada desert (flip side of Buzzard's Bay) with a woman he liked; when they came out of the desert to meet my bus, she didn't like him. The day I arrived, Dad was removed to an asylum and the miserable consolations of shock therapy, and so I spent that sad centrifugal summer translating Atlas Missile technical manuals from English into Air Force, eating franks and beans standing up at the kitchenette of a sunless and airless one-room apartment, visiting spaced-out Dad on weekend afternoons in an academy of laughter south of San Diego and a few miles north of the Tijuana whorehouses I visited weekend nights. (No débutantes after all.) Selfish me had figured for a long time, and with graceless petulance, that in exchange for *that* summer I was owed something, and now at last I meant to pay me back, with Nicholas trustee of the debt.

So I had an interest. My other interest was simpler to narrate:

if my son got *Blackwing* to the Bahamas, my wife and I would have a boat in the Bahamas.

He got her there. He and two college buddies provisioned her and prepared her for sea in September, while hurricane Hugo made its way up the East Coast from the Caribbean. When it passed, Nicholas gave them a crash course in the rudiments of sailing, and slipped our Jamestown, Rhode Island, mooring the first day of October. Block Island, Fishers Island, The Thimbles, Long Island, City Island, the East River, Sandy Hook, Mannasquan, Atlantic City, Cape May, Chesapeake City, Sassafras River, Annapolis, Smith Island, Norfolk, the Dismal Swamp, Elizabeth City, the Alligator River, Okrakoke, Oriental, Beaufort, Wrightsville Beach, Waccamaw River, Charleston, another Beaufort, New Teakettle Creek, St. Simon's Island, St. Augustine, Daytona, Cocoa Beach, Vero Beach, Fort Pierce, Palm Beach, Fort Lauderdale, Key Biscayne, the Gulf Stream, Gun Cay, the Bahama Banks, Chub Cay, Nassau, Allan's Cay, Hawksbill Cay, Sampson Cay, Pipe Creek, Staniel Cay, George Town, Eleuthera, Governor's Harbour, The End of the Road.

That road was six months unwinding, bristling with pitfalls and drug dealers and drug agents and anxiety and shoals and snags and reefs and the worst gear-busting winter winds ever recorded in the southern Bahamas. Priscilla and I had agreed to meet Nicholas and *Blackwing* at Governor's Harbour on the 100-mile-long island of Eleuthera on March 20. Such time-tabled rendezvous are laughably chimerical. On our end we had flu to avoid, blizzards to pray against, semi-tropical airlines with semi-tropical attitudes toward confirmed reservations and clockwork schedules. On Nicholas's end was a complex of nautical machinery, his body's machinery, weather systems, kismet. On March 20, we landed with Nicholas's brother Justin at Eleuthera's little airport, and took a taxi to the harbor. In the harbor, swinging from a mooring thousands of miles from home, our boat and our son. The boat was impeccable, the sun shining, the son tan and grinning, the family Wolff fused, trust repaid, the outcome agreeable. It was difficult not to feel smug: I'd told them so, and it was so.

With what mixed feelings Nicholas surrendered command of *Blackwing* might be imagined. With what mixed feelings I took responsibility for safely returning Priscilla, the boat and me to Rhode Island might be imagined. The idea was to take it easy, to laze three hundred miles through the islands of the northern Bahamas and back across the Gulf Stream; then to push more than a thousand miles up the Waterway to Norfolk; then to bring her the final six hundred miles home, reading the seabagful of paperbacks we'd brought, catching some good rays, watching the handsome world float by at five miles per hour—less, if we wanted to hang out. I had finished and revised a book; Priscilla was on leave from teaching. We felt we deserved this, and we knew we needed a jolt to our routine. Back home we were owned by a house, and trees, and gardens, and processes of maintenance that had become habitual, were becoming reflexive, feckless. We'd begun to sleepwalk through the seasons, constricting with work and relaxing with our eyes closed. I was beginning to look forward to figuring our income taxes: the novelty of the year was a story narrated by spreadsheet; had we done better or worse this year than last year? We had begun to worry ourselves. It wasn't a "rat race" we had entered. "Rat race" is too vigorous for how it felt; "Getting and spending we lay waste our powers" was too verby for how it felt. Pulling the covers over our heads was how it felt. We were past due for a sea change. I sensed a danger in the serene regularity our life together had become: what I happened to know at my age could too easily become all I thought I needed or wanted to know. I needed a good shaking up, wanted to see anew, with sharp eyes, beyond my accustomed range and field of vision. Not that I welcomed obstacles or difficulty, the friction that makes for good narrative and bad marriage. Let it not be assumed that my appetite for refreshment was mere mid-life crisis. No: I was well beyond the hammy clutch of crisis. I needed to sharpen my edge, and I thought I understood that a sea passage—scary, chancy, variable—was a sovereign honer. I would—by Neptune!—relax with a vengeance.

The Islands

During the transition week, we stayed in Eleuthera at a friend's beach house, and swam and played ping-pong and read and played ping-pong and walked on the beach and argued about politics and played ping-pong and played ping-pong. I guess I mean to say we had fun. Most mornings that week, Nicholas instructed me an inch at a time in the foibles of the boat I had taught him to sail. This felt less like usurpation than succession; call it evolution. When Nicholas took *Blackwing*, he had understood that to have the engine break down—and carelessness of many kinds could cause it to break—would be a tragedy of uninsured Force 10 magnitude, a five-thousand-dollar mischance. So, I had reckoned, Nicholas would not be careless with our engine, with what he seemed to regard as *my* engine. He was not careless, but his pinched means and pinch-fist ways had motivated him to learn certain ugly chores I had paid others to do. So now he taught me the perversities of the fuel filters, and how to change the engine oil without having to steam-clean myself and burn my clothes when I was finished. He showed me how to tighten the stuffing box, a duty so ghastly I don't even want to tell you what it is or how it's

done or why. A job I did once after Nicholas took me through
it a step at a time. A job I again pay others to do.

I felt like a stranger on our boat: not only because I was
being taught her ways as though I were chartering her, but
because *Blackwing* looked different. The boat looked better.
It had always looked good, I think, but Nicholas had made it
look better. He had finished the cherry interior bright, laying
up coat after coat of varnish. (And where did three six-footers
sleep while the varnish was drying?) Above decks he had taken
all the brightworked teak down to bare wood, and brushed on
eight coats. Below, the bilge was dry, smelled sweet. The sails
had been cleaned and spot-mended. You would not guess
looking into my son's bedroom at home that *Blackwing*'s icebox would have been scrubbed, but it had been scrubbed. (The
ice chest was also empty. Dry. Hot. They had sailed more than
two months in the Bahamas without ice. Ice cost money. Those
boys had been strapped for cash; cleaning out detritus from
Blackwing's forward shelf, I'd found a want ad torn from a
Florida newspaper: "Fair recompense paid to subjects offering
services for scientific study of Jock Itch." Six weeks ago Nicholas had phoned me from the Exumas. Overcoming my
terror of the cold and uninflected voice I heard when he
guessed I was meddling, I had asked him how his money was
holding up. "Great. No sweat. I've got almost a hundred dollars!" He's not a hedonist.)

He had made our boat sound and clean, and made us happy.
There was nothing more that he could do, except sail with us
and Justin twenty miles north up the west coast of Eleuthera
to Hatchet Bay, and say goodbye.

The day, like all Eleutheran days so far, was clear; the wind
was fair; *Blackwing* moved fast through twenty-five feet of
water. We could see the bottom—could we ever see the bottom! We could identify a thin dime on the bottom, but we

weren't looking at the bottom, pretty as it was; in the way of victims of vertigo, we disciplined ourselves not to look down. We instead stared ahead, trying to make out distinguishing features along what seemed to be an undifferentiated coast. But in less than the time it takes to tell, we were sailing through a hole in the wall, and making our way to a mooring of the Hatchet Bay Yacht Club. A few feet from the mooring pickup Nicholas said the water looked to him "thin," and I was on the point of requiring him to define his terms when I ran us aground in soft mud. I don't run aground. Ask anyone. Maybe I *used to* run aground, in Chesapeake Bay, but I DO NOT RUN AGROUND.

"Dad, we're high and dry. Tide'll ease you off in a couple of hours. Mix a Mount Gay and juice. Be mellow in the Islands, mon. Gotta blaze, Ma. Justin and I have a plane to catch."

This was what a father does when he throws his son off the deep end (I guess here the conceit would call for shallow end), and yells *Swim!* There was water enough to float the dinghy, and I rowed my sons ashore, and asked Nicholas how often this had happened to him.

"Well, that's a weird thing. Never, actually."

(Well, actually: would *you* believe him?)

After Nicholas rescued his brother and said goodbye—jumped ship, took French leave, abandoned his mummy and daddy—Priscilla and I had a long, hard look at our hole cards. Neither told the other then, but both wondered what did we think we were doing? We had loran, a pinpoint navigational device. I punched in Jamestown, Rhode Island, to see our range and bearing, how far and on what course was home from Hatchet Bay. The loran scratched its head, added sums on its fingers and said go north about eleven zillion miles. Uh-huh.

After Priscilla reminded me of our agreement, that she could jump ship whenever she was fed up with *Blackwing* or its crew, we decided to put a Zoot Sims tape on the deck, were pleased to have verifiable corroboration that a rising tide floats all ships, ate a fine meal. The harbor was snug and pretty, bordered by the little settlement of Alice Town. This Saturday night a volleyball game was being played under arc lights against a neighbor from the archipelago called the Family Islands. It was a sweet occasion: we could hear bellows of enthusiasm, and Priscilla and I smiled a private smile, happy to share (at a little distance) the Bahamians' pleasures, to hear their boisterous huzzahs.

We were moored beside a spanky new ocean racer of about fifty feet; she was named *Tranquility*, which is probably—after *At Last* and *Finally*—the John Smith of boat names. All was tranquil on *Tranquility*, just as you'd hope at bedtime.

The next morning we were wakened before sunrise. The anchor was being raised on the ocean racer. The anchor rode was chain, and to run chain through a windlass and into a chain locker is to make a satanic clamor, skeletons slam-dancing in Hell. But that heavy clanking was as nothing against the nasal, boyish whine, speaking Southernese, in response to the captain's invitation that his deckhand "get that fucking anchor off the bottom!"

"You fucking get the fucker up, Dad! The fucker's muddy!"

"Haul that fucker up now or you'll spend the rest of this fucking cruise down there with it, on the fucking muddy bottom!"

I poked my head up from below in time to see the deckhand's mom smile a joyless smile at the people of Hatchet Bay, and make a shruggy gesture of surrender (*Y'all know how it is, boys on boats*), and thus *Tranquility* slipped away before sunup.

In transit to Royal Island, trying with what would become comic inefficiency to get a weather forecast, we heard a news report. Dozens of people injured last night during a fracas at halftime of a volleyball match in Alice Town. A melee. Bottles had been thrown, police and ambulances sent for. The attention of the Government in Nassau had been drawn, and by today's executive fiat there would be no more volleyballs spiked in Alice Town; the arc lights had been snuffed at Hatchet Bay. How the world seems is not how the world is.

Royal Island was the jumping-off harbor for a tricky passage across Northeast Providence Channel to Little Harbour in the Abacos, the northernmost Bahamian chain. We anchored in a palm-fringed lagoon that resembled a movie set of Eden. Water as clear as crystal, abandoned plantation, coconut palms backlit by a Tintoretto sunset. Sixteen boats were anchored in the large, nearly landlocked harbor. The moon rose, showing its sharp-edged silver face like a cheerful, goofy neighbor peering over a fence: *Hey, guys, what's cooking?* The nautical almanac had said the moon would rise and it was so, the spheres in their regulated cycles, time and tide right with the world, natural law beside me in the cockpit. The night lavished softness, the moon spilling such unpolluted light that we could see by its beams our anchor dug into the chalky-white sand below our keel; as the breeze piped up, we heard the voices of wine and beer and rum drinkers float across the water, singing the songs sung in the backs of school buses ("Roll Me Over") and around campfires ("Row, Row, Row Your Boat"), and by God we joined in. Was this okay or what? We were gathered into the anything-goes euphoria of strangers sharing a discovery. Then it got rowdy, as though the whole harbor were drunk on liberty. Someone shot off a parachute flare, and we heard chivvying gasps. Bad Form. This Is Not Done. Flares were reserved for Mayday emergencies, to signal grave distress. To set off a flare back where we thought of as *back home* would bring the Coast Guard down on a mariner. Back home playing with flares was much deplored; horsing around with flares was a rum job, a hanging offense back home. But we weren't back home. For sure. So another boat lofted a parachute flare, and another, and soon the lagoon was bathed in moonlight, starlight, phosphorus. Phosphorus in the velvet water, phosphorus aloft. The harbor was lit, and so were we.

I went below, and spread out the charts. Again. I'd been studying the ungiving things since the night we met Nicholas in Governor's Harbour and, to my disenchantment, they weren't more inviting tonight than a week before. The dilemma was simple: we had to navigate the fifty-three miles in ten hours, from dawn till sundown. *Blackwing* could do 5½ knots under power in calm seas and neutral (or offsetting) current. We had to hit Little Harbour Bar on the button, and I spent the next several hours calculating courses and tidal sets. There were no buoys out there, and we'd spend most of tomorrow out of sight of land. At home I'd use tidal tables and current charts to calculate the effect of tides on our course. Here, now, I sought instruction from the *Yachtsman's Guide to the Bahamas* and was casually informed of an unpredictable phenomenon (cause unknown) of a powerful tidal set "at times," *either* northwest (onshore) *or* southeast (on our nose). It made a difference which. This tidal set had a reported velocity of up to three knots. Whether we could expect three knots or two or none of help, or three of hurt, this also made a difference.

If the wind (or tidal current) was on *Blackwing*'s nose, we wouldn't make it. On the other hand, if the wind was behind us, or abeam of us, we probably would, unless something went wrong. Moreover, if we *almost* made it, there was no escape hatch, no harbor of refuge. (A sort of anchorage, called Hole in the Wall, at the southernmost end of Great Abaco, was notorious for wretched protection from the prevailing wind and for an anchorproof bottom.)

The rum was beginning to wear off. I had shut down Jimmy Buffet for the night, and was playing a tape of Pablo Casals doing Bach solos. He was working his way through a threnodic patch, and I explained to Priscilla that I was "apprehensive." She cocked her head at me. I said I was "anxious." She asked me what I was talking about. I said it was going to be a "chancy" passage. Not "tranquil." In fact, I was looking at alternate routes back to the coast of Florida. An easy passage would take us home by way of Nassau and Freeport, shit-holes. Priscilla said she'd hang her head in shame. When it came down to it, Priscilla seemed always to be the one of us who put the thing in gear and stepped on the gas. She likes to know the pros and cons, but I'm not sure why; it takes a lot of cons to turn her off course.

So next morning we got our hangovers out of our berth an hour before dawn. While Priscilla made peanut-butter sand-wiches with Ritz crackers, and packed them in zip-locked bags, I tried to tune in Charley's Locker on the transistor radio. In the Bahamas, on weekdays, at 6:45 a.m., maybe, if reception was good, it was possible to tune in Charley's Locker from Coral Gables, Florida, to get a rough prophecy of weather in the Caribbean. This followed a roundup of sports news from Trinidad and Jamaica, and was preceded by a maddening hornpipe chantey, "Barnacle Bill the Sailor" or the like. It was possible—if the boat was pointed in just the right direction, and if the seas were quiet, and wind wasn't shrieking in the rigging, and no casuarinas blocked reception, and Priscilla remembered not to talk while I listened, and I kept alert despite a numbing chatter of cricket scores—to hear every third or fourth word. The velocity of Charley's weather report was re-markable; someone was paying by the second. He sort of seemed to bring passably okay news. Windsouthwest-some-thingknots-somethingelse-by afternoon. Then, slow and sure, every syllable enunciated: "Sat-is-fy alllll your boat-ing needs at Char-ley's Lock-er."

"Let's go," I said.

So we went.

It was a hairy passage. We jumped off at the first hint of light, got up in oilskins and wool caps and gloves. The wind was up and at 'em, twenty knots at first, gusting to twenty-five. The day was gray and ominous, with low clouds scudding in from the west-southwest. The rusted wreck of a fertilizer freighter at Egg Island cut was the last vessel we saw that day. We were headed due north, shoved by great cresting rollers; *Blackwing* is a notably dry boat, but as the wind increased, spindrift blew off the tops of the surge, spraying us with warm water. When a gust hit, it came from the west. The wind was beginning to clock around, and I was tense, racing the sun to cross Little Harbour Bar before dark, and safely.

Priscilla noted nautical miles accumulated on the log, an odometer that gives a roughly accurate account of speed through the water, which is (because of the effect of tidal and wind currents) less interesting than speed over the bottom. We seemed to be making six knots, and that was good. *Blackwing* is cutter rigged with a large mainsail and two jibs; we were sailing with a double-reefed (radically reduced) mainsail and the roller-furled jib, called a Yankee, and we were flying.

Priscilla kept me equipped with hot tea and peanut-butter crackers. I hadn't eaten peanut-buttered crackers since I was a kid, and neither had Priscilla; she reinvented them for this voyage, and this is why she's so smart: she knew that a quantity of those crackers, dry in zip-locked bags, would give our wind-swept, water-soaked cockpit a milk-and-crackers-at-recess comfiness. This passage was a trial for her. All these years she'd fought seasickness, and now we were trying a timed-release drug taken by way of a patch worn behind her ear, and either it was working or she was too busy hanging on and helping out to be sick. That was the good news. The bad news: I was working hard to keep *Blackwing* on course in those willful seas, with the wind building and coming more and more off her beam. Plus: beginning just after noon, past the line of no return, we could see lightning on the horizon, and hear thunder. Plus: the steering felt sloppy, and I heard the rudder creak when I adjusted it to counter the violent push of a roller on our port stern quarter.

Other than being stove in, or catching fire, there is no worse destiny in heavy seas than to lose a rudder. *Blackwing* is steered by a wheel that moves the rudder by stainless-steel cables rove through sheaves to a rudder quadrant, and I knew that our trouble was more likely the connection between wheel and rudder than the rudder itself. Nicholas had had a steering cable break a few weeks ago in the Exumas, navigating a tricky reef. I had an emergency tiller, but it would take all my strength to keep *Blackwing* on course with it, and I was cold and tired. I felt shorthanded; I *was* shorthanded, and I elected to keep my anxieties about our steering system to myself.

A simple truth we couldn't ignore: Priscilla—smart, brave and calm—is not strong. She has an unerring sense of place, so that she could thread us through a reef. She would cheer-fully go below and make food in wild seas. But to ask her to douse and furl a sail in huge seas, or to trim a sheet, or to wrestle the wheel out here where all was too big for our britches—this was to ask too much. Unspoken between us was an agreement: I sail, she thinks. Her will wasn't in question, or her nerve; she was overpowered, and I wasn't, quite. But there was only one of me (alas, alas!), and that one was now wearing out.

Thunder and lightning exploded at four in the afternoon, just after we'd caught sight of a landfall on Great Abaco. When the wind-driven rain hit us in horizontal sheets, we could see nothing but gray wet, and evil electric bolts, and the concussive thunder scared us silly. I wondered what it would be like, if I couldn't find Little Harbour Bar, to ride this out at sea, through the night, waiting for dawn, hoping to find my way across.

Wondering this, I heard Priscilla say, "That's it." The "it" she referred to was a reef, forbiddingly named The Boilers, a mile or so south of the bar. If "it" wasn't "it," all bets were off, and we'd rolled snake eyes, crapped out, bust ourselves. Time was short now. "It" *was* "it," and now all that remained was to follow the *Yachtsman's Guide*, which Priscilla read to me above the scream of the wind and the thunder and the smash of the sea:

> Little Harbour Bar should be negotiated with care, according to the following directions. Approaching Little Harbour Bar from the south, stand off the coast not less than one mile until Little Harbour Point and Tom Curry's Point are in transit. (See sketch chart of Little Harbour.) They will then be bearing roughly 305°. Alter course to port to keep them on this bearing until in mid-channel between the point and the line of breakers on the reef that extends south from Lynyard Cay. Then alter course to north, running parallel to the land for about 400 yards, in order to clear the reef that extends for about 300 yards north from Little Harbour Point. You will then be in 18–24 feet. As you alter course, rounding the reef, to the port a cove behind the lighthouse will open up. This will be easily recognized by the white sand beach and a group of coconut palms in the eastern corner. This is not a good anchorage.

See what I mean? Clear as mud? If you don't see what I mean, if you see instead what the *Yachtsman's Guide to the Bahamas* shows, if you see it with utmost clarity so that you could put a hand on *Blackwing's* wheel and guide her over the reef, then you're of Priscilla's tribe. We made it. The storm was passing, Priscilla grinning.

"Look," she said. "Look there!"

I looked, terrified what I might see. It was a pretty beach, our anchorage, a very good anchorage, pink sand beach. And over it, arched from way out at sea—near the ungodly depths called The Tongue of the Ocean, to the spot off Lynyard Cay where we dropped anchor—a rainbow.

I thought of it as her rainbow, and do. When I met Priscilla in 1963, she was temperamentally unlike anyone I'd known; I fell in love with her for the inexpressible reasons people fall in love but also for a character I can try to articulate, her unimpeded clarity of vision and expression. Of course Priscilla had understood the *Yachtsman's Guide*, and of course she had translated its dense instructions into a rational course of action, and of course she had seen how this coconut palm related to that coral head. If I couldn't have counted on Priscilla to continue to see and say unambiguously, we wouldn't have come to this place in this way. Imagine someone who sees things and systems whole, and who articulates precisely what she sees. Such a person can neither be fooled nor fool, and to live with her is to live with the recurring surprise of hearing a sane consciousness expressed with insanely serene candor. It is frightening to be wholly understood; it is bracing; it is fun; it keeps me off reefs. Because Priscilla's relentless good sense has no interest in prudence, only in knowing the odds so the odds may be disregarded; because her comprehension is a renewable resource driven by curiosity; because to see the world through her eyes is to see a misbegotten human comedy rather than a blighted human tragedy; because she said something crossing Little Harbour Bar that made me laugh; because I associate her with light, with warmth and buoyancy and illumination—that was her rainbow, and is.

It is worth feeling wet and cold to feel dry and warm. It is worth being scared to be secure. It is worth leaving sight of land to make a landfall. More than a few times, *Blackwing* had been an instrument of instruction in these lessons, but to be safe aboard her, with Priscilla, in the lee of those very reefs that caused such dread, was to feel the kind of gratitude that it is irrational to feel for inanimate objects. Perhaps this was why Priscilla—bringing a tray of rum drinks and cheese to the cockpit—found me below in the engine compartment, tightening the steering cable. It had been well secured and abundantly greased by Nicholas, but it had stretched, as new cable will, under the strain put on it today.

"Come on out of there," Priscilla said. "The sun's setting."

"I know," I said. "I need the last of the light to adjust her steering."

I saw Priscilla make that ancient sign of schoolyard and marriage, eyes rolled upward while forefinger circles ear clockwise.

"What's the matter with you?" she said. "What's wrong with tomorrow?"

The question was sensible, as far as it went. It failed merely to accommodate how I'd feel tonight leaving undone what ought to be done to thank our boat for bringing us safely to this place, whose rainbowed and sundowned glow I was missing to thank our boat for bringing us to this place. Well, it confused me, too.

We'd seen through our open hatch stars clear and sharp in the flawless atmosphere—Arcturus, Spica, Regulus, the Southern Cross—and the next morning came in clean and bracing. I had fallen asleep in my clothes, and by now was too funky even for me. Bathing on *Blackwing* was a trial: one squatted in the slippery gloom of our tiny head compartment, dribbling cold (and precious) fresh water from a comically forceless telephone shower. Conventional New England wisdom had it that soap and shampoo wouldn't clean in salt water. Nicholas had commended a Lemon Joy salt-water bath and shampoo (dip bucket in ocean, stand in cockpit, invert bucket over hair and torso), a plunge in the soft warm sea for a rinse. It worked; I was his student again.

Studying the charts, planning our next complicated passage, I noticed over the tops of my sunglasses an inflatable dinghy, pushed by an outboard, grinding toward us. The irritating noise (irritating when someone else was making it but not when I was making it) reminded me how quiet the world was here in these Out Islands. We were anchored off a pretty beach; when we were anchored, it was always off a pretty beach, so I'll describe the generic pretty beach now, and next time when I write "beach," you'll read, "talcy sand fifty yards off our bow, a deserted island, palm trees, great seas crashing against the barrier reef of pink and purple coral" . . . Not a boat or person in sight, except this one, nearing from Little Harbour. It was churlish to resent company; call me churlish.

Here he came: "Ahoy, *Blackwing*! Where's the cap?"

"I'm the captain. And owner."

"Oh." The fellow bobbing alongside, a little more or less my age, was disappointed. "Where's Nick?"

This question would be repeated all the way home: *Where's Nick?* To meet returning north the people he had met migrating south was an odd sensation. He'd made many friends, and these were not the friends I predicted he'd meet. The Inland Waterway is sometimes called the Blue Flag Expressway, for the blue flags flown from boats whose owners are not aboard. I had predicted that Nicholas and his friends would meet the paid hands of boats much bigger than *Blackwing*, crews of young men and women not much older than Nicholas. In fact, the boys of *Blackwing* preferred the company of people like us, oldsters looking for an adventure, middle-class couples (with an occasional remittance man or woman thrown in to raise the tone of the venture) who had cashed in their chips, sold the pencil factory or software patent or house in Shaker Heights, to quit the world and wander.

It was an oddity of many of these people that they brought with them vestigial Polonius- or headmaster-inspired wisdoms, so that many felt compelled, especially after a dinner served on their boat, to clear their throats over a glass of brandy and ask Nicholas and his friends when they were going to settle down, get with the program, start on their careers. They evidently detected no irony here. They may have been provoked to counsel by Nicholas's vague version of his recent history and his plans. He was less than forthcoming with newly met friends about the title to *Blackwing*; when asked who owned her, he knew he couldn't say he did, or he'd be mistaken for a drug dealer or—worse!—a rich kid. He also wouldn't for sure confess the plain fact, "My daddy let me have the keys." So he'd take on a cryptic mien, shrug, look at the night sky, say, "Some guy in Jamestown asked us to bring her south."

We met dozens, scores, of people along our way who told of kindnesses done them by our son and his friends (without telling us of the kindnesses they returned). We heard stories of Nicholas's ingenuity with tools, his eagerness to lend a hand, his seamanship, his curiosity, his friendliness. We heard about get-togethers, and especially a huge Valentine's Night potluck blowout in the Exumas for hundreds of live-aboards who'd convened at Staniel Cay, just up the beach from the Happy People Marina. These happy people had shared their food and experience and stories with Nicholas and his friends, and what other situation could have given our son a window—through which he wished to look—into the cluttered interior of American middle age? If the sailors hailing *Blackwing* displayed undisguised dismay to find us rather than our son, we could endure paling by comparison. If envy is the wasting sickness of the middle class, nature offered a remedy in children, teaching how good it can feel to wish for another better luck than one's own luck.

· · ·

The fellow in the dinghy, a long way from his home in Tulsa, declined our invitation to come aboard. He said to tell Nick he'd really done it this time.

"This one's worse than Wax Cay Cut; he'll know what I'm talking about. We screwed the pooch this time."

What happened: the sailor and his wife had bounced across the bar of Little Harbour lagoon at high tide of a full moon. Now they'd have to wait for the next full moon to bounce back out. We drew five feet, and it was too close a shave for us to try Little Harbour lagoon, so pretty it constitutes an attractive nuisance. Nicholas's friend's boat drew more than six feet, and he'd been using its keel to dig trenches in the sand during every daylight high tide of the waning and waxing moon. He left us to try again. We saw him later, motionless in the water, his mast at that telltale ten-degree angle we would soon have reason to recognize up close and personal.

The Siren who entices sailors across reefs has no seductive power over me. I plot a course for deep water, steer clear. Solo voyagers and racers court extremes; some cruisers enjoy the chest-cramping test of a shoal bar at high tide, or shave this side of a buoy meant to be taken on that side. The dare might save fifteen minutes, which isn't the point; the point is the frisson when the keel taps. For me the point is serenity, a limit to surprise. I shun ambush. *Have a nice day?* You bet, a nice day's just the day for me.

I trust nothing and nobody, including myself. I know a bit about myself, including what I don't know, so I ration trust miserly. I have my compass swung, update charts, tighten what's loose, reef too soon. A thirty-percent chance of thunderstorms is one hundred percent to this meteorologist. The only surprise I welcome at sea is a wind shift in my favor. *Uneventful* is my favorite notation in the log. I do not sail boats to pump adrenaline or to grow an ulcer. My desideratum at sea is elementary: to cause no harm. To cause no harm is no passive ambition. It requires an imagination for disaster; it demands that the master of a vessel not put his vessel (or his family, say) in harm's way, needlessly, improvidently. I expect to be surprised at sea—I am not a fool (I think)—but I want surprise to come of natural law rather than my carelessness. Wanting to do no harm, I discovered I had translated myself from the quondam Hotspur Priscilla had married into a very clerk of a sailor, fussy, a look-before-you-leaper. This fever of caution had alarmingly spread inland to other enterprises: I now balanced my checkbook, "maintained" my shoes, did a fall lay-up on my body, would have put a spring coat of varnish on the lawn mower if I could get the Z-Spar to adhere to grease. Sometimes I came to believe I was no yachtsman; I was a grunt laborer. I sailed a mop. Was this Commodore Wolff? White-flanneled skipper of a sailing yacht? On my knees in the head, scrubbing piss and puke from the moving parts of a plastic toilet? I had become a prig. I took cleaning and fiddling over the top. I became a master of the domestic arts: scrubbing, scouring, sanding, painting, varnishing, greasing, adjusting, worrying. If my car failed, I'd stick out my thumb. Boat: I'd inflate the raft, shoot off a flare. So I learned to test this and check that, looking for the bite-sized surprise now, at anchor, so there would be no great ugly surprise later, out there.

It seemed a possible dream, to comprehend the universe of a 30-foot boat, my 30-foot boat, possible even to control Blackwing's destiny, in a modest way. A 30-foot boat is not after all a five-ton timepiece. It could be got into, wrestled with, maintained, fixed. If, hanging upside down in the engine room to adjust something, I heard a little noise, the terrible plop of my Ray-Bans falling into the greasy and carnivorous bilge, I had a handy-dandy magnet with which to fish them out, at the expense of only a few hours. Of course the magnet raised hell with the compass, which then needed reswinging.

To keep *Blackwing* fit, I'd merely pretend I was Sisyphus and put my shoulder to the rock, or let Nicholas take *Blackwing* on a long voyage so he could put his shoulder to it.

Sailing the southern Abacos was a strained pleasure, more pleasure than strain, but a trial of attention. To sail is to attend: in New England the eye squints to pick out a buoy or the loom of a light. Here, as there, we watched the sea's surface for the telltale ripples of a shifting wind, and studied the sky for its lessons and warnings. But now we looked down as well as up; it is said of the Bahamas' shoals that the most valuable skill a navigator can bring to their successful circumvention is an aptitude to "read" the water. By this is meant an ability to distinguish between the dark blue of deeps, the turquoise and aquamarine of adequate depth, the green of a grassy bottom often safely deep, the milky pale yellow of sandy shoals, the white of a sandbar dry at low tide, the dark patch that looks like coral but is only a shadow cast by a cloud, the brown of coral that can tear a hole in a boat's bottom (not to be confused with the harmless brown of "fish muds," caused by bottom-feeders eating dinner, stirring up the marl). Nicholas, who is color-blind, nevertheless learned to read the water from *Blackwing*'s bowsprit or, in especially perilous waters, from up her mast. (The downside of that upside, he told us, was a clear view of sharks working the bottoms.)

Learning to read thin water is an incremental adequacy; the apt scholar of shoals depends not only on memory and common sense, but on sunlight from above and behind. Sailing into the sun, it is impossible to distinguish between the consequential shades along the sea's spectrum. So we had to plan our passages, which demanded snaky course changes through erratic channels, according to the sun's declination, which often warred with felicitous tides. (The tidal range in the Abacos was as great as four feet.)

If we came to distinguish between water that would float us and water that would not, I never accustomed myself to sailing fast, hour after hour, with three feet and less beneath our keel. Is it reliable that what we don't know won't hurt us, that ignorance is bliss? Or is it incontestable that seeing is believing? I don't know why we found it less settling to see the bottom beneath our keel than to sail by faith in charts, as we do in New England's murky brine; to see the bottom near Rhode Island is to be on the bottom. In the Bahamas, sailing at a hull speed of six knots, the unnatural clarity of the water gave us the willies, an illusion of boiling forward into decreasing depths, as though the bottom were rushing up at us. We trained ourselves to disregard our terror, to pretend to know better, to smile as we sailed into what seemed to be five feet, four, two. But I'd reach the end of an Abacos passage, strike the sails, line up a casuarina with a church steeple, triangulate that line with a line bearing 287° to the butt of a dirt road, dodge a sandbar, home in on a water tower (looking sharp for the submerged pilings of a wrecked pier), drop the anchor and uncramp my white-knuckled hand from the wheel and a dumb unfelt grin from my face.

What we have here is a point-of-view problem. Up close, through my eyes, the seascape looked one way. Passages were treacherous, and their timing required exacting precision. Our clock was still on northern time; I had crossed from Royal Island as though I were running to catch the 7:06 from Pleasantville. So what if the worst had happened, if we'd been holed up for a week or two in one Eden in place of another? Or the other worst: we had had to spend a night at sea, floating two and a half miles above the bottom of Northeast Providence Channel? After all, I wasn't a single-handed Joshua Slocum dodging growlers, icebergs and pirates in the Roaring Forties. I wasn't commanding a convoy escort on the Murmansk run. Seen from above, we must have made an enviable picture, sailing like gangbusters through pristine water under a warming sun. This was the Bahamas, as in the Sunday newspaper supplement ads. And if my keel hit sand? *Blackwing* would float off on a rising tide. And if she didn't? We'd wade ashore and phone Allstate.

As these verities sank in, we settled into what became (for a time) a tranquil routine. The sun would wake us; we'd drink coffee and orange juice; we'd laze in the cockpit waiting for the tide to do the right thing. We'd make a shopping list: this required much consideration. Not since we'd lived in Brittany twenty years before had we invested such prodigal gobs of time in the contemplation of what exactly we'd put in our mouths during the coming twenty-four hours. It wasn't as though a Brittany-like horn of plenty awaited us ashore: we were deliberating what we'd have with the tuna salad, whether taters or rice would go best with fried chicken. (It's an oddity of life aboard a small boat with a two-burner camp stove that it requires discipline to exorcise the temptation to prepare a meal of four or five courses, nuts to soup, fish to cookies. Priscilla and I were old enough to know better: we'd learned to eat lean.) Our lists made, we'd take the dinghy ashore to search for ice and bread and beer and fruit and cheese; we'd find what we came for. We'd take the dinghy back to *Blackwing* and laze in the cockpit; we'd observe that it sure was a nice day; we'd think aloud that it was almost warm enough to swim; we'd say we were thinking about taking a swim; we'd swim; we'd sit in the cockpit letting the warm air dry us; we'd notice it was coming on toward the lunch hour; we'd discuss lunch; we'd make lunch; we'd eat lunch; we'd say we were considering a little nap; we'd take a little nap; we'd pull up anchor and sail a few hours to the next pretty beach (see above); we'd drop anchor; we'd make rum drinks; we'd take the dinghy ashore for a dinner of fried or sautéed or grilled grouper or flounder; we'd bring the dinghy back to *Blackwing*; we'd put a tape in the deck, maybe Dave McKenna, maybe Thelonious Monk; we'd sit in the cockpit, looking at the night sky; we'd go below to our berth; we'd lie on our backs talking, looking at the night sky. We'd sleep.

If one island in the Abacos looked like another, the islands were culturally distinct: a vacation paradise, where it's safe to let Muffy and Biff roam with pail and shovel, can be one island over from a drug terminus upon which it would be worth your skin to stumble. Along the west coast of Great Abaco (whose east coast is as tame as a tourist) is the Bight of Abaco, whose mainland and island settlements, menacingly called The Marls, are so hazardous to outsiders that charts of the area carry notices that passages through the wilderness islands are "specifically N O T recommended." (Emphasis N O T added.) We met a sailor who had stumbled into the Bight of Abaco in search of solitude, who found greater solitude than he sought, and less. He was set upon by a clan of natives with whom he left his wristwatch, dinghy, outboard, transistor radio and blue jeans; these people titled themselves "the meanest people in the world" and shared a single Scottish surname, a name I'll refrain from printing not from vigilance against litigation but from dread that they'll bring their outboard-powered skiffs over the ocean to Little Rhody and find me tucked under a down comforter and murder me in my sleep.

These McKillers dwelt ten miles away as the buzzard flies, but at the antipodes from our destination, sweet Green Turtle Cay. We darted outside the protection of reefs to make our way north to Green Turtle Cay from Don't Rock Passage to Whale Cay Passage. Unsettled weather could have made this moment a trial: the unholy phenomenon of onshore winds piling huge seas onto shoal bars from the off-soundings ocean deeps (almost three *miles* deep!) is called a "rage." But today was fine, the wind light, and Priscilla read aloud to me from the *Yachtsman's Guide*: "Caution: Never pass close to the west of Whale Cay, where there are dangerous swells even in settled weather. Never underestimate this passage, as several boats and lives have been lost here in recent years." Talk about your wet blankets.

We gave the west of Whale Cay what I'd call a *wide* berth, and snuck into Green Turtle Cay's White Sound on a rising tide, and anchored. Now this was a pretty island. I'd describe it as having a pinkish-white sand beach beyond which casuarinas grew, and palm trees. But wait, Green Turtle Cay was different from the rest. Along its west coast were bluffs; these soared from the sea to a great height. We got the dinghy ashore; to achieve that summit was worth the risk of nosebleed, and so—without guides or bearers—we climbed past oleanders and hibiscus to the Bluff House and finally, on the roof of our immediate world, at eighty feet, we stood, Goombay Smash in hand, looking down our snoots at reefs and bars and sand bores and the sun, sinking. After trading a grand view for a bad dinner, we surveyed the memorabilia framed on the inn's walls, and the first to catch our eyes was a recent article from *Cruising World* retailing the loss of a sailboat out in Whale Cay Passage, within sight of where we stood:

> The breaker arrived completely unexpectedly. On this beautiful sunny November day in the Bahamas, with winds not more than 15 knots from the north, I could not have imagined that a huge wave could break right on top of us, throwing me against the steering wheel . . . bending the wheel, breaking my right upper arm in four places, and leaving me with a cracked rib, a black left eye and both hands severely bruised. . . . We learned later that a 30-footer had been lost the day before our misadventure.

In retrospect, I blame our coming misadventure on that cautionary narrative. Descending from the heights after taking aboard a quantity of rum and table wine, climbing with exemplary grace into the dinghy, I said offhandedly, "Let's have a drink over at the Green Turtle Club."

"We had a drink at the Bluff House."

"Well, I was thinking we ought to have a drink at the Green Turtle Club."

"Well, we had a drink at the Bluff House."

"I was thinking of prolonging the pleasure with a digestif."

"Oh boy," said Priscilla. "I was thinking of hitting the hay."

"We'll have our whole lives to sleep when we're dead. Come with me, we'll have a fine time."

Priscilla said, "*We'll have a fine time?* You sound like the jerk in 'Hills Like White Elephants.' " Priscilla teaches literature; she knows her modern American short story backward and forward.

"I think I need a drink to relax me."

"From what?"

"You've got a short memory," I said. "I just brought us through Whale Cay Passage."

"But it was as calm as a bathtub."

"So it seemed," I said. "To you," I said.

By Priscilla's silence I knew that she had come—most reasonably—to see the wisdom of my proposition. To motor us across the harbor to the Green Turtle Club, I got the Seagull outboard started (with ignobling difficulty), and we were necessarily silent in the din of its single piston banging like the hammers of Hell against its single cylinder. I began to brood: I had *never* liked the goddamned outboard; it had *always* been false, treacherous . . . selfish! I wasn't going to take it anymore. I would . . . *replace* it. My revenge fantasy was cut short by our arrival at the Green Turtle Club's docks, lit by twinkling oil lamps. Here was the place!

Priscilla had her back to me, where it had been since we agreed to have a fine time at the Green Turtle Club. She was climbing out of the little rubber boat. She was—oh-oh. This was an old story, and none sadder. She was pushing out rather than up with her legs. Her hands were fixed on the dock, her feet to the bow of the little rubber boat, which was moving away from the dock. When the little rubber boat was about as far from the dock as Priscilla is tall, Priscilla was very wet. I helped her back into the dinghy, ferried her back to *Blackwing*, helped her aboard, and left her. I had not spoken. I had a hunch Priscilla did not prefer that I speak ("Would you please please please please please please please stop talking?" says the woman in "Hills Like White Elephants." Ray Carver called his turn on *please* "Will You Please Be Quiet, Please?"). I was bound for the Green Turtle Club. It was what Priscilla would have wanted, if she'd thought about it.

In the open-air bar of the Green Turtle Club I found myself alone with a party of two badly sunburned men my age with two women less than half my age. I sat two tables away, positioned so I could see but pretend not to look. The men were drunk, I noted with disapproval as I took a long pull on my Beck's. I was in a tetchy humor. Any drinker or ex-drinker will recognize the symptoms: an exaggerated sense of what's now called "entitlement"—I Deserve a Better Time Than I'm Having sort of thing.

I eavesdropped. The young lady facing me was theatrically beautiful. Literally: she made references to her work on stage and screen. She was British. The men, and a woman hidden in shadows, were asking the starlet her analysis of contemporary films. The starlet's critical judgment was ever the same: "Boring." *Rain Man* was "boring" and *Robocop* was "boring" and *Predator* was "boring." The starlet would brush back her gorgeous black hair, as though she were hot. (She was hot, I'll admit, but the temperature hung in the 60s, and there was a whispery breeze.) By brushing back her hair she could arch her pale throat, and show off her arms and shoulders, and pucker her lips and blow strands of hair away from her mouth and eyes. She couldn't have been prettier.

"Oh, I walked *out*; it was so boring."

A gent asked her verdict on *My Left Foot*.

"Yuch! Talk about boring! Who wants to have your date buy you tickets to watch sick people gross you out?"

This made the party laugh. I recollected those snapshots of our erstwhile Presidential candidate and his friends on Bimini, dancing the limbo, wearing parrot shirts and those awful sunburns. What reminded me, *Monkey Business* had passed us a few days before, heading north. I wouldn't mention it, except the captain didn't slow down, and his wake near swamped us. On the stern, *Monkey Business* had been painted over, but you could make out the old name underneath—what Lillian Hellman calls "pentimento," a rethinking, a repentance of a still visible first instinct. Anyway, the tender still wore its name on its backside; *Monkey Shines*, I think it was.

"*My Life as a Dog* is extremely boring."

In the old days I would have ordered another Beck's; I would have dug in, leering, glowering, leering, glowering. Thanks for small favors, the old days aren't the new days.

When I came aboard, Priscilla said, "We're a couple of bozos."

So it would be okay.

And next morning it was okay; it was okay right up till we dinghied to the dock of the Green Turtle Club where we thought we'd eat breakfast. Priscilla's hands were fixed on the dock, her feet to the bow of the little rubber boat, which was moving away from the dock . . . There's nothing easier to break than a good mood or harder than a bad habit.

It was time to get out of the Abacos and across the Gulf Stream to Florida. North of Green Turtle Cay, casual yacht traffic thins almost to vanishing, except for live-aboards transiting from north of Palm Beach into the Bahamas in the late fall and

early winter, and back home in the spring. The northern Abacos are mostly uninhabited, with a desolate end-of-the-world
atmosphere, especially on a cloudy day during a blustery
northwest passage of twenty-five miles, driven by a northeast
wind of twenty knots to Allans-Pensacola. This was an abandoned Air Force missile-tracking station, populated by moray
eels in its reefs and barracuda in the mangrove flats. Oh, and
sharks. Did I forget to mention sand fleas? Sand fleas weren't
a worry when the wind gusted to thirty knots, but anchoring
was.

I use a heavy anchor called a plow, made in England by
CQR (*secure*: get it?). I swear by it; I swear by anything weighing twenty-five pounds that can arrest the drift of another
something weighing ten thousand pounds when another
something is being hammered by a north wind. The holding
power of an anchor is a function of physical properties that
can be mathematically calculated, once that anchor is set. To
set an anchor is an art I believed I had mastered. Priscilla
would bring *Blackwing* into the wind under power, and slow
her till she was dead in the water, and I would nonchalantly,
imperturbably lower the anchor to the bottom (no undignified
heaving, no tangling myself in chain); I would then aloofly pay
out anchor rode while *Blackwing* drifted astern. When five
times the water depth had been unflappably payed out in rode
(I had marked it in twenty-foot increments), I would snub the
rode to a cleat, and observe diffidently how, as usual, the anchor had CQRly bit into the bottom. I would then nod to
Priscilla an almost imperceptible nod (no wild oaths, please,
no despotic commands) to shut the engine down and start
chipping ice for the rum drinks. I would sit quietly in the bow,
triangulating lines of sight on various objects ashore—casuarinas, say, or maybe palm trees. Meantime I would casually
pay out more rode as *Blackwing* drifted astern, till I had
achieved the desired ratio of 7:1, rode to depth.

Except at Allans-Pensacola. We were dressed in oilskins,

weary, lonely, wet and cold from the front's spill of rain. It was late in the day, and the sun was too low to light the reefs that ringed both shores of the harbor, the only harbor within reach, a harbor said to be marginal ("a hard chance," in the idiom of cruising guides) in a northerly. Two boats were anchored close to each other, farther up the harbor, where we would like to have been. Priscilla brought *Blackwing* into the nor'east wind; I lowered the anchor; *Blackwing* drifted fast astern; the anchor bounced uselessly along the hardpan sand bottom. I could see it bouncing. It made me angry to see this, and to haul in rode and chain and twenty-five-pound plow also made me angry, and made me reflect on how lucky Priscilla was to have in her hands a varnished teak steering wheel instead of a muddy length of chain. This process was repeated for the next hour or so: the helmsperson, following the anchorperson's despotic commands, maneuvered *Blackwing* into the wind; the anchorperson lowered the anchor, which skipped along the hardpan bottom, provoking from the anchorperson wild oaths.

This routine did not proceed in solitude, unobserved. To watch a couple anchor a boat is one of the sea's great entertainments, way more satisfying than a world-class sunset or moonbeams filtered through casuarinas. It is proof of one's superiority to observe—from the CQRity of one's own steady state, with one's own vessel tugging fruitlessly at what holds it, with a beverage cooling one's hand and perhaps a dish of beernuts nearby on one's cockpit table—a couple less evolved hurling oath, command and anchor. The world at such a moment is starkly binary, split between the anchored and the would-be anchored. Up at the head of the harbor, one of the two anchored was pretending not very successfully to be not watching us. He was smoking a pipe! This pipe-smoking shook me to my rubber Wellingtons. It was not right. And then, as though that were not enough, the pipe-smoker turned toward *Blackwing*, languidly, and motioned *my* helmsperson, to whom *I* gave despotic orders, to approach. And then, as though that weren't enough, she did his bidding.

"Holding's bad down there," said the skipper of *Enshallah*, a heathen corruption of *que será, será.* "Anchor here, between us."

Priscilla commanded me, tyrannically, to lower the anchor, and I did, and it held. There was marginally room enough for our three boats to swing, if they swung together, without hitting. The skipper of *Enshallah* had violated a first principle of the Law of First Anchored: he had welcomed us to his sanctuary. This generosity was a breach of all anchoring protocols. I didn't know what to say, so I sulked. Priscilla said, "Thank you."

The skipper pulled on his pipe, which he smoked upside down. "I'd dive on that anchor," he said. "To make sure it's set."

To examine an anchor in the Bahamas was always advised, because in the clear shoals it was an easy chore, sometimes even fun. (No one dives into Block Island's New Harbor to counterfeit study of his anchor dug into mud and beer cans and shit.) I eyed the mangroves seventy yards from my bow, and mused on the barracuda feeding there, in competition with sharks. I wondered whether the little food fish that lived among mangroves ever toured seventy yards to sightsee a plow anchor, and whether the bigger diners followed them on such a safari.

"You think it's a good idea to dive on that anchor?" I said.

"Well, I do think it's a good idea," said the master of *Enshallah.*

"I think it's a good idea," Priscilla said.

"You want to dive on that anchor?" I asked Priscilla.

Priscilla looked at me; she cocked her head; she shook her head slowly. I had a hunch she was thinking about where she was spending her sabbatical and with whom.

"What I think I'm going to do," I said to Priscilla and to

her pipe-smoking friend on *Enshallah*, "I think I'm going to slip down there in the water and have a look at that anchor."

The water was warmer than the air, and the wind was blissfully uninteresting below the troubled surface. I stayed down, looking sharp for predators, glancing behind toward the reefs and eels. A dozen feet down, the anchor rested on, rather than in, the bottom; its flukes were tangled in a furze of eelgrass, and each time the wind blew *Blackwing* astern, the rode went taut, and the flukes strained at the grass, and held. I dived, and labored to dig the flukes in the bottom, and it was like trying to dig them into the surface of a parking lot. So I tangled them thoroughly in the grass, and broke the surface gasping, and told Priscilla and her best friend that I wasn't all that impressed by what I'd seen. I didn't want to lean too hard on this, because night was coming on, and I couldn't imagine anything I less desired than to raise anchor, go elsewhere and try again. This was weak of me, and imprudent, and in violation of all maritime usage and decorum, but I was of a mind to say *what the hell*, to say, as it were, *enshallah*.

Our neighbor pulled at his pipe and remarked that he had been in this very spot four days, diving among fish, and he sure hadn't dragged. "I'm dug in so deep I'll have to blast my way out."

I would have responded with appropriate awe, but his other neighbor, his friend, had just arrived at *Enshallah* for cocktails, having rowed a little dink into what was now a thirty-knot gale.

That night, all night, while the wind gave *Blackwing* a battering, shaking her mast, rattling her rigging, bringing her to the end of her anchor rode with a jarring shudder, I stood anchor watch. I didn't have fun. I wished I'd never examined the anchor on the bottom; faith thrives on blindness. I had lit an anchor light, in deference to doctrine, so we wouldn't be run down by anyone coming on Allans-Pensacola by night, which of course nobody would. Our nearby neighbors also showed anchor lights, and a few hours after midnight I saw *Enshallah* move to leeward, farther and farther astern. I watched, and wondered what to do. The pipe-smoking, among-man-eating-fish-diving, anchor-dug-in skipper surely knew what he was doing; he was no doubt paying out more anchor rode. He was not; he was dragging down on the reef, and as soon as I realized this, his neighbor began to shout and to blow a foghorn at his friend. The skipper of *Enshallah* was standing at his bow. No, that was the skipper's wife; the skipper was rowing his anchor and chain back upwind. It was an extraordinary feat, and he got it done, and got his anchor down in time, and did not lose his boat on the reef. No thanks to me. I made a mental note: next time you see an anchor light move, holler, the way Nicholas would. I made another mental note: no man is an island. And another: be nice.

The next afternoon, at three-thirty, within easy sight and less than a mile from our next anchorage at Great Sale Cay, two hours past low tide, we ran hard aground. Our loran had guided us flawlessly through the reefs and sand bores of the Little Bahama Bank. We were tired, as usual, and relieved to see a dozen masts at the anchorage just across a sandspit to port. We felt smug, probably, but we weren't so stupid that we didn't follow the guidebook's instructions to stay well off-shore of a sunken blue sedan (search me!), and to sail a couple of miles southwest of the entrance to the harbor before we turned northeast. This was to avoid a sandbar. The day was overcast, and I couldn't see the bar; I guessed I had sailed two miles; I had instead sailed *almost* two miles; the depth meter read eight feet, six, five, four; we hit.

This was not good: we were in open ocean, exposed to a high wind, bang up on what was said to be sand but felt like asphalt. I tried everything I knew: I lowered sails, of course, and attached our anchor to a halyard that ran through the masthead, and took the anchor to seaward in our dinghy. I brought the dinghy back, and cranked on the halyard run through a sheet winch. By this stratagem I hoped to heel *Blackwing* sufficiently to float her off. Might have, too, if the anchor wasn't skipping uselessly along the bottom. No dice. I sat in the cockpit and wondered if it would feel good to weep.

Meanwhile, Priscilla worked the radio, talking to sailors a couple of miles—alas, not quite a couple—distant in Great Sale's Northwest Harbour. Conversations on VHF radio are not private conversations; in fact, they give pleasure to strangers in just the way that listening in on a party line to parties discussing divorce or bankruptcy might give pleasure, and for the same *Schadenfreude*sque reason, with the added stimulus of legitimacy: maritime code rules that one is obliged to monitor, eavesdrop on, a sailor's broadcast misfortune. Priscilla's audience counseled patience; the tide was rising. Priscilla got advice from *Enshallah* and from others: *Soleil*: we recall you! *Leisure Gal*: what's ours is yours! Time crept; the wind built; the seas slapped; the sun fell. With an hour of rising tide left, Priscilla and I decided to ask *Leisure Gal* to relay a call from her powerful radio to B A S R A, Bahamas Air-Sea Rescue Association, to ask for a tow off the bar. This was complicated, because the nearest towboat was at Walker's Cay, fifty miles away. The colloquy was between Priscilla and her relay, her relay and B A S R A, B A S R A and a towboat with a piquant name. The discourse went like this.

"*Leisure Gal, Leisure Gal!* This is *Blackwing, Leisure Gal.* Get us *Love Bone.*"

"B A S R A, B A S R A! This is *Leisure Gal. Blackwing* wants *Love Bone.*"

Love Bone wanted five hundred dollars cash, "win or lose." We pondered this arrangement. *Blackwing* was beginning to pound against the bottom, and in my exhaustion I misread the meaning of that evil banging. I told B A S R A to bring on *Love*

Bone, and no sooner had this been arranged, night now, than I sensed I could power *Blackwing* off the bar, with a few lucky bounces. And I did, and *Leisure Gal* instructed B A S R A to take its payday another day from another sailor. And so we crept sheepishly and most cautiously up Northwest Harbour, lit by searchlights and mast spreader lights and foghorns and good cheer on the radio. The crew of *Soleil* sent over a casserole, and after dinner Priscilla said gently, "I think we better have a chat."

I guessed what chat was coming. Seven years before, we'd had a chat aboard *Blackwing* at the west end of the Cape Cod Canal the night before we were to go east through the canal, and thence a hundred and forty miles down east to Maine, a beeline to Monhegan, in the Gulf of Maine as much as eighty miles offshore. That chat was about navigational skills and our young crew—Nicholas was thirteen, Justin ten. Priscilla took one position on that adventure, I took another, I prevailed, we went. I sailed us beyond the Dry Salvages, beyond a pod of cavorting sunlit humpback whales and into the pure terror of a fog thick as buttermilk. What I recollect better than our dread lost in the Portland shipping lanes waiting for some tanker to crawl into our cockpit—and lost off Monhegan, and lost on the Green Ledges, and lost somewhere west of Portugal—was my shame, the awareness as sudden as stroke that none of it was necessary.

Now, before Priscilla had begun to make her gentle case, as soon as she began to wrap my pride (such as it was) in gauze, I cut her off: "I'll do whatever you think best. We don't have to do this. None of this is necessary."

Saying so, I knew that it was not, at a fundamental level, true. *Some* of this was necessary: it was necessary to get from this uninhabited cay to the next place. But the thrust of Priscilla's profound (as in *deep*, as in five feet of water below a

boat that draws four feet eleven) reservations about our situation was irresistible. This was supposed to be fun. Our imagination for discomfort and disaster, a prophetic inclination
toward doom and gloom that had turned us into stay-at-
homes, was supposed to be asleep now. Now our senses were
meant to be awake, and gleaning good vibes. We were to have
been sun-warmed and sea-bathed and easygoing. *Who needed
this?* It was a question any sailor will recognize. It is a question
impossible not to ask when the wind hauls around the wrong
way, when that same wind goes past the limit of "bracing"
into the Force 7 territory of "gale." When seas begin to break.
When a line squall appears on the horizon. Maybe, depending
on a sailor's limit, when the sun goes behind a cloud. When
a sailor grips the lee rail and pukes into the scuppers. When
the main halyard jams in a masthead sheave. When a sailor
is lost in fog somewhere near the toothy coast of Maine. When
a sailor spends an afternoon aground on a sandbar.

Priscilla said, "I think we should get Nick down here."

I didn't have to say how it would be for me to make that
phone call. And how would that phone call be made? It would
be broadcast by radio, patched into Freeport by *Leisure Gal,
Soleil, Enshallah*, whomever. The relay would tell an operator
to tell my son that he'd have to leave the job he had just started
in order to fly to Florida, and from there to Grand Bahama
Island, in order to help us bring *Blackwing* across sixty miles
of Gulf Stream, because we were scared, in water way over
our heads (figuratively speaking, of course), not sufficient to
the tame adventure we had set ourselves.

I said, "Whatever you think." And I meant it.

Knowing I meant it, Priscilla said, "Let's sleep on it." I knew,
and she knew I knew, that because I had meant "whatever
you think," what she now thought was *I think we shouldn't
get Nick down here.*

. . .

The next morning, warm and dry and sunny, we rested. Great Sale Cay abounded with sand sharks along the edge of its mangrove banks; here were rays and snapper and bonefish and barracuda. And here, seeing the benign world lit by benign sunbeams, doubt bleached invisible by the sun, I spent a couple of hours in the fishy world, cleaning *Blackwing*'s bottom; it was the last chance I'd have to see it in clear water before we crossed to Florida. Besides, it made me feel valiant.

After lunch we stowed deep in the bilge the library of paperbacks we had lugged to Eleuthera. We had now been aboard *Blackwing* almost two weeks and neither had read an opening sentence. Nor would we: keeping the boat afloat, plotting courses, casing hazards, shopping, cooking, cleaning, maintaining, staring at the bottom, squinting into the sun, napping, waking to check the anchor, studying cruising guides, studying charts, reckoning distance made good from Hatchet Bay and distance to go to Narragansett Bay, forecasting the weather, talking, remembering aloud, missing our boys, shutting up, listening to Pablo Casals or John Lee Hooker, laughing, fretting, beachcombing, sometimes sleeping—set against all this, reading cried uncle.

Our passage to West End across the Little Bahama Bank, in ten or twelve feet of water, had two jeopardies, one of which especially distressed me: reading about the jumping-off port for Florida in the *Yachtsman's Guide*, I had charted my way almost to our destination when I reached an italic passage regarding Indian Cay Rock: "*Important: Please see caution below regarding this channel before proceeding.*" Set off in a box, using boldface caps and italics, as typographically alarming as cautions get in the *Yachtsman's Guide*, was this ***"Caution Regarding Indian Cay Rock/Barracuda Shoal Channel:*** *At this writing all navigational aids for the Indian Cay Rock/Barracuda Shoal Channel are missing. We* *have no word as to when or by whom they might be replaced.*"

I mentioned a second jeopardy: mysterious tidal sets had been observed in the vicinity of Barracuda Shoal Channel. Yeah, yeah: I'd been warned before about tidal sets. Hadn't been bothered yet by a tidal set. *Blackwing* was tidal-set-proof.

We set out at first light on a perfect day, the last day before a front was due in from the west; we were headed west; if we didn't plunge now, we could be pinned down for a week by foul weather at desolate Great Sale Cay. We were out of ice and fresh food. We were low on water and, worse, Mount Gay. Now we had the sun at our back, where we wanted it. I hit my loran (an electronic navigation device) destination on the button north of Mangrove Cay; we were halfway to West End; in twenty-three miles, four hours, we'd be sitting pretty at Jack Tar Marina before the cocktail flag flew.

"Damned loran's on the blink."

Priscilla had heard me fret about the loran's waywardness many a time before; today she couldn't care less. We were navigating by what's called dead reckoning, observed landmarks (Mangrove Cay) checked against compass course and distance sailed. Two hours later the loran seemed to go crazy, telling me that I was far to the south of the rhumb line to Barracuda Shoal Channel. Occam's razor is a principle in rudimentary philosophy and science that holds that the simplest explanation of a phenomenon is the favored explanation. That is: if the loran has functioned with unerring accuracy, and it now warns that *Blackwing* is off course to the south, then the simplest explanation of this message, since the navigator wishes *Blackwing* to be right on course, is "Damned loran's on the blink."

Within view of West End, a couple of miles off course to the south of Barracuda Shoal Channel where I'd been set by the tide, in seven feet of water, surrounded by sandbanks drying out in the ebbing tide, I dropped anchor. We were afloat in a maze of sand bores, rocky shoals, coral heads.

We worked the radio, calling Jack Tar Marina, groveling for advice. We were advised to await high tide, and eyeball our way in, reading the water. I wondered aloud how that would work, since high tide would arrive a couple of hours after nightfall.

"Well, mon, you could get a pilot."

I had trouble understanding my interlocutor's Bahamian accent. I'm not being snotty here; they were his Bahamas long before they were mine, and how he chose to talk was his business. I mention my difficulty only to underscore the situation of a couple of folks with one boat between them, a single *Blackwing* to their name, floating in a little pool of water, their anchor dug into bone-dry sand. Such a couple longs to interpret, is avid to fathom, its choices.

"Please send us a pilot," I said.

I knew about pilots. In Julius M. Wilensky's *Cruising Guide to the Abacos and Northern Bahamas* (1980), a pilot is discussed in reference to a grounding at Fox Town on Little Abaco Island. This pilot had come with friends in an outboard to lead Wilensky and his crew to safe water. He had spent several hours at his work, and Wilensky notes that "he never mentioned how much he wanted. You should ask first, before you engage a pilot. The $5 we paid him might seem too much . . ." Well, not *that* much too much, considering the alternative. Making allowance for ten years' inflationary pressure, call it $10 or—let's shoot the moon—$25, I asked Jack Tar Marina how much a pilot would charge to guide us in. There was quite a long silence, and Jack Tar said we would have to negotiate directly. By hand-bearing compass I triangulated my position, got the pilot on the radio, gave my position, asked for help, and—almost an afterthought—asked how much he'd like from me. He said something that sounded like "fifty," and I laughed. I asked was that fifty *dollars* he wanted, to come a couple of miles to show me the way in? He said "two fifty," and I thought that inflation was slow to impact

West End if he wanted half what Wilensky had paid ten years ago. But you've guessed: that would have been "two fifty" as in two hundred and fifty dollars for half an hour's work. Not in a million years.

"Done," I said. "Come," I said. "Chop-chop," I said.

These negotiations were less simply sealed than reported. The more we talked to the pilot, the less we conveyed. He had asked our position, and he was meant to be approaching us even as his voice faded. He confessed, in a diminishing whisper of static, he couldn't find us. It seemed he couldn't understand my accent, and he was looking for us in another ocean, down the Atlantic coast toward the casinos and duty-free shops of Freeport. As an egalitarian enemy of hierarchy, I had trained myself to repudiate the commandment *know thy place*, unless the place I didn't know was near the coast of Maine, or on the Little Bahama Bank south of Barracuda Shoal Channel. My radio voice transmitted a high reedy panic until an intermediary with a familiar articulation and idiom contacted the pilot, and translated my urgencies into useful loran coordinates.

The pilot found us. He didn't lead us in. He towed us. He towed us with his brand-new twin 250-horsepower Mercury outboards mounted on the transom of a brand-new Boston Whaler Outrage fishing boat; he pulled us over sandbars, and through sandbars. He dragged us into the Jack Tar Marina basin, and didn't cast us off till I'd signed thirteen twenty-dollar traveler's checks. He didn't have ten dollars change on him (or a peg leg, or an eye patch or a parrot on his shoulder), but he did have a gold front tooth, and a great smile. Tied to slips in Jack Tar Marina, ringing us like pitlings around an arena stage, was an audience of sailors. It was the cocktail hour, and they were relaxed in their cockpits, listening to their ship-to-ship radios, regarding us. We recognized them: *Leisure Gal, Soleil, Enshallah*. Oh, and more, many more.

The skipper of *Enshallah*, lighting his pipe, said: "Now *that's* the way to travel. No wear and tear on the sails, no wear and tear on the engine, no wear and tear on the crew."

Jack Tar Marina, sixty or so miles from Lake Worth Inlet in Palm Beach, is a tight artificial harbor dug out to serve cruisers crossing the Gulf Stream. The hotel that owned it had gone under a week or two before we arrived; now high chain-link fences topped with razor wire bordered the marina; our only exit out of Jack Tar Marina was through a padlocked gate beside a security shed manned by guards bearing side-arms and shotguns. It seemed the hotel had abruptly shut its doors and laid off the huge staff that had been brought there and housed nearby in migrant camps. The staff, understandably desperate, had looted the larders. When security guards caught and punished them, the hotel was vandalized. The neighborhood was on edge. A couple of days earlier a huge chain had been laid in the water across the entrance to Jack Tar Marina; the chain had been removed this morning, but think of being towed into it by the pirate-pilot with 500 horse-power of Mercurys and a Boston Whaler Outrage.

At Jack Tar we waited out a front. Every afternoon we'd meet in shifting cliques at Baby Grant's, a little restaurant in the settlement strung along the westernmost end of Grand Bahama Island. Snugged into Baby Grant's, we'd drink beer and eat fried grouper or pork chops at long communal tables, and the crews stuck with us in West End would strike up deals, form flotillas to voyage in concert to Fort Pierce or to Cape Canaveral or to St. Augustine or to Lake Worth Inlet, where we were bound. These cohesions followed a good deal of throat-clearing and sniffing around; sailors wanted to be helpful, but no one wanted to be hindered by a sluggard or a fool during a Gulf Stream crossing. The Stream is a great river within the Atlantic, and between the Bahamas and southern Florida its axis moves north at six knots. A wind from the north, countering that swift current, builds seas of ferocious steepness and short periodicity. Put simply: a Gulf Stream norther breaks boats and sailors, and no one at Jack Tar considered crossing to Florida till the wind came around to south of west. We were smaller by ten or twenty feet, and slower by a knot or two, than any but one of the boats waiting to cross. And I had not forgotten how *Blackwing* had arrived at Jack Tar Marina, so I had no stomach to thrust us on anyone, and I have to confess that our new friends didn't work to convert us from standoffishness.

Nonetheless, we became friendly with the crowd piling in from the northern Bahamas to wait out the contrary wind. We ate potluck dinners at the picnic tables near our slips and heard great fish stories told with the eternal gestures of hands spread and spreading away. People used first names, and didn't mention the real world across the Stream. After a few days the crews began to rib us about our grounding at Great Sale Cay, so I told about the poor soul trapped in Little Harbour lagoon when we came over from Eleuthera, and someone said she knew that guy: "It had to happen, he never goes anywhere without bringing trouble with him, can't trust any place to have enough trouble to suit him."

And then the stories rained down of bona fide trouble out there in the Gulf Stream, and after a couple of days of those lurid tales of lost rudders, swamped dinghies, engines torn off their mountings by the pounding of Promethean rollers, fingers smashed by gear busting loose, drownings . . . The captain and crew of *Blackwing* waited to cross with opposing emotions of impatience and dread: I felt like a kid who, with his first electric train assembled and plugged in, throws the switch only to learn the electricity has failed. I also felt like a death-row prisoner strapped in the hot seat who realizes, just as they throw the switch, the electricity has failed. We began to wonder if we sold our house and cashed in our retirement funds, could

we hire that gold-toothed pirate to tow us home to Rhode
Island, or tow *Blackwing* home while we supervised from
above, from window seats on American Airlines?

On the fifth afternoon of our layover at Jack Tar, the weather
gave signs of breaking, and the group split up and each crew
went about its private business on the eve of battle, putting
affairs in order, double-securing secure gear, checking the
rigging for hairline cracks and the sails for unraveled seams,
cleaning and oiling weapons to combat the cruel sea. The
atmosphere brought to mind the anxious, quiet preparations
in the mountain hut on the Matterhorn, when climbers fiddled
with their axes and crampons and ropes while they looked at
the sky, wondering would they go up tomorrow?

Tomorrow dawned. We crossed a Gulf Stream as untroubled
as a goldfish pond. There was no confusion about the boundary
of the Stream, from the bright green of the Little Bahama
Bank into the deepest blue in nature, a saturated azure of
stunning clarity. The Stream is a warm river rushing north
from the Yucatán Channel, gathering speed from the Coriolis
force and from prevailing winds, bottlenecked between Florida
and Bimini, crowded with sea creatures. I remembered the
observation of a *National Geographic* photographer whose
dives had been frustrated by sharks: "When man enters the
Gulf Stream, he enters the food chain. And he doesn't enter
at the top."

Our worry—and we had to have a worry or it wouldn't have
been a day on the water—was being pushed so far north by
the Gulf Stream that we couldn't make (or *lay*, as navigators
say) Palm Beach. To take the influence of the current into
effect, I had charted a vector course, pointing our nose way
south of Palm Beach in order to be crabbed north and hit Lake
Worth Inlet on the money, which is the only thing you can hit
if you hit Palm Beach. The accuracy of this vector course
depended entirely on a constant speed forward through the

water. If something slowed or stopped us, we'd miss our land-fall.

I was the alpha wolf in a pack of three fools; the other two boats depended on the accuracy of my loran readouts, and on my navigational shrewdness. One skipper decided he didn't believe we had to point so far south, and so he veered off my course, heading closer to the rhumb line (straight line, loxo-drome, least distance between two points); he drifted north of Palm Beach and was last seen bobbing toward Labrador. (We were in radio contact until he declared he was resigned to his destiny; *enshallah.*)

There was lightning on the western horizon, but I didn't care about lightning. I cared about the United States Coast Guard. Let me tell you, sailing in the Gulf Stream is like sailing into a war zone. Coast Guard vessels were evident at all points of the compass. I mean big ships, ghostly white, with anti-aircraft batteries, and machine guns and cannons. My dread was to be approached, stopped, boarded and searched. Not that I was running cocaine or weed or guns or—bank on it—money: if we were boarded near the axis of the Gulf Stream, we'd be driven north at six nautical miles per hour, and that would make us sad. I intended to make us inconspicuous, nonchalant; I did this by looking casually in the direction of the Coast Guard vessels—on the theory that they'd be sus-picious if we pretended not to notice them—and by talking to Priscilla about poetry. I assumed they could hear us through their directional microphones, and I'd never heard drug deal-ers discuss poetry with Sonny and Rico on "Miami Vice." Live-aboard sailors had ascribed to the Coast Guard and DEA uncanny deductive powers, and I hoped that the Coast Guard had deduced that drug runners would on no account discuss poetry running drugs across the axis of the Gulf Stream.

Nicholas had been boarded by plainclothesmen in Key Bis-cayne's No Name Harbor. This didn't surprise us. He and his friends and *Blackwing* fit a provocative profile: they were too young to own the boat except with ill-gotten gains, and *Blackwing* was too small to be a professionally crewed yacht. Nicholas had taken the dinghy ashore and was walking the beach at Key Biscayne with a bad case of cabin fever. He noticed an overdesigned and overpowered and undermuffled speedboat bearing down on *Blackwing* at anchor; he watched a couple of slick customers come aboard wearing fancy sunglasses and carrying fancy automatic weapons. He saw his friends point ashore, at him; he watched the speedboat come toward him, and he told us he was pulled in quite a few different directions, and one of them was not toward the bow of the speedboat. Before he could run like crazy, they were on him; he was ordered to return to the boat of which he was the putative captain; there he watched while *Blackwing* was searched, though what she might have been smuggling *to* the Bahamas (except beer, which sells in the Islands for thirty dollars a case) was a mystery. The boys were lucky: the DEA chose not to tear her interior apart. So when the *federales* hopped in their speedboat and roared off in a tidal wave of wake, all hands felt relief. Until Nicholas remembered the dinghy.

"Who's swimming ashore to get it?" ordered Cap'n Nick.

"I guess you," volunteered one of his crew.

"That would be my guess," volunteered the other.

"How do you figure?" commanded the captain.

"Well, it's your dad's dinghy," conceded the first mate.

"And you took it ashore," offered the second mate.

Leaving Governor's Harbour, we'd been boarded and delved by the Royal Bahamas Defence Force. Half a dozen uniformed men bearing automatic weapons had materialized in a fast inflatable runabout. They'd made a thorough search, opened a few tins of food, studied the bilges, looked through our duffel bags. This had been courteous: the enlisted men had teased

Nicholas about the Boston Celtics; when they left, the officer in charge had wished us *bon voyage*. Courtly, but with locked and loaded firepower at port arms.

We knew we were being watched. Unmarked planes flew frequently and low over our anchorages; it was conventional wisdom that the blimps we saw every day were equipped with high-resolution cameras of the kind used in satellites, and that if we were questioned by the Coast Guard where we had cruised, it was best to remember exactly, since the feds had our itinerary thumbtacked to their bulletin board. It got to be a drag, drug stories shouldering aside a more human-scale Island mythology. We wanted to hear sweet stories, funny stories, stories out of the repertory of human comedy. Instead we were warned about yachties being shot or burned to the waterline for poking a bow into the wrong cove, and we were told of hijackings and unsolved murders and beatings.

We would stand foursquare against the drug scourge, but please not along the axis of the Gulf Stream. In the event, we were left in peace until we were coming through Lake Worth Inlet in a thunderstorm, zero visibility, and a Coast Guard patrol boat radioed us and the other boat in our mini-convoy (the third having been set a little north of Greenland by now). We were naughty: we had entered the territorial waters of the United States of America without flying a quarantine flag, which is a little yellow triangle beseeching the Coast Guard to come aboard and rummage for contraband. Nicholas had warned us to fly that flag, and now the Coast Guard was cross with us even before we'd touched home plate.

Life is a crapshoot: the Coast Guard decided to search one rather than both of us. In the rain. And the wind. Under thunder. And lightning. Half an hour before night. The pointer pointed to our companion. *Adiós, amigos!* We were out of there. Home. Home?

The Ditch

Come what came, we were safe. Snugged down below, drinking tea, we felt as smug as Magellans. We'd mounted a snapshot of Nicholas and his friends just above the loran readout, and I was studying it. Priscilla was reading Nicholas's log of his passage down the Intercoastal Waterway, an eleven-hundred-mile-sequence of rivers, lakes, bays and land cuts vulgarly titled The Ditch, an inland waterway (protected from the Atlantic mostly by barrier islands) from Norfolk, Virginia, to Miami. We were eighty-three statute miles north of Miami, at Mile 1017. Powering at five knots (the Waterway is too narrow and tortuous most places to sail), we had two hundred hours of travel ahead of us. And that was just to Virginia. Beyond Virginia lay Chesapeake Bay, Delaware Bay, the New Jersey Coast, the East River, Long Island Sound, Fishers Island Sound, Block Island Sound.

It was raining hard now, and I'd lit the kerosene lamp to give us some light and warmth. *Blackwing* has a wood-burning stove that extends the cruising season in New England, but here in Florida a candle cut the damp cold. I liked being below. I thought we'd feathered our nest quite well. Our house is a rambling Victorian, too big for us, with spare rooms and redundant outbuildings. The place is stuffed with stuff: book cartons that haven't been opened since the mid-1960s, tools and machines to maintain the yard, ancient tennis rackets, closets of clothes held like Confederate war bonds in a profitless speculation that they might make a comeback (bell-bottoms, wide ties, white flannels); I've stored variant versions of manuscripts, students' short stories and essays and grades; I've stored empty shoe boxes in case they might be useful for storing something smaller than empty shoe boxes. You know; who doesn't know? But down here, below on *Blackwing*, the concept *necessary* was subject to ruthless revision. What I brought aboard, Priscilla would trip over; things stood trial for their lives. It was comfortable, and comforting, to strip down, to experience what could be lost in a burglary or foreclosure without diminishing us. As the weeks had passed, we had cleaned up our act, and we had learned the acrobatic tricks that made it possible to move with a show of practiced grace from the forward vee-berth (as big and as comfy as a queen-sized bed), through the main cabin (with opposing settees, a drop-leaf table between them, a small galley aft on the port side), to the head (tucked tight behind the companionway steps, and under the cockpit's bridge deck). The main cabin was white and clean, with varnished cherry doors and trim, a varnished teak and holly cabin sole, plenty of light. We knew the inches and dark corners of the place where we lived, and cleaned what was dirty, fixed what was broken, polished what was dull. Our boat was simple, and within the tiny universe we inhabited on *Blackwing* we had the experience rather than the dream of control and competence and—sometimes, now, protected from the driving rain—perfection.

We'd expected, living days and weeks in close quarters, that we'd get on each other's nerves. Nicholas had confessed to feeling cramped and corked, and so had his crew. Three had made a good number of friends to share confinement; one could always break off from two to brood, or sulk, or silently scream at the (a) inconsideration, (b) incompetence, (c) imperfect hygiene of the other two, who would not notice, or could pretend not to notice. Pretty soon the surly tired one, the furious one, would pop a cold beer or tell a joke or see a funny sight, and the little storm passed. Now, silent below, watching Priscilla read, no place to go other than the place we had chosen as our prison cell, I wondered how we'd do.

"We'll go right where he went," Priscilla said. "It's all here in the log; he'll tell us what to do. It'll be perfect. If we follow where Nick leads, we'll do just fine."

It was so. Nick had been where we were going. Talk about displacement, reversal of customary order. A father says, "Here are the keys. Drive carefully." Nicholas, in Governor's Harbour, had said, "Here are the keys, be careful with the boat." In fact, Nicholas's log was more explicitly cautionary than most fathers would dare. A father might say, "Watch out for speed traps in Connecticut." Nicholas's log said: "The chart shows that Green #45 should be left to port northbound; the chart is *wrong*; beware a shoal spot fifty feet northeast of #45." If we didn't beware, we'd hit it, and that was a fact. There were encouragements, too: "Went to old hotel near Cocoa Beach Bridge and had a few. Funky joint, like hotel in *The Shining*. Check it out, but don't try to write a book there." It was pure pleasure, taking Nicholas as our guide; it was relaxing to let the son become the father, not to resist this inversion. He had been where I had not been, and he knew what I did not know: where to anchor, what bridge tender would open the draw on request, who grills a good hamburger, where to keep an eye open for otters, or laughs, or beauty. From this place forward, Palm Beach to Jamestown, we were in his hands. How did we feel to follow rather than lead? We felt swell.

We spent a day tied to a pier at Sailfish Marina on Lake Worth. We'd thrown in our lot with sportfishermen; marina life had its busy charm: we gaped at heavy-metal sportfishing boats, 60-foot Bertram killing machines as sleek as F-18s, gleaming white fiber glass and gleaming stainless steel and gleaming varnished hardwood. These showed off Brobding-nagian rods and reels set near audaciously complicated fighting chairs; aloft rose monster tuna towers, up and up, as high as follies. The boats rumbled with twin-engined Caterpillar diesel throatiness through Lake Worth Inlet from the Gulf Stream; approaching Sailfish Marina, they'd gurgle at low rpm to the weighing dock, and dump bravura loads of swordfish, tuna, marlin, sailfish and shark. While paid hands performed a three-hour wash-down of salt and scales and blood and gore from the sportfishermen, Priscilla and I, like kids, like a couple of retired geezers, would gawk at a deckhand slitting open the belly of a shark, and we'd take pictures of each other gawking, and, in unison with everyone else gawking, cry out *jeez!*

Priscilla said, "Let's phone Justin and tell him a college sophomore slid out of that tiger shark's belly."

Justin had a special relationship with sharks, since seeing *Jaws* as a little boy, against our better judgment. So we phoned Justin at Bowdoin and told him we had watched a college sophomore slip out of a tiger shark's belly. He laughed politely. It was a worn-out joke. He'd heard us report sharks in whose guts were found college frosh and high-school juniors and seventh-graders. He asked, sounding anxious, "You guys showing each other a good time?"

What Justin meant: What do you find to talk about when you don't talk about us? What Justin meant: Take a vacation from your boys, The Boys, our boys. Justin, we heard you loud and clear. We suffered the (maybe) benign disorder of nonstop recollection. Priscilla and I put too many hours into riffling the pages of memory's scrapbook, and the pictures were forever the same: The Boys. For them it must have become an oppression; for us our fixation with recall was ceremonial. Like most ceremonies, it gave pleasure. Like most habits, it limited what we did because we did it instead of something else. We were never-endingly doing our sons' biographies: remembering them, analyzing them, telling their fortunes. This was a way to escape the self, to look elsewhere than at the here and now.

But the here and now was the purpose of this voyage. We were here to respond to now. Moving through the water, finding the channel, looking immediately ahead, responding to what we saw . . . This was not a prophetic enterprise, nor retrospective. The Waterway, in its slow unwinding, had no narrative thread evident to me then. Winding north, I forgot how to write, literally: my minimalist log of our progress is barely decipherable. I memorialized our voyage by notes on wind direction, tides, weather (put down "sunny," and add "ibid." to each change of date), bridges and mile markers. The miles were marked on stakes laid out at frequent intervals, port and starboard, marking our course, our biography.

Leaving Palm Beach, floating past people's front yards, peering into their kitchens and bedrooms from a distance of yards—this was a hoot. Americans—even the marginal fortunates living waterside—make a motley cohort. North of Palm Beach along the Gold Coast, fools-gold coast, we saw expressions of preening grandiosity that decorated the concept of kitsch. In this Xanadu—where gators dwell in the water traps of golf courses and catfish stroll the boulevards—were decreed by arbitragers and Subaru distributors pleasure domes, monumental humps of pink stucco; into the extravagantly watered lawns edged by flamboyant (I'll say!) trees were cut little canals, to float motor yachts as grand as the caretaker's house. We couldn't escape the privileged sense that this silliness was arranged for our entertainment, that we would be discourteous and ungenerous not to stare frankly at what had been set port and starboard to refresh our senses.

Palm Beach's swank displays were merely predictable, as old-money Hobe Sound's affectedly unaffected Attic restraint was predictable. We were on the lookout for the capricious, and we found it everywhere. In Eau Gallie, on the tip of Merritt Island along the Banana River, we came upon an immense green concrete dragon guarding the homeowner's front lawn. The day we passed, the dragon's mouth was belching smoke and sparks and flame, the outcome of a barbecue cooking in the beast's torso. Did you ever?

The Intercoastal Waterway, ICW, completed an uninterrupted hookup from Norfolk to Miami in 1935, though portions had been undertaken as long ago as Colonial times. It was dug to excite commerce, but meanwhile barging along The Ditch was overtaken by trucking along the interstates. Now it was used by pleasure boats as an alternative to offshore passages along the mid-Atlantic coast, especially to escape killer shores between Cape Hatteras and Cape Fear. Seven thousand boats a year transit north and south along the ICW; seven thousand are too few for a crowd, just enough for company; most are powerboats.

Powerboaters and sailboaters are trapped in a Tom versus Jerry cartoon of reflexive mutual antipathy; to powerboaters, sailors are snobs and eccentrics, inconsiderate slowpokes absurdly insistent on exercising their right-of-way in accordance with the finest of fine print in seagoing Rules of the Road. To sailors, stinkpotters are boorish speedhounds indifferent to the huge wake they churn roaring clamorously through narrow channels, swamping sailboats and eroding the fragile shoreline and chewing up defenseless manatees. In fact, the powerboaters we passed bow-to-bow, who passed us from astern, were almost invariably considerate and friendly; it is unsettling to surrender a prejudice to experience, but if we'd brought anything to the party, it was a willingness to be surprised.

We were surprised most by the navigational exactions of traveling up The Ditch. When we'd planned the trip, we'd noticed a fallacy of logic in our dream to upset the uniformity of our home routines. What could be more sleep-inducingly uniform than to rise at dawn and plow north till dusk, along a narrow waterway, the diesel turning a steady 2700 rpm, following the magenta line on the chart, measuring progress by counting off regularly spaced channel marks, even numbered reds to port, green odds to starboard? Looked at narrowly, our would-be experiment in ultimate cohesion and attention had merely exchanged a regularity of days ashore (from which we fled) for an extreme regularity of days afloat (to which we fled); in this model a monotony of gardening and writing became a monotony of five-point-five-knot long-haul trucking. But it wasn't like that. Our senses were engaged: if negotiating the Bahamas without navigational aids was by inference and eyeballed best guess, navigating The Ditch meant understanding not only where we were going (to a spot between green stake #3 and red stake #4), but whether we had been set by current out of the narrow line connecting where we were going with where we had been (a spot midway between green stake #1 and red stake #2).

Priscilla had a swell feel for our situation, studying it on the abstract environment of a chart; I had a feel for *Blackwing*'s tangents and drifts. Priscilla knew where was center channel; I knew how to steer us there, and feel our way through deep water. Together we worked our way ahead, and I mean *worked*. Happy work, though, and Priscilla knew how to feather our nest: she had bought us a yellow beach umbrella rigged by a patented contraption to the steering station. She was expert in fetching and raising this at the first blush of discomforting sun. Iced tea materialized one beat before iced tea was desired. If I had been silently calculating our day's run to Fort Pierce, Priscilla had made an itinerary, subject to her daily revisions, home to Jamestown. Some micro for me, macro for her; some vice versa for vice versa. So we were team players, but we were also characters in what Hemingway believed was our first and last novel, Americans on a raft. We were a precious and privileged distance off the everyday verities of our crazy quilt of a gorgeous and tacky country; we believed we could see our country fresh from that little distance offshore, and so we looked sharp, and looking sharp we did not sleepwalk; we felt alive to that narrow band of our country, and to ourselves, and to each other.

Our routine aboard became regular—a hum of conversation, shared responses to the passing circus (or from the passing circus, depending again on point of view), shared silences that we didn't mistake for brooding or discomfort; ashore we were often surprised, when I had the sense to look beyond what I believed was inexorable. It's an ironist's vice, it's this ironist's vice, to look for discord, error, the good idea gone bad: looking along the Waterway, I found confirming evidence of botched design, of will opposed and impeded by circumstance. So now I read in my notebook a notation regarding Fort Pierce's grim and seedy downtown, where competing office-supply stores, facing each other on the main drag, were boarded up, had evidently driven each other out of business. I must have found in this joyless sight some confirmation of barbarous human nature: then I thought it would be of use in a piece of writing; now I think it's of no use.

Our best moments were unanticipated. We had docked in Vero Beach on a hunt for supplies. Back when, waiting on the shoals short of West End for the pirate-pilot to lead us toward the Gulf Stream, I had noticed a dreamy look in Priscilla's eyes. Later she told me it wasn't that distant a dream; it was a sixty-or-so-mile westward conjury of the U S of A, home waters, asphalted terra firma. She was thinking safe dry land, but she was also thinking supplies. It had been satisfyingly simple to find the thin rations we sought in the Bahamas, because Bahamian bakeries and icehouses and liquor stores were clumped in harbor settlements (and if they weren't, who minded the walk?), or perhaps because we expected to find so little. Stateside, by contrast, industrial-strength foodstuffs were out along the highway at the Publix and Winn Dixie, and we had to settle for convenience stores, and so our quality of life had been much depressed by the change of waters to bountiful America, even though we were well trained to eat lean aboard *Blackwing*. This afternoon we had walked from the Vero Beach municipal marina to buy beer. Along the way we'd passed a codger walking his foppish little dog. *Walking* isn't exact: the old man was mounted on an electric tricycle equipped with a high whippy mast topped by a bright orange flag. He controlled his yippy wee pooch by the agency of a kite string. The animal, no doubt practiced in the synergistic arrangement, was nevertheless unresigned to it, and strained vainly against the half-pound-test line.

"That's quite a system you have there," Priscilla said.

The old man said, "You must be tourists."

Priscilla said, "How can you tell?"

He said, "You're kidding!"

He asked where we hailed from, and when we told him, he said that was one hell of a coincidence, his son lived there too, "in Delaware." Easy to believe he required remedial tutelage in geography, but I came to adjust my view to his, and to understand that a neighborhood of weensiness was as good an association as a proximity of latitude and longitude; whatever brought us together was jake by me.

The old man had directed us to a fish and bait shop on Bethel Creek, where we would find "good, cold beer." Priscilla asked the rough-looking tattooed counterman lurking in the dark cave of his fishing shack where we might buy milk and orange juice. He stared at her, and threw something toward her.

"Here's the keys. It's the Dodge in the lot."

He told us where to shop, and what sights to see along the way, and I believe if we'd let him he would have come with us to pay for our groceries and bag them and carry them to *Blackwing*.

We learned to assume that people would be other than we assumed. It is a term of opprobrium among live-aboards that a novice boater is so poor a mechanic he can't screw the cap on a bottle of Mount Gay without crossing the threads; he "can't even adjust his stuffing box." In a Florida marina I hired a mechanic to adjust my stuffing box. He was a rougher-looking customer than the fellow who gave his Dodge to strangers off the street: similar tattoos, a Harley T-shirt with its sleeves torn off, a patina of grease on his exposed skin, a fine full belly of the sort termed "Milwaukee goiter," a plumber's wrench in his back pocket. As soon as he came aboard, he demanded a beer, and when he finished the beer he crunched the can one-handed, and if you don't believe me, if the crunched can's too perfect for words, I'll understand. Then he fixed things. He dived back into the tight engine compartment, and while he called every part of *Blackwing* a bad name, and hammered those parts with his wrench, he fiddled and adjusted and tuned and advised. I asked him a couple of times how much all this was adding up to, and he said, "Gimme another beer." When he was finished, he said, "Nice boat. Very pretty boat." When he said "pretty," the word sounded pretty. And then he began to reminisce about our home port. He asked us if we drank in the Narragansett Café; he asked if we knew Nick, who owned Central Garage. Sure we knew Nick; he worked on our cars, worked also on the conveyance I now drove instead of sports cars and Norton motorcycles, a Wheel Horse riding mower.

"Tell Nick Nigger says hello," said our new friend.

Priscilla said, "What a world."

Our new friend looked hurt: "That's what they call me. That's my nickname."

Restaurants were museums of human unpredictability. In a Daytona waterfront restaurant with ambitions of refinement, we stumbled on pre-dance senior-prom-goers from New Smyrna High. They gave good value. Watching them was like doing an exegesis of the *National Lampoon Yearbook*. The prom queen wore a ball gown and a rhinestone tiara and smiled every second; we heard her say to a fat boy in a white dinner jacket a lot too tight on him, "You look great! You look *so* cute!" (To put her prevarication in context, a girl about her age said of my Reef Runners, silly rubber shoes meant to protect the tootsies against nasty coral, pebbles and hot sand at the beach: "Those are the *cutest* shoes! I got to *get* me some!") The seniors had found their places: at the jock's table were crew-cut boys and clear-skinned girls with a lot of bouffant to their dos. At the literary magazine's table were unclear-skinned, pallid, angry, cigarillo-smoking boys and girls who wore no evening gowns or dinner jackets: black turtlenecks for her, black leather for him, sour misery vibes coming off the poached bass. The rich kids looked bored, jaded with the Chart House and its Polynesian drinks with umbrellas sticking out of them; the rich kids ordered Wild Turkey, "straight up, and, honey, ask the bartender to give me a twist." How did they get so young? How did we get so old?

Maybe not so old. Daytona gave me an odd baseline reference for "old." I got carded in a convenience store that catered to golden-agers. I was essaying to buy a six-pack of beer, and the young lady behind the counter asked me for ID. I said, "Look at me. You can't be serious." She was serious; she showed me a notice that said she'd be checking the age of anyone who purchased beer; she'd have proof that I was twenty-one-plus, or I'd put the beer back in the cooler. "But I don't have ID with me." She said that was too bad for me. I said, "Look at my white beard. My bald head." She looked. She saw a guy nineteen, maximum twenty. Either she'd seen many a guy older than I, or she'd seen some twenty-year-old carrying around a monster load of worry and bad luck.

In Titusville, along the Space Coast, we tied up with a mess of boats that had come north and south to watch the first shuttle launch after *Challenger* went down. The boaters' kids clustered around a couple of manatees that floated around the gas dock, drinking water from a hose. The animals' backs were scarred from propeller cuts, and you could see their lassitude was ill-adapted to powerboaters in a hurry to get from one Chart House to another; the manatees had cute whiskers going for them, and the boaters' kids photographed them, and exclaimed over them. The scene was busy for our taste, so when we saw an ad for the town's "finest Italian restaurant," Lorenzo's, to which we would be carried by courtesy car, I got on the telephone. Lorenzo said to get myself and my wife out in front, "the limo's on its way."

In Southern California I'd come to associate conveyance in limousines with dashed book-into-movie dreams, with the snapping shut of checkbooks and the awful putting away of billfolds. I associated limousines with broken promises, and when I saw this stretch limo, white and waxed, I felt a little premonitory hitch. Along the way to Lorenzo's the driver complained bitterly about the *Challenger* "trouble." The "media" had "blown it out of all . . ." Out of all *what* would you guess? You're right, out of all "proportion." Spin again: the Shuttle "trouble" had been "a bummer" for . . . Right you are, for "business." Lorenzo's was in a shopping center next door to Chicken Delight. It was not a stretch-limo kind of exterior presentation; inside was in keeping with outside. This was a shopping-center Italian restaurant, with cannelloni from Weight Watchers and garlic bread from the microwave.

Driving us home, our uniformed and becapped driver said, "I've got one question. How do you figure the mayor and our fair city council?"

"I'm sorry," I said.

"I don't want to butt in," the driver said. "Your opinion is your business, but me—I got to believe someone's on the take."

"We don't know what you're talking about," Priscilla said. "We don't live where you live."

"I read you loud and clear," the driver said. "You're entitled to your private opinion. And if you're not into politics, that's also your right as a citizen. In my opinion."

"In my opinion," I said, "they're both on the take."

"I catch your drift, Cap."

We had a fight at a Greek pizzeria near the St. John's River. The dinner began well, with a carafe of retsina; the only warning bell to ring was Priscilla's uncharacteristically pugnacious insistence on ordering for us not only a large Greek pizza, but two large Greek salads. She's a light eater, and I'm not. I amended the dinner order, instructed the waiter to bring me a small rather than large salad; I said my wife, despite her initial order, would also prefer a small salad. My wife said, "Mind your own business." She told the waiter to bring her a large salad.

We'd had a good day, had put many miles under our keel. I congratulated us for owning such a swell boat. In fact, having ordered a second bottle of retsina, I toasted us for having ten years ago had the perspicacity to purchase such a commendable vessel.

Priscilla's face abruptly clouded: "It was outrageous the way you bought the boat. Unpardonable."

"Huh?"

"You didn't even ask me my opinion."

"Of course I did!"

"You did *not!* You didn't receive my permission. You just said, 'I am *going* to *buy* that *boat*, and that is *all* I have to *say.*' Like some macho jerk."

"Priscilla!"

If retsina was talking on her behalf, she was also fed up with the delicate courtesies required of our relentless proximity. She was fed up with me. Later, walking home, Priscilla let me have it again, for allowing her to order about twelve pounds of Greek salad as a side dish to twelve pounds of pizza.

"You're such a wimp!" she said. "A mouse!"

"I thought I was a macho jerk."

A block later I caught her smiling, then laughing. "Think of it," she said. "This is the best fight we can come up with. A grievance ten years old."

In fact, there was a strain between us. During the several years before we treated ourselves to this escape, I had finished a novel, had accustomed myself to writing rather than to publishing, to baking bread rather than to casting it upon the waters. It had always been my professed desire to toss a book like a bomb over my agent's and editor's garden wall, and run for my life, and this time I had done just that. Whether my work gave good vibrations, or bad, or none—I was beyond vibrations' range. No small part of Priscilla's willingness to undertake this journey was my implied promise that while New York cast its various verdicts on my value, I'd shun telephones. If I was a mendicant (and I was, despite cloudy title to a pocket yacht), I might as well be a tramp.

But recently I'd begun to hang on telephones at the dockmaster's shed and outside supermarkets called Piggly Wiggly. Would X buy the French rights? Did Y just love it to death? What I heard over the wires gave no joy, and too soon I was traveling the Waterway with my upper lip curled down and my lower lip stuck out. This made Priscilla angry. To check the temperature of work over which I had surrendered control was to her self-indulgent, and perverse, and profitless. It was one thing to do something irrational (write); it was a different and truncated thing to expect strangers to do something irrational (buy it, love me). When I feel sorry for myself, Priscilla takes it as her mission to give me even better cause to feel sorry for myself, so that in time I might learn that it is happier not to feel sorry for myself. At the most improbable moment —watching a baby porpoise learn to dive by swimming loopy "S"s so close to its mama they touched, hearing them catch their breaths with a unison theatrical chuff like health enthusiasts swimming laps—I'd let my thoughts drift to the advertising budget, first print run, advance reviews. Priscilla said this was a sickness; she was right.

They call the Georgia portion The Big Wiggle, because the Waterway snakes through wetland creeks in byzantine loops and oxbows, so that *Blackwing*'s stem might move in an hour through all points of the compass. So twisted is the route that a great distance over the water might represent a tiny distance over land; we might see the mast of another boat less than a straight-line mile distant, and eight miles by water, as though the water route we traveled were the stretched rubber twine wrapped around a baseball's core. Navigation through those marshes was taxing: creeks and bayous and sloughs and cul-de-sacs branched off the narrow main channel. The tidal range was great, nine feet in places, and to go aground at high tide would make a monument to high-and-dryness.

The Florida Waterway had been crowded with local boaters and with snowbirds migrating north. Now the crowds thinned out. We journeyed entire mornings without passing another boat or seeing a human being or habitation. The grass was pale green and yellow, and unfolded to the horizon, and the spring dawnlight was filtered through patchy fog. We saw otters swimming on their backs, cracking open mussels, being cute; when a water moccasin, convoluting alongside *Blackwing* (and to my inflationary eye near half her length) put itself on a course intercepting the otters, we called out a warning. Our alarm sounded intrusive and silly hollered into that wilderness silence; the snake and otters went about their business. Meantime egrets and blue herons waded on the marsh banks, and ospreys, nested atop channel stakes, brought fish to their fledglings. We saw wild horses running the beach at Cumberland Island, and at low water birds lined the water's edge waiting for the tide to drive small-fry fish to them, while smaller birds stood behind, waiting for the bigger birds to finish their lunch:

the Chain of Being. One afternoon, just as we anchored in the bend of New Teakettle Creek, a golden eagle glided to the water surface right in front of our bow, and got what it had come for.

But Priscilla's eye was elsewhere: "It's one of them. Look! Look there on the bank!"

Priscilla's manner is laconic, unless she's laughing. She wasn't laughing, and her manner was not laconic. She had spotted, napping on the mud bank of the narrow creek, a very adult alligator. Alligators down here were, if not a dime a dozen, no more than a dollar the half dozen, but not to Priscilla. I'd like to avoid superlatives, but I've never seen Priscilla so excited by anything. She wanted to watch that alligator do something. I'll be plain: she wanted to watch that alligator eat something—a ship's cat, or a skipper, whatever alligators like to eat.

The alligator wearied of Priscilla's attentions, slid off its bank, swam under our stern and took up a position on the opposing mud bank, slightly more distant from my wife. All through that night, whenever we heard the wild sounds of a wild place—an owl screech, a heron cluck, a rabbit shriek—Priscilla would nudge me.

"There it is. It got something!" she'd say. And I did not think about the advertising budget, or first printing, or advance reviews.

During a tornado watch, we waited at Lanier Island for the front to pass through. It was Saturday; the marina bar's parking lot was filling with muscle cars and black Jeeps with roll bars and dark blue Volvo wagons bearing family initials on nautical semaphore badges and carrying golfers from Sea Island, two islands to seaward. This was a mixed gang of weight lifters, fighter pilots, nabobs; old salts danced with chipper youngsters to a local rock band's fave raves. I don't care if southern ease is faked; I'll take it. Way off to the west, even as the moon lit us from above, I saw electrical storms. The horizon crackled like cluster bombs, and set the world's edge ablaze with menace, and while the dancers danced looking at one another or down at their feet or above at the moon or east or south or wherever, I stared off to the west and wished I were jollier, easier, better fun.

I heard a woman behind me, with a honey Georgia accent: "Are you a Christian?"

I turned east. She was pretty. "I beg your pardon."

"Are you prepared for the hereafter?" No menace: a sweet patient smile. I had been asked that same question three years before, so at that rate I guessed I'll be asked it seven times again. It was time to have an answer, and I explained that I cared too much for the *here* to fret about the *after*. She nodded sadly, serene in her disappointment; where was Priscilla's gator now that I needed him?

"Take care now," she said. I promised to try.

Beyond Moon River (as in "Muuuuune *Riii*ver, dah dah dah dee dah, dah *dah* dee dah dah dah, dah *duh* . . .") we tied up at Thunderbolt, and got a taxi to Savannah. The fare was seven-fifty; I gave the cabby a twenty-dollar bill, and asked him to keep nine.

"I can't make change, pardner."

"You have no change?"

"Just a ten and three ones."

"Tell you what: take my twenty, and why not give me a ten and a one."

"Well, how do I come out there?"

"Well, I give you the twenty to keep, and you give me a ten and a one to keep."

"All right! That's mighty generous of you, pardner."

Set beside the wide Savannah River, Savannah had been

overwhelmed by a seven-story Mussolini Modern convention Hyatt, and inland had a desperate bombed-out character: an impeccable antebellum townhouse sat next door to a Western Auto. Hustlers panhandled the unkempt public parks, store windows were protected by metal mesh and doors by a locksmith's inventory of dead bolts and chains and padlocks with hasps as thick as my wrist. We were reminded: the Waterway is not the real world's way. Despite its riverside situation, this city was inland, with interior preoccupations.

Back along the riverbank we were on the point of dining at the Shrimp Factory when a drummer spotted us looking at the menu and reached for my elbow.

"Come on in. Come on, now! You won't regret it! We got the best food in Savannah and we got the food in our kitchen to prove it!"

"Isn't that a non sequitur?"

"*Argumentum a fortiori*," said Priscilla. "Let's go home to *Blackwing*."

Nicholas had warned us; the log said of Savannah, "Savannah: wait for Charleston."

Southeast of Charleston, we hit Elliott Cut on the last of a flooding (favorable) tide. The *Waterway Guide* warned us: "If you're in a sailboat with only auxiliary power, don't try to buck these currents; it could put you out of control." At three-fifteen we were shooting for a restricted bridge that would be closed from 4 p.m. until evening, when I did not want to navigate Charleston Harbor. As usual, we were tired. A Coast Guard runabout with five crew members aboard passed us, and I waved a distracted greeting, calculating whether we'd make the last bridge opening. The runabout did a U-turn and came alongside; four young men climbed aboard *Blackwing* wearing brogans and the damnedest life jackets: the life vests made Mae Wests look like Audrey Hepburns. An officer asked questions while three enlisted men searched below; as I tried to answer questions, the current slacked and turned immediately against us. (". . . it could put you out of control.")

I laid it out: "I'm not running drugs. I've got no weapons aboard. If I'm lying, you can throw my wife in prison."

"Sir, we've got a problem down here."

The young officer stared at me, smiled and went below. He soon poked his head up as I bucked the current whipsawing *Blackwing*'s bow; we crept toward the bridge soon to close, trapping us in the narrow cut, without an anchorage.

"Captain," asked the teenaged officer, "where is your Pollution Control Placard?"

"My what?"

He explained: I was meant to have posted a placard "in the vicinity of any overboard discharge mechanism"; the proclamation on this placard was to condemn in the strongest (and Coast-Guard-approved) idiom the jettisoning of oil—what tankers do when they blow their tanks. "You're in violation here, Captain."

Scolded by authorities, I'm tame. But this was a pissant offense, and I was climbing on my high horse when I heard an enlisted man whistle from the engine compartment.

The pre-adolescent officer, a cub of a boy, a rosy-cheeked Sea Scout of a law-enforcement person, said, "I'm afraid we have an explosive situation down here, Captain."

There was a slight skim of diesel fuel on the bilge water. This was no big deal: diesel fumes do not explode, which is why we have a diesel auxiliary. I had found and plugged the fuel filter leak. But the Coast Guardsmen, finding no cocaine in our eggs, no hashish in our beer cans, decided to save our lives. They climbed back into the cockpit, where we were now half a dozen, plus four engorged life jackets.

"Your vessel could explode at any moment, Captain. We're going to accompany you to your destination at Ashley Marina."

"Why, if we could explode at any moment, are you all so calm and friendly?"

"It's our job, Captain."

The bridge closed. I said, "Shit." No: I said, "*Shit!*" The Coast Guardsmen looked at one another, and at Priscilla; that kind of cursing in the company of a lady was deplorable. They were darned disappointed with me. I said, "The bridge just closed. We're stuck here. The current's running so hard against me I can't keep a good course. The odds of an explosion must be gaining on us."

The enlisted men turned to the baby officer, and he seemed to be turning the enigma forming in his mind this way, and then that way. "We've got an emergency here," he said. "I'd better get that drawbridge opened."

And he did. We entered Ashley Marina horsed violently by a sideswiping current; Coast Guard regulations forbid boat-handling, I guess, because they didn't help us maneuver alongside our neighbor at the pier. This was a powerboat named *Black Knight*, which is the committee boat for the New York Yacht Club during America's Cup racing in Newport, two miles from our home mooring. *Black Knight* is the handsomest powerboat in the world, and its crew is not the boat's crew to whom one most would wish to present a forceful impression of having been confiscated by the Coast Guard under Zero Tolerance provisions of controlled-substance statutes. The crew aboard *Black Knight* made a show of looking elsewhere, as though to spy on our infamy were shameful.

"I don't know that we can handle this kind of thing here," said the dock boy.

Priscilla explained our situation while the infant officer worked up my ticket for reckless driving. The explosion potential seemed to have been forgotten.

"Eyes?" asked the toddler officer.

"Brown."

"Weight?" asked the suckling officer.

I told him. He looked at me, at my sunburned and very high forehead. He smiled. "And what should I put down for hair?" asked the fetus.

As the gang clomped across my deck and dropped to the pier, I said, "This was a Mickey Mouse bust. You could put a fire out with diesel, if I had enough diesel in my bilge to get a fire wet."

"Happy trails," the embryonic officer promised.

The dock boy at Ashley Marina said, "You people don't look like drug dealers, but smart drug dealers wouldn't look like drug dealers. Would they?"

We passed awful hurricane damage north of Charleston; along Isle of Palms the cabbage palmettos had been swept clean, and at McClellanville remnants of the shrimp fleet were aground, and passing this devastation made me protective of our boat, aware how lucky we were to have come so far unscathed. I was considering our good fortune as we approached Georgetown Landing on the Pee Dee River when suddenly, coming up fast from astern in a runabout, the United States Coast Guard, five men and an officer, life-jacketed and sturdily shod. When they drew near, I shouted at them to bug off. Priscilla was alarmed, and the Coast Guardsmen seemed dumbfounded.

"I've *been* boarded! I'm a good guy! I'm not a drug smuggler! I'm a citizen! Get off my case! I'm middle-class! I'm a prudent mariner! I'm . . ."

"Probably fucked," said Priscilla, under her breath.

They were alongside. I said, "Look at me. Do I look like a drug smuggler?" I explained to The Law that I'd just been put through the wringer in Elliott Cut, and the officer, a mature and reasonable man, asked to see the citation I'd been given, and when Priscilla produced it, the officer asked whether I had installed an anti-pollution placard, and when Priscilla said that was definitely an affirmative, Sir, because it was, because she had insisted we track down and install the stupid thing, the officer saluted her:

"I'll take your word for it, ma'am. Have a real nice day, Captain. At least you know we're out here."

But the day's bad luck hadn't begun. While Priscilla and I were food-shopping, the wind came up. We realized we'd tied *Blackwing* hastily to a badly protected pier, and by the time we ran back to move her the hurt had been done. Waves and wind had worn her hull against an exposed nailhead in the pier, cutting deep ugly gouges in her topsides. It had been dead calm when we'd tied alongside, and we'd been in a hurry to tie up, shop, get on our way; we'd let our guard down just for a moment, just once. Here, charged against my account, was the only damage done to that boat since she'd sailed from Jamestown more than seven months ago.

"What can we tell Nicholas?" Priscilla said.

"How can we tell Nicholas?" I said.

We sailed downwind and up the Waccamaw River to Prince Creek, and if there was a lovelier patch of Waterway, we didn't see it. The river was wide and deep, the color of hot chocolate; along its banks canals had been cut into abandoned antebellum rice fields. First-growth forests of live oaks were bearded by Spanish moss. The river was quiet and unthreatening, and I couldn't stop thinking about what I had let happen to *Blackwing*, and every ten minutes or so I'd lean over the rail and look at the hideous scars, and rub them, as though I could make them go away. Priscilla doesn't like to brood on what's amiss, but she wasn't immune.

"Do you think we can fix it?"

I said I guessed it could be fixed.

Priscilla said it would be nice to make the injury right before Nicholas saw it.

Shortly before dusk we anchored in a deep narrow creek, under cypress trees. The sky was clear; the wind had died and we could hear every creature on the riverbank. The low sun was casting pastels on the glassy water. Or so I was told; I was upside down in the cockpit locker trying to reach a broken electrical switch. The switch controlled our running lights, needed only when we moved at night, and we planned no night sailing south of Chesapeake Bay, so there was no need to repair that switch today.

"Why are you doing this?"

It was a question Priscilla had asked back at Lynyard Cay, after we crossed Northeast Providence Channel. "I have to fix it while I've got sunlight."

"What's wrong with you?"

I explained that I wanted to make a little right what I had made a lot wrong; I explained that if I had broken something, I could at least fix something.

"You're hopeless," Priscilla said, eating in the near dark. "You don't know how to take pleasure from anything. You've spoiled Prince Creek, and I'm not waiting for you to finish your dumb project; you've let our bucket of fried chicken get cold."

"But we bought it four hours ago."

"Don't be a small-print artist."

The next day we negotiated the ugliest and most treacherous stretch of the Waterway, Pine Island Cut, called by its many enemies The Rock Pile. The narrow land cut had been imperfectly blasted by the Corps of Engineers, which left rock ledges below and just above the water. The channel bristled with snags and deadheads and submerged logs. So narrow and dangerous was this stretch that to meet a tug towing a barge through it would be to kiss *Blackwing* goodbye. There was no room to spin around and turn back or to pass: southbound train and northbound train on one track. Edging The Rock Pile were shacks with wood or plaster statues in their yards—life- or bigger-than-life-sized grizzly bears and zebras and giraffes and dinosaurs; the displays had been put there to give passing boaters pleasure, to astound, to up the ante on the neighbors' bestiaries. There were other likenesses: seated cast-iron statues of lazybones black boys equipped with make-shift fishing poles, angling from the ends of The Rock Pile's docks; these astounded, too, and gave no pleasure.

"How far to Wrightsville Beach?" asked Priscilla.

When Priscilla was ashore, she'd stop in front of every garden she met, and stoop to study and smell, and take on a faraway look. Measurably far away: two hundred and eighty-three miles of Waterway, plus the distance to Rhode Island, James-town, Narragansett Avenue, her flower beds. Since he left us in Eleuthera, Nicholas had been living at home, and when he and his mother talked while I waited a discreet distance from the phone booth, I overheard mulch and weeds and diagnostic consultations and corrective remedies. We had put in bulbs the autumn before we left, and I knew Priscilla was unhappy to be far from home when the daffodils and snowdrops and tulips—some of them annuals—poked through. As long ago as his second-grade year in Vermont, Nicholas had planted gardens with his mother, and he understood her aggravated feeling that to be elsewhere when her plants bloomed was to have slipped a cycle; he had been making time-lapse stills and videos of Priscilla's flowers.

Now, in Wrightsville Beach, they switched places. This was no mutiny or MAYDAY; it was not unforeseen. We had planned as far back as the Florida–Georgia border to make what is bloodlessly termed a crew change in the middle of May. It made sense. Priscilla knew, or believed, she wasn't physically equal to the marathon Waterway runs and nonstop offshore passages that lay ahead to put *Blackwing* within striking dis-tance of home. Because she sensed she was approaching the end of her leash, and because she trusts what she senses, and because her flowers were newborn, and because (so far) what one wants both want, this part of our voyage was done now. We wanted to quit the game winners, take chips from the table. I had always believed that interesting stories were necessarily about failure; this story was not about failure, but it interested me. I had no illusions about the obstacles we had mastered: shallow water, reefs, treacherous anchorages, storms, the thin skin of fiber glass between us and the bottom of the sea— these were what Herbert Gold has named happy problems for happy people. On the other hand, we had overcome difficulties more interesting than trouble at sea; we'd behaved well to each other; we had hung in together day-to-day; we had hung, as they say, *tight*. This had required attention, not exactly the kind of attention required to maintain and navigate a boat, but akin to that kind of care.

Nicholas flew to Wrightsville Beach the day before Priscilla flew home. While she was packing, I busied myself paying the bills Nicholas had delivered. Maybe that was all there was to it, the dumb facts in dollars and cents of our intractable responsibility to a life of first-of-the-month obligations, or maybe it was the logistical exaction of manipulating checkbook and calculator on the little table better used for navigational reckonings, or maybe it was the concrete metaphor of watching Priscilla's locker empty, and become Nicholas's, but whatever provoked me, I felt more solitary in the company of Nicholas and Priscilla together than I felt with either alone.

My first boat was an 8-foot Penn Yan dinghy with white canvas topsides and varnished mahogany strakes and seats. To be free of land and landsmen has always figured in my fever for boats. At ten, living on the Connecticut shore of Long Island Sound, I'd row as far off Point o' Woods beach as my parents would allow, to an imaginary line connecting one headland of the

little bay with the other; I'd rest on my oars and wonder what
it was like beyond the line, one bay over. When I was not
languishing over my oars, I'd row as though in flight from
danger, backwater abruptly, spin in circles—the demented
ballet of a kid in a rowboat. I was a would-be passage-maker,
and a single-hander. I single-hand *Blackwing*, and it's bracing
to manage alone, to show off in the anchorage at Block Island
or Cuttyhunk, getting down the sails, setting the anchor by
my lonesome. But the point of it isn't to get away from home;
the point is to get home away from land. To behave well in
front of witnesses: Justin, Nicholas, Priscilla. To have them
aboard is to feel in my bones the imperative of care, the good
fun of good will; the point is to take pleasure from taking
pains.

Priscilla said goodbye at dawn from the marina dock, waving
us up the Waterway. She looked envious; she looked relieved.
Without her I felt incomplete, as though a sail had bust out
along a seam. But I felt, if I couldn't then articulate, consolations. We'd just written much personal history together. I
was sure of us. Now I was ahead of where I'd begun when I
pushed the Penn Yan off from Point 'o Woods alone: I had
company; we could go to sea, and float.

The night before Priscilla left we had had a snug night aboard;
Nicholas is tall, the boat is tight; Nicholas was proprietary,
and self-consciously considerate. Priscilla was proprietary, and
self-consciously considerate. *After you; no, I insist, after* YOU!
In no setting other than prison can the concept *my space* have
such manifest substance. I was surprised to catch myself re-
senting Nicholas. It hadn't been his choice to displace his
mother; he'd seen the Waterway; he had business elsewhere.
I knew all this, but during our first day and night together I
heard myself saying, "Priscilla doesn't stow the cushion there"
or "Priscilla likes to lash the boom more to port" or "Priscilla

says the beer's coldest on the other side of the ice chest."
Nicholas held his tongue, managed not to remark the obvious:
then was then, now is now; she's there, I'm here. Our first day
together I was too solicitous of Nicholas's judgment; I'd ask
him if he agreed with actions and courses that were unam-
biguous. Nicholas wisely kept his distance.

At the end of May he was to fly to Alaska to work as a
wilderness ranger in Wood-Tikchik Park; he could give me
eight days, and wherever we'd got to then, he'd trade off with
Justin. If *Blackwing* was to be brought within reach of home
by June 1, we had long legs to make, dawn-to-dark long legs.
Priscilla and I had thought we were doing well to put forty
miles under us, but I hadn't cruised the turnpike till Nicholas
came aboard. He had the preposterous notion that I could
deliver *Blackwing* from the south coast of North Carolina to
Rhode Island in two weeks. I knew I couldn't.

We did seventy miles to Beaufort. Sail hard, shop hard: we
tied *Blackwing* to the town dock and went in search of a hand-
held urinal. This was of value beyond calculation to a helms-
man taking long watches at the wheel, especially offshore night
passages north of Delaware. (A large fraction of the sailors
lost at sea go overboard pissing over the stern rail; you can
look it up.) We'd had a urinal aboard since I came home from
heart surgery a few years before (waste not, want not), and
Nicholas was disconsolate to learn it had been blown overboard in Northeast Providence Channel. He was determined
to replace it, and along the waterfront we found a pharmacy
where my son invited me to ask for, fetch and pay for the thing
we desired. I put the mission in his capable hands, because I
stuttered, because my stutter made it difficult to express some
classes of desire, because I was his father and because I had
money and he didn't. Nicholas looked, Nicholas found,
Nicholas slid to the cash register. He wanted this to go
smoothly, quickly, quietly, but, like a boy buying his first rub-

ber, he faced a venerable checkout clerk. She began a colloquy with the pharmacist: "The urinal doesn't have a price on it, Roy. How much for the urinal?" Roy said, "That urinal is four-ninety-five." She said, "I'm charging you boys four-ninety-five for this urinal. You want me to wrap this urinal for you boys?" Nicholas said that would be nice. "Well, son, the thing of it is I don't have a sack the right size for this urinal." So Nicholas had to tote it, its hinged lid poking out of the sack. We visited a bar. Shop hard, play hard. Between racks of 8-Ball, we sat at the bar of the Royal James Tavern eating ninety-nine-cent chili burgers, and drinking frosted mugs of Bud. The bartender tried to break my son's heart: "Hey, who belongs to this plastic pisspot in the paper sack?"

Nicholas said, "It's mine; I hate to leave the stool when I trade liquids."

The next day we motorsailed sixty-six miles to make the final seating of the legendary buffet at Belhaven's River Forest Inn. The morning after, we woke to dense fog, and at five-thirty pushed out into it, with a lift from the tide and the wind. By afternoon we reached Albemarle Sound; it had an ugly reputation for steep seas, but wind and tide had shifted, again to our favor, and we were piling up miles. In the Alligator River, Great Santinis flying Marine Corps Harrier jets, simulating bombing and strafing runs, came in low over the water and wingwagged us. We tied up to the last free berth in Elizabeth City half an hour past nightfall: we'd logged eighty-five miles in fourteen hours. Whatever you called what we'd done, you wouldn't call it cruising; call it people-moving; call it hauling ass.

We'd missed the evening cocktail party. Elizabeth City is the layover town for boaters entering or leaving the Dismal Swamp Canal; George Washington designed and underwrote the twenty-two-mile canal to open trade (rice, white-cedar shakes) from the Carolinas. Perhaps to endear the town to visitors, perhaps just another of the irregular courtesies offered all along the Waterway, the Elizabeth City Chamber of Commerce began long ago the custom of a nightly wine-and-cheese party hosted by the mayor in honor of transient boaters at the docks; this had been Nicholas's first taste of Waterway life when he came south, and he missed chatting up the town's personages. An Australian family on the motorsailor beside us, returning their boat from South Carolina to a Maine harbor a couple of miles from Bowdoin, urged ale on us; we sat in their pilothouse telling adventure stories. Or I did; Nicholas preferred hearing to talking.

Nicholas woke me before dawn. Maybe it was the ale, maybe it was my pollen and sap allergy, maybe it was too much distance covered too fast, a kind of five-knot jet lag—whatever it was, I felt rocky when we backed out of the slip to make the first opening of the Dismal Swamp Canal's locks. The system of locking through was complicated, and if we missed the early opening at eight-thirty, there was little chance we'd make it today to Norfolk, Mile One. I was fuzz-headed, so I gave the helm to Nicholas. He asked some small favors—to get him coffee, to switch the battery banks, to put sun lotion on his nose—and I didn't execute them well.

We missed the opening by five minutes: the lock tender at South Mills saw us coming and shut the lock at 8:28 a.m., and we had to throw the engine into reverse to avoid hitting the lock bulkhead. The next opening would be in two and half hours; we were in a narrow throat of the Pasquotank River. We knew that boats would come up behind us, jamming the river with traffic. Sailboats do not maneuver predictably in reverse. The morning was humid and hot, with a strong breeze blowing across our beam, setting us toward the riverbank; Nicholas needed my help, and I couldn't keep my eyes open. He was perplexed and irritated with me, and I was irritated

with me. We weren't supposed to let each other down. I felt
light-headed *and* heavy-headed, and my muscles ached. I was
too tired to drink water. I told Nicholas I guessed I had spring
fever; Nicholas said that was a great pity, he was spending the
least enjoyable morning he had ever spent on *Blackwing*, so
he might as well make it sepulchral and adjust the stuffing
box. He anchored; I asked if he thought we could retrieve the
anchor from the river bottom dense with snags; when I said
"we," he gave me a look, and shrugged. He stained himself
with grease in the oven of the engine compartment, cut his
hand banging and adjusting. Boats were stacking in around
us, and the sun was hot, and I didn't care about anything.
When Nicholas came up to the cockpit, the wind died, which
was nice; when the wind died there was a fly hatch, which
wasn't nice. The flies had materialized from nowhere, sticking
to every exposed surface of sail and hull. They were in my
ears and nose, and I saw them annealed to Nicholas's lips. He
didn't bother shooing them away.

When the canal opened, we had to be lifted eight feet by
water flooding into the lock, and to avoid damage to the hull,
the boat's lines had to be expertly tended. Nicholas was trying
to do this alone, running from bow to stern and back; when I
stood to handle a line, I went dizzy, and had to sit. The lock
tender wouldn't help, and Nicholas found himself single-
handing *Blackwing*, and shouting (he *never* shouts) at me and
at the lock tender. We got through, and into the canal. We
heard thunder, and I knew Nicholas was speculating on the
physics of a fifty-knot gust taken broadside in a canal forty
feet across. I guessed Nicholas wished he were in better company. I tried not to take this personally.

We squeezed through the lock chamber at the other end,
and fifty miles after Elizabeth City, Nicholas was piloting us
through Norfolk Harbor, coping alone with charts, draw-
bridges, barge traffic, Navy traffic, a marina reservation. He

had his eye on an oxford-gray anvil of thunderhead, and when it burst he piloted us through the squall and asked me a final favor: to tie him a bowline at the end of a dockline he'd have to use tying up. I can tie a bowline in the dark, but not that day. I held the stupid line in my hands, and studied it, and said, "Sorry. Can't." So Nicholas did that too, and, at the marina, the dockmaster made the mistake of suggesting that Nicholas turn the helm over to "the captain there." I said this was not a good idea. As soon as we were alongside, Nicholas jumped ashore. He said he wanted to take a walk, alone. I said get us a hotel room. He said, "Cool." I said buy a thermometer. He said, flushed with anger, "Cool."

A couple of hours later Nicholas wanted to call an ambulance. My temperature was above 104°; he was scared. We got a cab from the Holiday Inn to the city hospital; the taxi driver played a rap tape and smoked a stogie. Nicholas asked if he'd snuff the cigar, and the driver said, "Walk."

Nicholas said, "Please. Just get us there."

The driver cranked the volume, rolled up his window and took a huge hit off his Dutch Master. We'd come north, the way I saw it. The climate had changed. The idiom had gone from *what cute shoes* to *walk; fuck yourself.*

It was a weekend night; the emergency room was crowded with people having a hard time of it, but the reception nurse took a look at me and said, "This guy's in shock."

Nicholas explained my St. Jude heart valve, certain medications. The nurse was a comedian; taking my temperature, seeing it spike 105°, he told Nicholas that Jim Henson, the man who brought "you kids" Miss Piggy, had died of something like this just the other day.

"Wait a minute," Nicholas said. "Knock it off now."

The nurse was leading me back to the doctors, and Nicholas was trying to hold my hand, and the nurse said, "You stay, Junior."

"Not in your lifetime," Nicholas said.

They ran IV fluids into me, cooled me with alcohol. I was out of it. Nicholas told me later some things he'd heard waiting. A bloody patient was on the gurney beside me; he'd been shot in the foot and ankle with a shotgun, and a nurse and police officer kept asking, "Who did this to you?" The victim kept answering, "How the fuck would I know? I'm drunk, in case you didn't notice."

Nicholas heard a mother deny kinship with her son dying of knife wounds. She wanted to know: suppose the bleeding kid *was* her bleeding kid, and he was underage, what was her financial exposure in such a situation?

While that boy waited for surgery, Nicholas overheard a surgeon on the telephone, shouting above the mayhem to his contractor: "I want a *real* doghouse. Not some bitty peewee shack, but something I can *stand* in when I visit my animal. Don't let me down, now—I've got a temper."

Nicholas realized after midnight that they'd lost a heart-attack patient. Not *lost him* euphemistically, *lost him* lost him. It was the principal conversation back there among the trauma unit. The Desaparecido's wife had sent him by ambulance at teatime; now it was coming on morning and they had his paperwork but no one could find him. "Try the morgue," an orderly suggested.

They let me go after seven hours. It was a viral infection, good news. It wasn't a big deal; I was merely sick and in debt five hundred dollars to the hospital.

After a couple of days in bed I was returned to myself, weak, chastened and cast down. We studied the charts of Chesapeake Bay. We looked to the right of the chart, to the east, and had the same idea at the same time: "Let's go outside," Nicholas said.

And so it was decided. We'd scratch Chesapeake Bay from

our itinerary, sail along the Atlantic coast the hundred and sixty miles from Norfolk to Cape May, New Jersey. That was a lonely ocean out there; we were shorthanded and could expect to be exhausted; if anything went wrong, there were no deep-water harbors or safe inlets along the Maryland–Delaware shore. But we would cut many miles off our trip, and we could sail through the night.

After breakfast, at the fuel dock, just before casting off, Nicholas said, "I've got bad vibes about this passage, a creepy feeling." I tried to pin him down; he wouldn't amplify. I felt stretched, as though I couldn't calculate either my reach or my grasp. I took a deep breath and listened to the weather radio. We seemed to be promised twenty-four hours of unsettled but manageable weather.

"Let's go."

Coasting Home

It's an experience familiar to anyone who's dived off the high platform, who's put an arm around a first date at the movies, who's dropped an angry letter in the mailbox, who's told the boss "I quit." Once begun it's okay. Sailing into the Atlantic that afternoon, settling into the mostly wordless groove of competence that keeps a boat on course and out of harm's way, we were happy. It wasn't until dusk, off the Maryland coast, that Nicholas called up to the cockpit from below: "Dad, bad news; I've got a fever. It's only a hundred, but I don't feel great."

Of course. It made sense; we'd talked about what we'd do if it happened. So Nicholas took the helm while I slept in the cockpit; he'd stand watch for four hours or until he felt too

sick and wasted to steer, whichever came first. As the sun set
over Virginia, we scanned three hundred and sixty degrees to
note the range and bearing of shipping we'd have to beware.
We didn't have radar, but we hoped they did, and that our
radar reflector lit it up bright and clear. I saw nothing; Nicholas
said he could make out a fishing boat on the horizon, way
astern.

I slept uneasily, worried about where I'd brought my son. I
questioned my own judgment; we were out here tonight because six months ago I'd promised a stranger I'd show up in
San Francisco on a certain day to expatiate to other strangers
on a topic titled by strangers "World Literature," a notional
genre without existence or reason to exist. What would I say
in San Francisco . . . ?

"Dad, you're on watch." Nicholas was shaking me gently.
"You were snoring."

"I was dreaming about a literary conference." He offered a
mug of coffee. I saw that the sky was clouded, the wind light
from the southwest. We were gently lifted and gently dropped
by greasy groundswells. We were motorsailing. "How do you
feel?"

"So-so," Nicholas said, helping me into the safety harness
that we attached by carabiner to a cleat when we sailed offshore, or at night, or alone. "If anything, my temp's a little
lower."

I didn't believe him. I asked him to take his temperature
and to show me the thermometer.

"Don't treat me like a kid, Dad. Okay?"

"Okay."

Shortly before midnight I heard Nicholas ask from below, "Is
that boat still following us?"

I had noticed running lights astern, but they seemed far
away, and we were running along a kind of loran highway,

following the rhumb line between sea buoys; it didn't alarm
me that other boats followed this obvious route. Truth was, I
wasn't practiced enough at night sailing to distinguish between
running lights on a huge ship far off and running lights on a
small boat close by. Nicholas came on deck. I pointed astern.

Nicholas said, "He's following us."

I doubted this, and said so. Nicholas suggested I change
course to the east and see if the boat changed course. I did; it
did. Nicholas said he was going to call the Coast Guard.

"Oh no! Not them! It probably *is* the Coast Guard. Call the
boat astern of us; ask its course; say we want to keep clear."

Nicholas went below and got on the radio to the Coast
Guard. I could hear his voice low and steady. A pearly light
mist was coming off the water, nothing that deserved the name
fog, but it was eerie, like the steam-machine atmospherics used
as props in horror movies. The rigging dripped. My eyeglasses
clouded; they were greased with wet, and the gray seas seemed
oiled. It was chilly now, and I shivered; not for the first time,
I wondered who I thought I was.

Nicholas was in the companionway, looking astern through
binoculars. "Bring us into the wind and cut the engine," he
said. I did as he said. We were dead in the water, locked in
silence except for the gently shaking mainsail and staysail. We
looked astern, saw above the low mist a red light, green light,
white light; the lights didn't move. "I think we're in trouble,"
Nicholas said; he went below to get the flare gun. I took it
from him, and wondered aloud if we were being shadowed by
the DEA. Nicholas said they wouldn't dick around with us;
they'd approach and board us. But he got on the radio again
to the Coast Guard, and I could hear him ask if the mystery
boat might be the DEA.

Now I heard alert care from the Coast Guard's end; they
assured Nicholas they had no knowledge of any official vessel
in our area. They asked our position, and when Nicholas gave

it, they said they'd send a patrol out to us, and as soon as they said it, the lights astern winked off. Whoever was back there had either moved or shut off their lights.

Who was it? Maybe a fishing boat, thinking it was following another fishing boat to a good haul? (Nicholas said they'd know by our masthead light we were a sailboat.) Okay, someone playing a game with us, for fun? (Nicholas said, "Does that make sense to you?") Maybe the DEA, after all? (Nicholas shrugged; why would they flee?) Then who? The Coast Guard never came. We moved on in anxious peace.

Justin arrived in Cape May to take over from Nicholas. He'd just finished final exams at Bowdoin and was dead beat after the long drive from Maine. A cold rain was sweeping us. Who cared? It was a supercharged occasion; the brothers are distinct but tight. It's what anyone would wish for sons, an uncanny intimacy between them, together with a capacity for surprise. They had each other's number; they perplexed each other. Except for our short stay in Eleuthera, Nicholas and Justin had not seen each other for almost a year, and I could see them measuring each other, marking growth the way fond parents record kids' height on a storeroom wall. I took satisfaction from this reunion: because I'd made us all sail boats, and had engineered this adventure, I had given myself the power to command us to join together. We'd been having a high old time, chatting up barflies and shooting pool with fishermen. Thinking my smug thoughts about my wizard synthetic powers, I had a hunch I was thinking through my hat, that my reasoning was circular. That we were happy tonight owed nothing to my calculation; what we had tonight was as fleeting as a fair wind with a fair tide on a fair day, and all we could do with it was run with it. We had blundered on a wake for a Cape May fisherman lost that week at sea, and the fisherman's comrades bought drinks for the house, and challenged my sons to a game of pool. It was time for me to go home to *Blackwing*, chart our course for the next day's sail alone with Justin. Tomorrow morning Nicholas would drive home, and fly away to Alaska. Much later that night, half asleep in my berth, I heard my sons walking down the dock, talking. Often they communicate in a slurred, breakneck idiom as inaccessible as code to outsiders and parents, but now they must have believed I was asleep.

"You'll have a swell time with him," Nicholas said.

"Of course," Justin said.

"Just be patient," Nicholas said.

"I know Dad," Justin said.

"Of course," Nicholas said.

Justin and I beat into a cold easterly, forty-four miles up the coast to Atlantic City. Like his mother, Justin was resigned to being made miserable aboard *Blackwing* by seasickness, but now the prescription ear patch rescued him too, and he was in a jolly mood as we thundered past the breakwaters and up to the marina that serves Harrah's. Justin was a gambler. The look in a gambler's eyes is a gorgon look: get out of my way; don't think of standing between me and that jackpot.

So how was it that a few hours later we glanced at each other and shook our heads? We'd done hard time at the slots: it was like making five knots through the water against a five-knot current; at the end of several hours our little plastic buckets held about as many quarters as they had held when we began, and our arms ached. So we tried the wheel, but it was crowded; we had to hurl chips in the general direction of our birthdate numbers. After four hours we were eight dollars down, maybe up. And if up, how long at such rates to become high rollers? We looked at each other, nodded and made our way, dodging wheelchairs, into the mob of golden-aged sports.

"Let's bag it, Pa. It would take forever to make a couple thousand. Easier to write about it, don't you think?"

It was cold out in the shipping lanes converging on Sandy Hook. We kept warm with mittens, ski caps, sweaters, parkas, tea and jokes. We saw the Jersey shore lit up, but we were well off it, avoiding fish traps that could catch our rudder and foul our propeller. Justin had sailed aboard *Blackwing* since he was nine, and he knew his way around her. But till now I'd felt his enthusiasm for sailing had often been dutiful; seasickness explained more than I could know, of course, but he'd been willing, not always eager. He'd deferred to his older brother's sometimes fraternal authority, had distanced himself from the underlying system of sailing, had come along for the ride, doing what he could to make the ride safe and pleasurable. But now, out there in the shipping lanes, he was different. Now he was soaking it up, asking questions, laying courses, entering data into the loran, trimming sheets. He showed the exhilaration of someone who—long after comprehending gyroscopic theory—suddenly realizes for the first time he's riding a bike without training wheels.

At dawn, a hundred and twenty miles later, *Blackwing* swept us into New York Harbor, past the Battery, up the East River to Hell Gate and beyond, dodging tugs and ferries. We cruised up the East Side at rush hour, pushed by a fair tide. Helicopters buzzed around the UN Building. Justin had the helm.

Twenty-four hours after leaving Harrah's, we were in Huntington, north of Cold Spring Harbor. As soon as we were snugged down, the sky opened, the wind howled, we lit a fire in the Tiny Tot fireplace, changed into clean clothes, cooked a pot of soup, put Lightnin' Hopkins in the tape deck, broke open a fresh deck of cards, played.

Nicholas had commended an anchorage on the Connecticut side of Long Island Sound, near New Haven, west of Sachem

Head, a collection of Maine-like rocky islands called The
Thimbles. Justin and I anchored midafternoon in deep water
tucked in the alley between two islands. We were alone in our
anchorage, except for teenagers water-skiing and showing off
for each other. Justin said to watch them made him feel like
an old-timer. It was a wonderful day. The pressure was off;
we'd get *Blackwing* home before June. We lazed in the cockpit
reading. Justin was reading a novel; I was reading *A Cruising
Guide to the New England Coast,* and he suggested I put the
cruising guides away for a while. It wasn't like Justin to tell
another what was best, but I took his suggestion as a thrust
with purpose, took seriously what he might have noticed about
my narrowed field of vision.

Later, we grilled burgers and dogs on a hibachi that hung
off the transom, and watched a perfect sunset. The moon came
up, and we lay in the cockpit looking at it. We played music,
trading tapes back and forth, listening to his Van Morrison
then my Billie Holiday then his Eric Clapton then my Bucky
Pizzarelli. In the silvery wash of moonlight he told me things
I'd never guessed before, and I told him things. We were in
a free zone together, out of range of our entrenched lines of
authority and privacy, not facing off but facing the same sky,
same moon. Such concurrence is rare; I'd experienced perfect
concord with my sons far from home, or driving at night lit
by the sea green of dashboard lights. Kin can wait a lifetime
for whole intimacy, and to have it once is to keep it. Credo.

We sailed in freezing rain to Saybrook Breakwater, up the
Connecticut River to Essex. We played gin rummy in the rain,
swinging from a rented mooring. In the rain we went ashore,
and ate at the Griswold Inn, shad with roe. We shopped in
the rain for groceries and the bag tore and emptied itself into
a gutter before we got to the dinghy. We played gin rummy.
We tried to nap; the rain beat us awake. The boat below
smelled of wet wool and of us. The rain fell. We drank beer
and played gin rummy. We took the dinghy ashore and ate at

the Griswold Inn, shad with roe. We got a good soaking going back after dinner in the dinghy. We drank beer and played gin rummy. (Later I found our gin-rummy scores penciled into a wet notebook; I owed Justin a couple of thousand dollars, or a couple of million, depending on where to put the decimal. There's an observation below an interim score: "This man can't be for real; is he hustling me?") Justin put Van Morrison on the tape deck. I'd heard Justin's Van Morrison tape. I put Billie Holiday on the tape deck. Justin had heard my Billie Holiday tape. We went to bed and listened to it rain. When we woke up, it was raining. The wind was howling from the northwest.

"Let's eat a fish lunch at the Gris," I said.

We were less than an hour from home by car. "Let's get out of here," Justin said.

It wasn't prudent to leave our mooring in such conditions. "In my considered opinion," I said, "weighing probability against experience, let's get out of here."

It was foul out there. We banged into the biggest seas I'd faced since we left Eleuthera. We were bucking a tidal current, making good 2½ knots, but way off in the distance was a ribbon of clear sky, and if the current was against us now, it would be with us later. And then it turned with us: we screamed up Fishers Island Sound to Stonington, dropped anchor at dark, rose at dawn, sailed past the Texas Tower into Narragansett Bay at the lunch hour and turned the corner at The Dumplings and tied up to Conanicut Marina at the foot of Narragansett Avenue, the street where we live. Justin ran home to get Priscilla, and by the time she raced down to the dock to greet *Blackwing*, I was cleaning our boat. We ate a picnic in the cockpit, and traded sea stories, tales of legendary groundings and gear-busting gales in a far-off chain of islands where the moon was full thirty days a month. Soon I returned to scrubbing, and Priscilla said to our son, "Let's leave him to it." She said this patiently. I scoured and fussed and oiled and adjusted and mended and prettied *Blackwing*. She had been good to us, and we had been good to us.

At the end of the day I took *Blackwing* to her mooring; she swung into the wind, facing south. I covered the sails, tied off the running rigging, locked the helm amidships, closed the hatches, shut her up tight. If, as she tugged on her mooring, the sense of an ending was a romantic illusion, it was a benign illusion. So too the illusion of having done something valuable by taking a boat to sea, and bringing her home to port. Maybe I had felt no more, no less, than any layabout in a beach chair? Was it a trick I played on myself to regard this draining of my mind as healthy? Of course what I felt wasn't the whole point, was it? I hadn't been alone out there. Sailing up Narragansett Bay, Justin had said, so quietly I could just make it out, "I think I'd like to take our boat on a voyage."

Born in Los Angeles in 1937, Geoffrey Wolff is the author of *The Duke of Deception: Memories of My Father*. He has also written a biography of Harry Crosby (*Black Sun*), as well as five novels—*Bad Debts* (1969), *The Sightseer* (1974), *Inklings* (1978), *Providence* (1986), and *The Final Club* (1990). He lives in Jamestown, Rhode Island.

A NOTE ON THE TYPE

The text of this book was set in Walbaum, a type face designed by Justus Erich Walbaum in 1810. Walbaum was active as a type founder in Goslar and Weimar from 1799 to 1836. Though letterforms in this face are patterned closely on the "modern" cuts then being made by Giambattista Bodoni and the Didot family, they are of a far less rigid cut. Indeed, it is the slight but pleasing irregularities in the cut that give this face its human quality and account for its wide appeal. Even in appearance, Walbaum jumps boundaries, having a more French than German look.

Composed by PennSet, Inc., Bloomsburg, Pennsylvania
Printed and bound by The Haddon Craftsmen, Inc., Scranton, Pennsylvania
Designed by Mia Vander Els